C

The Case for Development

United Nations, Centre for Economic and Social Information

with an introduction by Philippe de Seynes, Under-Secretary-General for Economic and Social Affairs

The Praeger Special Studies program—utilizing the most modern and efficient book production techniques and a selective worldwide distribution network—makes available to the academic, government, and business communities significant, timely research in U.S. and international economic, social, and political development.

The Case for Development
Six Studies

PRAEGER SPECIAL STUDIES IN INTERNATIONAL ECONOMICS AND DEVELOPMENT

Praeger Publishers   New York   Washington   London

PRAEGER PUBLISHERS
111 Fourth Avenue, New York, N.Y. 10003, U.S.A.
5, Cromwell Place, London S.W.7, England

Published in the United States of America in 1973
by Praeger Publishers, Inc.

Library of Congress Catalog Card Number: 72-94557

Printed in the United States of America

Contents

Introduction
Imperatives to Development

On October 24, 1970, the twenty-fifth anniversary of the founding of the United Nations, the General Assembly voted unanimously to proclaim the Second International Development Decade and to adopt the International Development Strategy, one of the most remarkable documents to issue from the world organization. The Strategy is exactly what its name implies: a large-scale perspective with an action plan that, if fulfilled, could lead over the next 20 years to a doubly improved standard of living in the two-thirds of the world now living largely outside of the modern economy. The Strategy is neither a utopian nor a poetic vision, but a hard-headed, practical document supported, with some reservations, admittedly, by a total of 127 countries.

Readers of the Development Strategy—an 18-page booklet with more than 80 paragraphs—can find many faults with it. Whatever one's viewpoint—free-enterpriser, planner, socialist—one is likely to conclude that those thoughts one approves are insufficiently elaborated, and those one does not like are treated at undue length. The sentences are long, the clauses are many, and the prose is often awkward. But to the experienced diplomat and international civil-servant the lumbering paragraphs, with their involutions and qualifying clauses, have a particular kind of beauty. They testify to that victory of reason over interest that is won only after long and arduous negotiation and long nights spent in committee sessions. An international consensus is not easily arrived at.

But it is worth having. A United Nations consensus is not like a law passed by a national government that immediately sets to enforcing it by printing up the necessary regulations, devising lengthy forms the citizens must fill out, and, if necessary, alerting the police to track down possible offenders. It is more like the Quakers' "sense of the meeting"—a general agreement after grave deliberation—that each is then free to carry out according to the dictates of his own conscience.

Nowhere was such a consensus more needed than in the field of development. This many-faceted task, as broad as life itself, of bringing the benefits of indsutrialization and world trade, with all the concomitants in health, education, social security and justice to some 2½ billion people who have so far not shared in them. Efforts at development through national action, through trade and foreign aid of individual donor countries, and through international agencies affiliated with the UN had, of course, gone on a long time—as had intellectual enquiries about the development process. But never had the two been fused in such a manner that governments representing many different interests could agree on serious measures involving trade, aid, and international development policies that, in principle at least, were recognized by all as desirable and necessary courses to follow.

The Development Strategy accomplished this and more. It made it possible for nationals of different countries, speaking different languages, following different ideologies, pursuing different ideals of personal freedom and social justice, to meet on completely common ground when entering the sphere of development policy.

This remarkable unanimity on essentials is well illustrated by the six excellent essays in this volume. Five were prepared as Executive Briefing Papers by the Centre for Economic and Social Information of the United Nations; the sixth was also issued by the Centre, but apart from the series. The authors come from diverse backgrounds: two are Englishmen, the remaining four are, respectively, Polish, Santa Lucian, American, and French.

Economists predominate (there are four of them), but, as the essays make clear, their interests have carried them into many different fields—history, sociology, political studies. Two are not economists: one is a writer on scientific matters; another, a well-known editor with a philosophic bent, a moralist, at least by avocation. Each treats the subject of development from his own professional point of view, but also—and this is important—from his own experience of the problems encountered as administrator, consultant, or observer, as the case may be, and predominantly as a human being. Although written from different viewpoints, often dealing with different subject matter, the essays proceed from broadly similar philosophical premises, through different technical considerations, to closely related general conclusions. This is what gives them their interest: our authors do not argue; they illuminate.

Arthur W. Lewis (now Sir Arthur Lewis), originally of Santa Lucia, has been a doughty fighter for development as a teacher (Princeton, N.J., London School of Economics), administrator, president of the Carribean Development Bank, and high UN official. His argument is that of a man who has seen much and analysed what he saw with an unusually sharp mind. Of course, he says, rapid economic growth is possible; of course, the process of growth must take place in many directions simultaneously; of course, development requires many institutional changes and, almost needless to say, there must be international action. Let us get on with the job.

The late Max Millikan has similar sweep. For many years one of the leading figures at the Massachusetts Institute of Technology, he combines historical perspective with a taste for the new mathematical economics. He is essentially a searcher for hidden keys, for the critical action that will start the development process and bring a country to the take-off point. His essay is, in fact, the testament of a rich and fruitful career.

David Wightman, professor of international economic organization at the University of Birmingham, and frequent consultant to governments and UN organizations, has followed the evolution of international cooperation in Europe and Asia. His essay on the economic interest of the industrialized countries in the development of the Third World is one of the most succinct summaries of international action in the development field that can be found in the literature.

Joseph Pajestka, who writes of the social dimensions of development, is director of the Institute of Planning of the Polish Government and has represented his country in many international negotiations. His primary concern is with the development of the individual in a social setting that will help to make him into a self-confident and productive participant in the development process.

Robin Clarke, author of "The Great Experiment," and the second Englishman, deals with the role of technology and science in development. The youngest of the group (he was born in 1937), Clarke, who started out to be a scientist but switched to writing because of social concerns, recently announced that he and some friends would henceforth live on a farm where they would devote their energies to the development of "soft technology"—i.e. simple labor-saving methods that could further development without causing ecological damage.

This leaves Jean-Marie Domenach, who writes about our moral involvement in development. I will deal with his thesis at somewhat greater length, not because he is a fellow Frenchman, but because all of us should become more concerned about the moral imperative as a motive-force in international action, particularly in the field of development.

There was a time in the 1960s when it was possible to be optimistic about the prospect that well-conceived, aggressive international action would raise the living standards of the emerging nations. This broad movement culminated in the passage of the International Development Strategy. Unfortunately, some of the momentum that led to this statesmanlike and potentially far-reaching action has begun to be lost. The events of the last year, particularly the difficulties that beset the Bretton Woods monetary system, and the uncertainties of the future have caused individual governments to look apprehensively at the immediate self-interest of their countries. Mercantilism, always latent, has been on the rise again. This is not a climate of opinion in which long-term plans of international betterment, such as the Development Strategy, tend to flourish.

Clearly, we need a new imperative to propel us to action. All the authors of the essays in this book deal in some measure with the arguments for the industrialized countries to act in international concert to promote the development of the Third World, and all touch at one time or another on the moral imperative. But Domenach elaborates most illuminatingly on the moral aspect of our involvement and (rightly, in my opinion) sees the need for development as an essential step to a world order based on law. I know of no better way to conclude this introduction than to quote him verbatim:

A world order within the context of classical diplomacy is no longer imaginable; it supposes progress on the part of each and all nations. Conversely, the security of each state no longer depends simply on a peaceful balance of power, or the respect by each of the rights of others: it implies a positive relationship and mutual assistance.

Philippe de Seynes

Philippe de Seynes
Under-Secretary-General for Economic and Social
Affairs of the United Nations

The Case for Development

A Strategy of Development

MAX F. MILLIKAN

As we approach the decade of the 1970's, many calls are being heard for a new strategy of development. In 1961, the General Assembly of the United Nations resolved that the 1960's would be termed the Development Decade, a period in which the world community would devote itself to the problem of generating in the less developed countries that constitute two-thirds of the world's population a process of accelerated economic growth that could in time lift the world's less affluent out of grinding poverty and provide the wherewithal for a marked improvement in the quality of life of the mass of the world's peoples. The quantitative target set was an annual average growth rate of the economic output or gross national product (GNP) of the less developed world by 5 per cent. The hope was expressed that the countries already more developed would assist this process by resource transfers amounting to at least 1 per cent of the national incomes of the developed group.

As we approach the end of the 1960's, it becomes apparent that while the target growth has been approximately achieved and resource transfers have fallen short of the goal by only modest amounts, the progress of development is inadequate. Accordingly, it is proposed that the world community should adopt new targets and new strategies for the decade of the 1970's to be called the Second Development Decade. In order to analyze what should be included in such a strategy, it is necessary to consider a number of aspects of the problem. Since a strategy involves decisions by a number of actors about matters for which they presumably have some responsibility, it is first necessary to decide whose strategy we are talking about. We must then outline rather more precisely the variety of goals toward which it is hoped the strategy will

3

propel us. In other words, what are the dimensions of the development we are attempting to promote? The measures to be recommended will then depend on our diagnosis of the principal obstacles to their accomplishment and our prescription of the best means available to the various decision-making actors already identified to remove those obstacles. It is to this analytic task that this paper is addressed.

Whose Strategy?

There are essentially three sets of entities to whose strategies this paper is addressed. First, there are the organizations, chiefly governmental, that determine the policies and programs of the less developed countries themselves. It is commonly and correctly observed that the bulk of the task of promoting economic development rests with them. They must determine, among the manifold functions of the modern state, what priority is to be given to development, how resources including capital, skilled manpower, technology and science, foreign exchange, and organizational and administrative talent can best be mobilized, how these various scarce resources can be most effectively allocated, and how the fruits of development can be most equitably distributed to their peoples. A good part of what follows will be devoted to a discussion of the strategies they might pursue.

But a good part of the case for a world-development strategy rests upon the perception that the effectiveness of the measures that the less developed countries can take to promote their own growth is importantly determined by the economic environment established by the acts and policies of the developed countries that, while they represent only a third of the world's population, control five-sixths of its output. These wealthier countries, which we can take as roughly comprising all those with per capita incomes of more than $1,000 per year, must provide some of the financial resources in the form of aid, loans, and private investment that are required to fuel development, must help to establish a world trading environment in which the less developed countries can find markets for the exports they must sell to pay for their essential imports, and must make available to the less developed countries through technical assistance and institutional collabora-

4

tion some of the knowledge, skills, and research results on which their own continued development is based. Virtually all of the developed countries have in one fashion or another accepted a responsibility to assist the development process in all of these various ways, but there is still debate as to what the key characteristics of their development strategies should be.

Finally, all of the many institutions of the international community must sort out the respective roles they are to play in world development and design strategies appropriate to those roles. One historically significant novelty that has characterized the decade of the 1960's has been the rapidly expanding role and number of these international organizations and institutions. These include, in addition to the United Nations and all of its specialized agencies, the International Bank, the International Monetary Fund, the General Agreement on Tariffs and Trade, the Organization for Economic Cooperation and Development (OECD), the various regional organizations, and the regional development banks. For a variety of reasons, we can expect that these international instrumentalities will grow still further in importance over the decade of the 1970's, and their development strategies must therefore be a part of our concern.

Strategy for What?

Before we can outline a strategy for development, we must be clear what it is we are trying to achieve. Development means many things to many people, and the manifold dimensions of the process lead to a wide variety of emphases in prescription. A casual examination of what are normally thought of as more developed countries and those we would all class as less developed reveals a wide variety of differences, each of which suggests a different definition of the development problem and appears to imply a different prescription for dealing with it. The most obvious and the one most commonly noted is that the underdeveloped countries are poor. The development and popularization over the past twenty years of the concepts of national income accounting has given a somewhat illusory precision to this notion. We are all familiar with the huge gap between the gross national product per capita of the more advanced countries and that of the less developed ones. The former range from an average yearly product per person of $1,400 in Japan to over $4,000 in the United States, while in the latter, the figures for most countries lie in the neighborhood of $100 or $200 a year. There are so many more people in the countries at the low end of the scale than in those at the high end that it is perfectly clear that no feasible simple redistribution from rich countries to poor countries can add enough to the incomes of the poor to improve significantly the welfare of the underprivileged. For most of mankind, the problem is perfectly clearly one of production rather than of mere distribution. Thus, the central purpose of resource-transfers from richer to poorer countries is not to equalize the distribution of existing world output but rather to make possible substantial increases in productivity in the poorer countries.

How is this to be done? A key structural difference that was early observed between the more developed and the less developed countries, and from which incorrect conclusions about development strategy have sometimes been drawn, is that in the poorer countries the majority of the labor force is engaged in agriculture and an even larger fraction of total output consists of the products of agriculture, while in the richer countries manufacturing and other nonagricultural activities play a much larger role. This led some countries to conclude that industrialization was the key to development and that development strategy should be concentrated on this objective. More recently, another observed difference between more and less developed countries has led to an opposite and equally incorrect strategic conclusion. This is that in spite of the much greater importance of agriculture in the economies of the underdeveloped countries, the peoples of these countries are much less well fed than those in the developed world. In most low income countries there are too few calories available to supply minimally necessary human energy, and in virtually all, the diet is grossly deficient in some elements, such as protein, essential to sound human growth and effective performance. It is also observed that, while in the developed countries generally, population growth has stabilized at relatively modest rates between 1 and 1½ per cent per year, in the developing countries, improvements in public health unaccompanied by any corresponding decline in birth rates have led to an explosive expansion of population at two or three times this rate. Thus, looking forward, some observers have described the core of the development problem as a race between population and food supply and have urged that development strategy take as its two priority elements population control on the one hand and the stimulation of increased agricultural productivity on the other.

Meanwhile, as improved social indicators have provided increasing information about aspects of societies not covered in the usual economic accounts, such as literacy, communications patterns, aspirations and values, and social mobility, other differences between developed and underdeveloped societies have received increasing attention. Because educational levels are much lower in the poorer countries, and because education is seen as a prerequisite to the expansion of opportunity associated with development, some would give it the leading role in development strategy. Employment as the economist traditionally views it is a means to the end of higher output and not an independent goal of development in its own right, but increasingly employment opportunities are coming to be seen as having sociological and psychological implications for the quality of life not comprehended in the economist's usual calculations. A characteristic of many less developed societies, including some with very impressive records of economic growth, is persistent unemployment of large fractions of the labor force, amounting to 10 or 15 per cent, including many whose aspirations for new opportunities have been sharpened by education. Thus, in some development strategies, the provision of employment is viewed not merely as a means to other development objectives but as one of the ultimate goals of the development process itself.

More generally, there has been increasing concern in recent years with the extent to which the development process offers opportunities to all classes in the developing societies to participate integrally in the modernization process. The usual economic indicators tell us a good deal about national levels of output, but they reveal very little about how the life styles of individuals in different segments of the population are affected by development. Opportunities for education and for employment are only two of the many dimensions in which the choices open to most citizens of developed countries are wider, more diverse, and more satisfying than those available to the average man in a less developed country. In this consideration of the breadth of participation of the

7

people in development, three objectives are distinguishable. First is the classic goal of spreading as widely as possible in the adult population opportunities to participate meaningfully in making the decisions that determine the directions in which the society will move. This participation in decision-making is much broader than participation in politics, though that is a very important element in it. It includes participation in the decision-making processes of all institutions, public and private, national and local, that affect the lives of the citizens. Developed societies differ from the less developed ones in having a much wider range of institutions in existence, a much greater breadth of options open to those institutions, and the involvement of a much larger fraction of the population in their activities than is the case with older, more traditional societies.

The second type of participation is participation in the fruits of the development process itself. This has to do with how widely and how equitably the extra goods and services produced by development are shared among the various elements of the population. While many developed societies have recently been discovering serious inequities to some of their less advantaged members, it is nonetheless probably true that inequity has been somewhat reduced in general by the development process. Nevertheless, the goals for which development strategies are designed must clearly include explicit attention to the equitable distribution of the fruits of the development process.

The third aspect of participation is participation in the key activities through which development is implemented. People want to share not only in the decisions that affect their lives and in the things that development produces but also, perhaps more importantly, in the constructive and psychologically satisfying activities that development comprises. The most important illustration of this type of participation is employment opportunities, but it is much broader than ways of earning a living as these are narrowly conceived. Economists frequently make the mistake of implying that because development is measured by its product in goods and services, its sole purpose is higher consumption, however achieved. A little introspection suggests that our major gratifications come as much from the acquisition and exercise of creative skills as from the consumption of goods and services, and that it is therefore appropriate that development strategies should, at

8

least in part, be directed toward maximizing opportunities for such human creativity. Thus, in considering the goals of development, we must add to the usual indices of higher productivity and larger output per capita increased participation by the peoples of the developing countries in decision-making, in the fruits of development, and in the processes of its implementation, as well as the elaboration of an institutional structure that will make such participation both possible and fruitful.

Given this complex of interdependent objectives, which, as we shall see, are in some circumstances mutually reinforcing and in other circumstances competitive, how can we generalize about economic development strategies? The problem is not rendered easier by the diversity of circumstances that characterize the less developed countries. They range in size from some, like Guyana and Mauritius, with less than 1 million inhabitants each, to giants like India, with over 500 million. They differ in economic structure from predominantly subsistence economies, like Somalia and Paraguay, to those with an important industrial component, like Brazil and Turkey. Some, like Venezuela and Libya, are blessed with an easily marketable international resource that gives them ample access to foreign exchange, while most, like Jordan and Pakistan, have to struggle mightily to earn less than enough foreign exchange to keep their development moving. Some, like Chile, have a common language and a reasonably homogeneous culture, while others, like the Congo, speak so many tongues and are composed of such diverse tribal elements that a national identity is very hard to establish. In political structure, they are not arrayed along any simple spectrum from left to right but include a bewildering variety, some with power centralized and others widely dispersed, some with one dominant party and others with many, some with attempts at tight governmental control over the economy and others with freer reign for private activities, some, like contemporary Indonesia, open to assistance and influence from almost any part of the international community and others, like Burma, somewhat withdrawn and resistant to counsel from abroad.

In the light of the complexity of the interrelated goals of modernization—virtually all aspects of public policy are involved—and of the bewildering variety of circumstances, economic, social, political, and cultural, in which the countries of the developing world find themselves, one may well ask whether the hope of outlining a general development strategy broadly applicable to the developing world is not a vain one. Is not each case *sui generis* calling for its own specially tailored set of instruments and measures, whereby national and local officials and those in the world outside who would help them can attempt to make progress toward the particular set of values that for them have priority. Certainly much of the development literature suffers from the effort to apply oversimplified models that pay inadequate attention to the peculiarities of each complex economy and culture. Nevertheless, there are enough common elements both in the purposes that development is designed to serve in different countries and in the economic and structural changes that will make it possible to justify what can be called a general strategy of development, recognizing that its application in particular cases requires sensitive adaptation and adjustment. What follows here is perhaps not so much a strategy as a framework to insure that individual strategies will be both comprehensive and compatible.

Looking first at economics, the most important feature of the more developed economies, which distinguishes them from the less developed ones and from which most of the other economic distinctions logically follow, is not their relative affluence but rather the fact that they have exhibited over a period of several decades a capacity for sustained, built-in, and reasonably steady annual growth in economic output per head of the population, amounting on the average to 2 or 3 percentage points per year. Production in both developed and traditional economies fluctuates from year to year, in response to fluctuations in weather, accidents of history, variations in the business cycle, wars and political upsets, and the like. But over several decades, the trend in the developed economies is steadily upward in per capita terms, while in the underdeveloped ones it has historically not been so. This regular self-sustaining economic growth of the developed economies is historically a relatively recent phenomenon. While our information on the economies of earlier centuries is totally inadequate, a little simple arithmetic will demonstrate that this must be so. For the last fifty years, per capita incomes in the United States and Western Europe have been growing at around 2 per cent a year, with rates substantially higher than this in some countries, like Russia and Japan, and a bit lower in some others. Arithmetic tells us that something growing at an annual rate of 2 per cent doubles

10

in about a third of a century, multiplies eight-fold in a hundred years, or sixty-four-fold in twice that time. The highest per capita GNP in the world, that of the United States, is now a little over $4,000. The value at current prices of the minimum consumption required to sustain human life is something between $50 and $100. Thus, it is clearly impossible for per capita growth rate of the kind the developed world has experienced for the past half-century to have been with us for more than a couple of hundred years.

On the other hand, since many of the developing countries have average levels of income only slightly higher than the minima required to sustain human life, it is equally clear that these countries must at best have experienced relatively static trends in per capita income. During the past decade, to be sure, the less developed countries as a group have achieved an average rate of growth in per capita incomes of nearly 2 per cent. But this has not been self-sustaining in the sense that a significant fraction of the resources that have made this growth possible has been supplied by the developed world in the form of foreign aid. Some writers, notably W. W. Rostow, believe that it is possible to identify in the history of each of the presently developed countries a period of two or three decades during which these countries made the transition from a relatively static long-term trend of per capita income to one of self-sustaining economic growth. They have labeled this transition phase the "take-off." In the terminology of these writers, the central goal of international development strategy can be described as bringing the countries of the less developed world through the take-off and into a stage of regular economic growth that can be sustained at a rate of 2 per cent per year per capita or better, without a continuing infusion of outside resources on concessional terms of the sort that foreign aid provides. While there is continuing debate in the academic community as to whether a transitional period such as the take-off can, in fact, be historically identified, what its structural characteristics are, and how applicable the historical experience is to the present problems of the developing world, few would dispute the empirical observation that the developed countries, in fact, exhibit regular built-in growth, while the underdeveloped countries do not, or the conclusion that the core of the development problem is the achievement of regular long-term growth without external subsidy by those who do not now exhibit it.

11

While self-sustaining economic growth will not in itself of necessity bring with it adequate progress toward all the other goals that countries seek in their modernization programs, it will facilitate many of them, and it can, I think, be persuasively demonstrated that in the absence of per capita growth, significant progress toward most of these goals is impossible. Without growth, there can be no lasting alleviation of poverty, no industrialization, no important improvements in agriculture, no real amelioration of malnutrition, little progress in education or the spread of employment opportunities, and very low prospects for increased citizen participation in any of the senses we have discussed. With growth, progress toward these other goals is not automatic and requires strategies designed to reinforce it, but, for reasons we shall be exploring, without growth, it is impossible.

A commonly stated development objective is to narrow the gap in living standards between developed and underdeveloped societies. If, as there is every reason to expect, the developed societies continue to grow, the gap cannot be narrowed unless the growth rate of the less developed countries is greater than that of the developed ones. In my own view, this narrowing of the gap, which could be achieved as well by slowing the progress of the developed countries as by accelerating that of the less developed, is not an important objective of international development strategy. If the less developed countries not now able to sustain regular per capita growth at a reasonable rate of 2 or 3 per cent per year were, with the aid of the international community, enabled to achieve that capability, most of the other developmental goals they seek could sooner or later be brought within their grasp. It would be nice if some of them could at least partially overtake the earlier starters in the race, but this does not seem to me a useful way to formulate a key objective of development strategy.

Critical Bottlenecks to Growth: The Economic Anatomy of Take-off

While simple models of social and economic processes may be dangerously misleading, we can start our analysis with the elaboration of such a simple model that focuses our attention on the central role of capital accumulation in growth. The output of any

economy consists of a major part, which is goods and services currently consumed by the population, and a minor part called physical capital formation, which consists of additions to the stock of
productive assets that the economy has at its disposal. The fraction
or percentage of the national product devoted to capital formation
we call the rate of investment, or r.*

It is a characteristic of regularly growing developed economies
that their rates of investment are much higher—two or three times
as high, or more—than those of underdeveloped countries before
they have begun to grow. In developed economies, net investment
rates are 12 to 15 per cent or more, while in traditional economies
not yet developing, they are seldom higher than 5 or 6.

We need two more numbers for our simple model. The first is
the capital-output ratio, which tells us how much additional capital we must have to add one unit per year to the stream of output
that the economy can produce. If it takes an additional $3.00 worth
of productive assets to turn out an increase of $1.00 worth in the
annual stream of outputs, the capital-output ratio is 3. Clearly, this
number depends on the kind of output we are talking about and
the kind of productive assets it requires to produce it. In some sectors, like housing and electric power, capital-output ratios are quite
high, and in others, like agriculture and many services, quite low.
We can, however, find an average for a whole economy by dividing
the value of increases in all kinds of capital assets by the value of
the increase in total production associated with them. Interestingly
enough, when we measure this national average capital-output
ratio in both developed and underdeveloped economies, it turns
out to be a very similar number, usually somewhere between 2
and 4. It may, of course, be very much higher, if a country has
engaged in the wasteful accumulation of expensive and unproduc-
tive assets, and it may occasionally be lower, if a country has the
good fortune to turn out a large amount of additional product
with very little increase in its capital stock, as may occur, for in-

* Since some capital assets wear out or are used up during a year, part of
any year's production of capital assets is required merely to keep the stock of
assets constant. This part is included in what we call gross national product
and gross investment but must be deducted to arrive at the net product, which
is available either for consumption or for increasing the stock of productive
capital. Since we are interested in the role of capital formation in generating
growth in output, the r we are using here is *net* investment as a fraction of
net product.

stance, in agriculture in a bumper harvest year. But empirical studies suggest that, allowing for exceptions due to special circumstances, a trend of capital-output ratios will average out over the years, in both developed and underdeveloped countries, somewhere between 2 and 4. We can now find the growth rate of total output by dividing the rate of investment by the capital-output ratio. If the rate of investment is 9 per cent and the capital-output ratio 3, then the national product will grow at 3 per cent per year.

But this is not quite the end of the story. We are interested in a growth in per capita incomes, and if the population is expanding, some part of the growth of product will be required simply to supply the additional population with the same miserable standard of living that the present population already enjoys. We can now find the annual growth rate of per capita incomes, which we may call g, by subtracting the growth rate of population from the growth rate of national product given us by r divided by c/o. Our model is now complete and can be written in an algebraic formula as follows: *

$$g = \frac{c/o}{r} - p$$

It is important to note that this formula and the model it symbolizes is a tautology that, by itself, tells us nothing about the real world. It merely divides all the innumerable factors affecting per capita economic growth into three logically related segments, population growth, rates of capital formation, and everything else that is implicitly included in the productivity of capital expressed in the capital-output ratio. Since economists have come to believe that investments rates are one of the crucial variables, this separation is useful so long as it does not mislead us into forgetting all the other important factors of which we must take account. What the model suggests is that strategy to accelerate the rate of per capita economic growth should include three elements. There should be measures to increase the investment rate r, measures to

* Strictly speaking, it is more correct to divide the growth rate of product by a population index rather than to subtract the population growth rate, but for population growth rates of less than 5 per cent, which virtually all of them are, the result is nearly identical and the computation in the formula in the text is much simpler.

reduce the capital-output ratio or to prevent it from rising, as it has a tendency to do when investment rates expand rapidly, and measures to reduce the rate of population growth. In each of these areas, while the crucial requirement is policies and programs of the developing country itself, both the developed countries and the community of international institutions have an important part to play. We will take them up in turn.

There are two ways in which investment rates in developing countries can be increased. The country can increase the fraction of its own domestic production that it devotes to capital formation by reducing the fraction currently allocated to consumable goods and services; in other words, it can increase the rate of domestic saving. It can also acquire additional resources for capital formation from abroad, either by borrowing these resources from foreign governments, international institutions, or private holders of capital against future repayment, or by securing grants of resources on concessional terms, that is, foreign aid. What we have here called "borrowing" should be interpreted broadly to include equity investment by foreigners in the capital assets located in the developing country. We can thus think of r as composed of two parts. One part, which we can call s, consists of net domestic savings, and the other part, f, is the ratio of net capital resources transferred from abroad to the net national product of the recipient country. Thus, r is the sum of s and f. In order to get some reasonable numbers in mind, let us, for the moment, take a reasonable estimate of the average capital-output ratio for developing countries to be 3 and their population growth rate to be 2½. Then to raise the per capita growth rate to 2½ per cent per year, we must achieve a net investment rate of 15 per cent. For a country whose traditional savings rate has been 5 or 6 per cent, not enough currently even to maintain living standards constant, this is a difficult task.

There are two reasons why countries at the lower end of the income scale find it difficult to achieve self-sustaining growth entirely on the basis of domestic savings, that is, without any infusion of capital resources from abroad. The first is what is known in the literature as the low-income trap. If consumption for the bulk of the population is already barely above the subsistence level, it is not possible to reduce it to release resources for investment without severe human suffering. If a growth process can

15

once be launched and a significant fraction, perhaps 20 or 30 per cent, of the resulting increase in per capita income can be recaptured for plowback into capital investment, the savings rate can gradually be raised until, after two or three decades, the process can become self-sustaining. But in the initial stages, few countries can lift themselves by their own bootstraps.

The second reason why capital resources from abroad are needed to launch the development process does not emerge clearly from our model. Development requires a large supply of specific types of capital equipment and raw materials, which most underdeveloped countries either cannot produce at all within their borders or can produce only very inefficiently, with very high capital-output ratios. If the resources released by higher domestic saving could be converted into goods easily salable abroad, the country could earn the swelling volume of foreign exchange it requires to finance the imports associated with a development program. But for most countries in the early stages of the development process, a rapid expansion of exports encounters special difficulties. Markets for their traditional raw-material or tropical-product exports are not easily expanded, and the development of new export industries requires a transitional period of structural changes, capital investment, much of it imported, and the acquisition of new organizational and technical skills, which cannot be accomplished overnight. A few countries, like Venezuela and Libya, are fortunate enough to have a readily marketable natural resource that relieves them of this specific foreign-exchange bottleneck, but most are not so lucky. Thus, even if they were able to double or triple the domestic savings rate to release resources for investment, they could not earn the foreign exchange to buy the imports that such investment requires.

This review of the rate of investment as one of the key factors affecting growth permits us to identify two crucial bottlenecks whose elimination must be a key feature of development strategy. The first is the rate of domestic savings, which must somehow be substantially increased, and the second is the country's foreign-exchange earning capacity, which must also be raised to new and much higher levels. In other words, there is likely to be both a gap between the resources required to sustain a target rate of growth and the domestic savings available for this purpose, sometimes referred to as a savings gap, and a gap between the country's actual

16

and potential export earnings and its minimum requirement of imports to sustain a target growth rate, frequently called the foreign-exchange gap. The relative importance of these two gaps will vary widely from country to country, but measures by the host-country government to close both gaps are likely to be called for in most cases. Measures to raise marginal rates of saving include appropriately designed taxation, the restriction of both public and private consumption expenditures, the improvement of private capital markets and the adoption of a variety of incentives to higher levels of both business and individual saving, and appropriate pricing policies for government-operated and regulated industries. Measures to close the foreign-exchange gap include import-substituting investments, a variety of devices to promote the expansion of exports, skillful management and regulation of the foreign-exchange market, and a correct design of tariffs and subsidies on imports and exports of both goods and services.

There is a dilemma here. For a variety of reasons, to be explained shortly, measures to increase both the domestic rate of saving and net foreign-exchange earning capacity are both easier to take and more likely to be successful in an environment of rapid growth in per capita GNP than in a more sluggish economy. On the other hand, such rapid growth itself requires, as we have seen, both high levels of investment and burgeoning supplies of foreign exchange. It is this paradox that gives rise to the need in the early stages of development for substantial resource transfers from the developed countries to close both the savings gap and the foreign-exchange gap during a transitional period of years, until rapid self-sustaining economic growth can be assured. Since the justification for foreign aid on concessional terms is to provide the residual resources required after host countries have made all reasonable efforts to maximize both domestic savings and foreign-exchange earnings, the measures they have taken to this end are an appropriate concern of donor countries and of international agencies supplying capital resources for development.

With respect to capital transfers, in addition to foreign aid, or, to use the language of the Development Assistance Committee (DAC) of OECD, net official transfers, both developed and underdeveloped countries have a responsibility as part of their strategy to adopt measures to facilitate the flow of private foreign investment. In recent years, this flow of private capital from developed to underdeveloped countries has amounted to more than a third of the total resource transfers. While it is naïve to believe, as some do, that this ratio can be dramatically and suddenly increased, since privately and publicly supplied resources perform somewhat different functions, it should be an objective of the strategy of the international community gradually to raise this ratio over time, until, hopefully, the requirement for public transfers at concessional terms has disappeared.

How large should these financial transfers from the developed to the less developed countries be during the decade of the 1970's? During the 1960's, they have amounted to a little bit less than 1 per cent of the national incomes of the developed countries and to a fifth or a sixth of the total capital formation taking place in the less developed world. This, together with some improvement in capital-output ratios, to which we shall turn presently, has permitted an average growth of about 5 per cent per year in the gross product of the developing world. Calculations made by the U.N. Secretariat, by the U.N. Conference on Trade and Development (UNCTAD), and by various other analysts have suggested that, provided the developing countries make substantial efforts to raise their own savings rates, their foreign-exchange earning capabilities, and the productivity of investment, an increase in transfers from the developed world to 1 per cent of its gross national product, which is about 25 per cent higher than its national income, could make possible an acceleration of average growth rates of gross national product in the developing world to between 6 and 7 per cent, which would amount to growth rates of from 3 to 4½ per cent in per capita incomes. From two-thirds to three-quarters of these transfers might be in the form of official transfers, that is, aid both bilateral and through multilateral institutions, and the remainder might be private capital flows. This does not seem an impossible target at which to shoot.

How long might we expect such official transfers would have to be continued before the developing countries were able to stand on their own without extraordinary concessional assistance? It depends on a great many things. A large effort will do the job both more quickly and with less total resources than a half-hearted one proceeding at a slower pace.

Much depends, perhaps more than is often realized, on what

18

happens to both labor and capital productivity in the developing countries, that is, on all the things affecting the capital-output ratio that will be discussed in detail in the next section. The policies and strategies of the developed world on matters other than aid are also crucial. As development proceeds, it is probably generally the case that the importance of the savings gap as a factor limiting capital formation declines and that of the foreign-exchange gap rises. Thus, the possibilities of an early termination of aid depend increasingly crucially on export performance. This is determined partly by the strategies of the developing countries themselves but is importantly affected by the trade and foreign-exchange policies of the developed countries. While, for most of the transitional period, trade and aid policies are more fruitfully regarded as complementary parts of a common strategy than as alternative ways of achieving the same result, it is nonetheless true that policies to facilitate the access of underdeveloped country products to developed country markets can greatly accelerate the speed with which aid can be tapered off without interrupting development.

The geographical pattern of the resource transfers required to sustain development momentum will, of course, shift over time. Some of the large countries representing an important share, maybe half, of the population of the less developed world, like India, Pakistan, Turkey, and Brazil, should, with good management, be able to free themselves from dependence on concessional aid by the end of the decade of the 1970's. Others, further behind in the development process, like Indonesia and many of the countries of Africa, may require significantly longer. Continuing growth, even of the developed countries, can never be assumed to be automatic or assured, and development strategies, both national and international, will always be called for, but, insofar as the goal is self-sustaining growth without resource transfers on a concessional basis, this should be achievable for most countries by the end of the century at the latest.

While earlier diagnoses of the growth problem by economists tended to emphasize the obstacles to higher investment rates posed by the savings gap and the foreign-exchange gap that we have been discussing, there has been increased recognition of late of the importance of a wide range of elements in both national and inter-

19

national strategy designed to increase the productivity of resource use in the less developed countries or, in terms of our simple tautological model, to reduce the capital-output ratio or prevent it from rising as investment expands. Recent analyses of the sources of growth in the developed countries have suggested that a good deal less than half of their per capita growth can be accounted for by increases in capital employed per man with constant technology, and that the major part results from technological progress, improved education and skills of the labor force, exploitation of economies of scale, and improvements in the effectiveness of operation of a whole range of institutions from individual firms and farms through all kinds of markets, government organizations, and regulatory bodies. There is increasing recognition of the fact that the relative observed constancy of capital-output ratios means not that the productivity of capital and other resources has been relatively static but rather that a number of factors tending systematically to raise capital-output ratios as growth proceeds have been more or less offset by other elements tending to reduce them. In the first category have been such things as shifts in the composition of output toward more capital-using activities, the exhaustion of available land and other natural resources, and the substitution of capital for labor in a growing range of economic activities. Offsetting these on the other side have been improvements in technology resulting from invention and research and development, improvements in human capital brought about by education and training, economies resulting from large-scale production, and increased efficiency in the management of enterprises.

The offset has been only approximate when averaged over long periods, and the constancy of the aggregate capital-output ratio should not be exaggerated. Even what appear to be small changes can have large effects. Thus, a reduction of the aggregate capital-output ratio from 3 to 2 with an investment rate of 15 will raise the per capita growth rate by 2½ per cent per year. While there was wisdom in the early insistence of economists that growth cannot be changed solely by technical change or effectively promoted from outside by technical assistance alone without capital transfers, since the implementation of technical change usually requires substantial investment, it is equally true that without constant and systematic attention to increases in productivity rapid increases in investment rates are likely to bring offsetting increases in capital-output ratios. This is what is frequently meant by references to limitations on the absorptive capacity of an economy for increases in its rate of capital investment. Absorptive capacity can be raised by serious attention to productivity improvement, though there are, of course, limits to how far this is possible.

Recent developments in agriculture provide a good illustration of this relation between capital investment and productivity increases. Without the technological transformation made possible by the new miracle seeds in wheat, rice, and other grains, large increases in the agricultural output in many less developed countries could have been achieved only with an exorbitant investment in irrigation, fertilizer, and the like. While the new agricultural technology also takes large amounts of new capital, it produces so much new output that the resulting capital-output ratio can be held within tolerable bounds.

It is very much harder to generalize about strategies for productivity improvement than about ways to increase the investment rate, which is perhaps why economists are more prone to the latter type of generalization. Factors on which it is important to concentrate for productivity improvement depend intimately on the particular circumstances of the country in question and on the stage of the development process that it has reached. A checklist of the factors to be included as candidates for priority strategic attention would be something like the following:

1. The allocation of investment resources among major economic sectors such as agriculture, housing and construction, manufacture of consumer goods, production of intermediate and capital goods, improvements in such elements of infrastructure as transportation, communication, and power. For reasons to be explained presently, incorrect allocation can sharply reduce the average productivity of capital.

2. The adoption of technologies appropriate to the country's resource base. Thus, if, as in many countries, capital is very scarce and labor in superabundant supply, productivity can be increased by adopting labor intensive and capital-saving technologies.

3. Research, as, for instance, in agriculture, to develop new technologies particularly suited to the conditions prevailing in the country.

4. An appropriate balance between activities designed to replace imports with domestic production on the one hand and those intended to generate exports on the other.

5. Education, training, and the development of human resources.

6. The promotion and improvement of a wide variety of institutions, public and private, whose smooth functioning is important to the development process.

7. The right balance between excessive governmental efforts to regulate, control, and manage economic activity and inadequate attention to such regulation and control in areas where it is important.

8. The provision of a framework in monetary management, tax and fiscal policy, and the control of markets that will maximize the incentives for productivity improvements.

Virtually all these types of productivity improvements are related both to the level of investment and to the availability of external capital resources. Changes in structure, improvements in technology, expansion of education, the elaboration of new institutional forms are all much easier to achieve in a growing economy with high investment rates than in a sluggish economy with low ones. Thus, productivity improvement is not a growth-strategy alternative to one of increasing investment but rather a necessary complement.

The various measures to promote productivity increase categorized above are obviously primarily the responsibility of the governments of the developing countries themselves, and the priorities to be accorded these measures will vary widely from country to country, depending on its particular circumstances. Nevertheless, the international community has a double interest in these measures. First, since they affect in important ways the effectiveness of the capital transfers supplied by developed countries and international institutions, these bodies have a legitimate concern with what otherwise might be regarded as purely domestic responsibilities of the recipient governments. Second, the effectiveness of many of these productivity-promoting activities will be powerfully conditioned both by the technical assistance that the outside world is in a position to supply and by the international economic environment that it creates. While the cost of technical assistance to the developed countries has been modest relative to that of capital transfers—for the DAC countries, it has recently been running at 12 or 13 per cent of total transfers or 20 to 25 per cent of official transfers—its importance is much greater than this cost would imply. Both donors and recipients have a great deal to learn about how to make technical assistance more productive. There has been a tendency for these activities to be selected on the basis of targets of opportunity or of the special interests of those involved rather than on the basis of a country program worked out jointly between donors and recipients that identifies areas for priority attention on the basis of a systematic examination of the conditions in the country in question. While these conditions vary so widely that it is difficult to lay down general technical assistance strategies, it is clear that more attention must be devoted during the 1970's to the design of such strategies on a country-by-country basis.

Turning to the last element in the model, population strategies, there has been a rapidly growing recognition of their importance. While as recently as ten years ago very few countries had governmental programs for the promotion of family-planning, and technical assistance programs both bilateral and multilateral generally avoided the subject, there are now more than thirty countries with such programs and the list is growing rapidly, and technical assistance in population control has become an important and accepted part of many bilateral and multilateral aid programs. We should not exaggerate the contribution we can reasonably expect these programs to make to accelerated per capita income growth in the decade of the 1970's. Even when vigorously and effectively pursued they are, at best, very slow acting and will yield results only over the course of a good many years. Beyond this, in the absence of a vigorous strategy, there would be reasons to expect a considerable increase in population growth rates in a good many countries during the 1970's as death rates decline still further and the fraction of women of childbearing age in the population increases. This means that, at best, we should regard ourselves as successful in our efforts at population control if, by pursuing them vigorously, we are able to prevent a marked increase in growth rates by 1980. Important as prompt and effective population control measures are for the longer haul, the bulk of any increase in per capita growth

23

rates that we hope to achieve during the 1970's will have to come from a combination of higher levels of investment and increases in productivity.

Three Requirements for Take-off and Their
Implications for Strategy

There are three requirements that must be met if take-off is to occur, that is, savings and investment rates are to grow enough and capital-output ratios are to be kept low enough to make self-sustaining economic growth possible.

First, there must be a minimum level of effort across the board in all development activities, or what some writers have described as a "big push." Just as an airplane must acquire a certain minimum velocity to get off the ground at all, so for an undeveloped economy there is a threshold of investment and other types of activities that must be exceeded if development is to proceed. Above this threshold, the bigger the push both the better the chances of success and the shorter the period during which a foreign-aid booster will be required. Our simple model would suggest that results would probably be roughly proportional to effort, but, for reasons we shall explore in a moment, this is not the case. Low growth rates tend to be self-defeating, and high growth rates feed on themselves in a reinforcing way and generate still further expansion. Development is a perfect illustration of the Biblical paradox that to him who hath shall be given and from him who hath not, even that which he hath shall be taken away.

The second requirement is that it is necessary to undertake a great many growth-producing activities simultaneously. It would be much easier if we could find the key to growth in one or two leading activities like agriculture or education or steel mills or exports or transportation or power, concentrate on one or two priority sectors, and be confident that everything else would somehow take care of itself. There are some writers, like Albert Hirschman, who come very close to recommending this kind of an unbalanced growth strategy on the grounds that it alone will create the kinds of tensions that will motivate the correction of the imbalances. Unfortunately for this doctrine, there are a good many instances in the growth history of the last two decades in

24

which what started as promising but unbalanced growth has been brought to a halt by emerging bottlenecks in neglected sectors. Perhaps in the long sweep of history these will be viewed as transient episodes that ultimately change priorities in the right direction, but for many countries, time and their own internal dynamics do not permit the kind of learning by disaster that this prescription implies. If there is any promise in the notion of a conscious strategy to promote accelerated development, it surely lies partly in our capacity to see this as a systematic interaction of a large number of elements, to predict those that will become critical at later stages of the process, and to take steps now in anticipation of these future problems that will reduce their severity when they occur. Some imbalances are, to be sure, a necessary condition of growth, but when any leading sector gets too far ahead of the other sectors that must support and reinforce it, the result is likely, for reasons we shall explore presently, to be an interruption of momentum that may be very difficult to recapture.

The third requirement for take-off into self-sustained growth is a growth rate of exports and of the foreign-exchange earnings they make possible substantially larger than the over-all growth rate of GNP. In most economies, at the beginning of the growth process a substantial part of economic activity is of the subsistence variety dependent to a very limited extent on exchanges with other sectors of the economy or with the outside world. As development proceeds and an increasing fraction of economic activity is commercialized, the ratio of trade both domestic and foreign to production inevitably rises. Whatever the success of import substitution, the increasing complexity of production requires an increase in the ratio of imports to value added for the economy as a whole. This can obviously be sustained only if exports likewise represent a rising share of GNP. There are, of course, exceptions to these generalizations in the special circumstances of particular countries, but strategies that fail to recognize them adequately are unlikely to succeed.

Four Things to Watch—Reasons for the Three Requirements

These three requirements for take-off, a big push, reasonable sectoral balance, and a rapid expansion of foreign trade are related

25

to four characteristics of the development process that planners and strategists must bear in mind as they monitor and attempt to influence its progress. These are the rate of saving, and particularly the marginal saving rate, what we may call input-output balance, supply-and-demand balance, and the achievement in some kinds of production of economies of scale. We shall take them up in turn.

If total production expands only as rapidly as population, there is no rise in per capita incomes. Any rise in savings rates can then be accomplished only at the cost of an actual reduction in average levels of consumption. In very low income economies, this is physically difficult, and in democratic systems, usually politically impossible. While with rising per capita incomes some portion of the increase can by a variety of devices be captured for reinvestment, it is much more difficult if the rise is slow than if it is rapid. Widely announced development programs give rise to expectations for rising standards of living, which politicians are under strong pressure to meet. On the other hand, the intensity of these pressures is not closely related, especially in the short run, to the actual rate of growth of production. This means, in general, that the higher the growth rate of the economy the larger the fraction of the annual increment in per capita output can be captured for reinvestment, in other words, the higher the politically achievable marginal rate of savings. This is, of course, true for separate segments of the population as well as for the population as a whole. Thus, a modest over-all growth rate may permit high marginal savings rates if it is the result of very high growth in a limited sector of the economy accompanied by virtual stagnation elsewhere. Thus, if, for instance, a modest rate of growth in agriculture is achieved by averaging very rapid expansion of output and profits by a few farmers with a persisting low productivity of the majority, the marginal savings rate on the concentrated increases in income may be quite substantial. Or if, in a prosperous industry, general wage increases can be avoided and a large part of the growth in revenues channeled into profits, high marginal savings may be achievable even with modest over-all growth. But an explicit policy of a high concentration of income increments in the hands of a few violates the ethics and contradicts the politics of a democratic society. Thus, if development strategy is to be dedicated to raising savings rates while preserving a reasonably equitable distribution of the fruits of development, it has much better prospects at high aggregate growth rates than at low ones.

This is but one illustration of a series of conflicts between equity and productivity confronting development strategies, to which we shall return. Thus, on the assumption that there is a big push and that, for reasons of both equity and productivity, the growth in output and income is widely distributed over many sectors, strategy must be devoted to insuring that marginal savings rates, both public and private, are as high as possible. Public savings rates can be elevated in a number of ways. First, the tax structure must be designed to be as income sensitive as possible. Property and land taxes are poor from this point of view, income and excise taxes are much better. Second, the expansion of current public expenditures, especially those not directly related to productivity improvement, must be resisted in order to free resources for public capital investment. Educational expenditures, many of which are regarded in conventional budget practice as current, fall in a special category, since their purpose is frequently the expansion of human skills that should properly be considered a particularly valuable form of capital. Certainly the pricing policies of public enterprises, which in a number of less developed countries are quantitatively quite important, should, in general, be such as at least to cover full cost and may in some cases appropriately yield substantial net revenues. Public measures to encourage private savings include the design of taxes to inhibit consumption and reward investment, the development of institutions especially designed for the small saver, the promotion of insurance and pension schemes, and the systematic improvement of capital markets. Unless, by these various devices, marginal savings rates are raised to at least two or three times the level of average savings rates, the prospects for take-off are dim.

The second thing to watch is input-output balance. It is characteristic of an advanced economy that a large part of its product consists of intermediate goods or, to put it differently, that many producers produce outputs that are then purchased as inputs by other producers. These intermediate goods include all kinds of raw materials, many finished products, production services like transportation, communications, and power, and tools, equipment, spare parts, and factory buildings. In developed economies, producing units in agriculture, industry, and services also rely on

27

financial, legal, informational, commercial, and other services supplied by other organizations. In primitive economies, these intermediate transactions, apart from trade, represent a very small part of total economic activity. One way of characterizing development is by the growing importance of intermediate activities and the increasing interdependence of economic units that it reflects. This is revealed by what the economist describes as input-output analysis. In a developed economy, a fairly full complement of intermediate goods and services can be presumed to be available, and a new economic activity is seldom inhibited by shortages of critical intermediate goods and services. In rapidly developing economies, on the other hand, the proliferating demands for these intermediate inputs are frequently not properly anticipated and plants may stand idle for some time for want of raw materials, power, or transport; new agricultural techniques may not be adopted because farmers cannot obtain the requisite fertilizer, seed varieties, or pumps; or factories or power plants run short of fuel.

In developed economies with highly organized markets, the market process rapidly takes care of most of these adjustments, but in rapidly developing economies, the bottlenecks are not always recognized and, when recognized, may take a long time to overcome. Fortunately for the underdeveloped countries of the modern world, many of these deficiencies can be overcome, at least in the short run, by international trade, which is one reason why import requirements grow more rapidly than GNP. But they cannot all be dealt with this way. Many things like domestic transport, power, and some materials and services cannot be imported, and, in any case, as we have seen, the total import capacity of the less developed countries is severely limited. This means that in a development program a good many activities must be pursued simultaneously and also that development planners must keep a careful eye on input-output balances so that, making due allowances for foreign trade, future physical bottlenecks that might seriously interfere with growth can be foreseen and avoided before they occur. Much of the planning literature in both Western and socialist countries is concerned with how this input-output balance can be both correctly estimated and assured. The problem is rendered more complicated by the fact, elaborated further below, that some producing activities can be carried on effectively and

28

at acceptable cost only on a scale larger than the market of a poor underdeveloped country can justify.

The third thing that development strategists must watch is balance of a slightly different sort between the supply of and the demand for a variety of kinds of final goods. In a primitive economy, the bulk of economic activity is devoted directly to meeting the subsistence needs in food, clothing, and shelter of the producers themselves, and a relatively small fraction of output enters into the process of exchange. As development proceeds, many new commercial activities are launched in agriculture, industry, and services that both generate additional physical products available for exchange and additional purchasing power for the producers. In a smoothly functioning market economy, the pricing system operates in such a way as to call forth additional supplies of the things that are demanded with increments of income, or, looked at the other way around, it insures that income is generated sufficient to support effective demand for the new production that results from growth. Unfortunately, in a developing economy, where markets are imperfect and the pattern of investment decisions is affected by government policy and other nonmarket forces, these supply-demand balances cannot be taken for granted.

As with input-output imbalances, distortions tend to generate forces that will in time correct them, and some imbalances are necessary engines of change. Shortages create price increases that both reduce less essential demands and stimulate increases in supply. Surpluses reduce prices, encouraging consumption and discouraging further increases in output. Elementary texts describe how this is supposed to work and how it does, indeed, approximately work in large areas of developed economies. In underdeveloped economies undergoing rapid changes in structure and institutions as well as in policies and programs, these forces either sometimes work inversely or too slowly to prevent imbalances from causing crippling interruptions in the national growth process. Here, too, foreign trade is a partial safety valve. If shortages appear, they can be tempered by imports, and if, as frequently happens, capacity excess to domestic needs has temporarily been created, it may be possible to exchange products abroad if domestic costs are not too high. But for a variety of reasons too lengthy to catalog here, foreign trade is only a partial corrective to the kinds of supply/demand imbalances that imperfect policies and the strains of the development process almost always generate. For this reason, planners must watch for signs of these distortions, forecast their probable emergence, and be prepared to take prompt corrective action when they occur.

The fourth thing to watch, closely related to the other three, is how, in a variety of kinds of activities, efficiency and productivity vary with the size and scale of the individual enterprise. If the nature of technology were such that all commodities could be produced as efficiently in very small quantities as in large ones, many of the most serious problems of the early stages of development would disappear. Input-output balance and supply-demand balance could be relatively easily achieved, even at very low levels of income, by initiating a large number of initially very small-scale activities. The tonic of competition would be operative even in fields where the total level of production was modest. Beyond this, the equitable spread of new kinds of economic activity to insure wide participation in both the process of development and its fruits, both geographically and among all classes of the population, would pose relatively few dilemmas.

Unfortunately, technological reality is not like this. A railroad between two points must carry a minimum amount of traffic to be worth constructing at all, power from small generating plants is several times as expensive as from large ones, a telephone network serving many people is inherently cheaper per person than one serving very few, and there is a minimum scale of output for which, for technical reasons, most manufacturing operations must be designed if costs are to be kept low. This is partly a matter of history. Much modern technology has emerged in relatively large, relatively developed economies with markets big enough to provide little incentive for small-scale innovation. There has been much talk of the need for research on small-scale technology, which would be efficient for low-income countries. But there are facts of nature that make this an uphill battle at best. A large pipe inherently requires less steel per gallon of capacity than a small one. Moving assembly lines cut average costs, but only when a certain volume of production has been reached.

Economies of scale that resist efforts to remove them by ingenious innovation in small-scale operations pose serious dilemmas for development planners. There is a point in a rapidly growing

30

domestic market when it is worth shifting from imports to domestic production, even though initial sales will be considerably smaller than the output of a plant of optimum size because, in time, with the growth of demand, its capacity will be fully utilized. What this point is depends on the real costs of foreign exchange, on the behavior of production costs with output, and on the rate at which domestic demand is expected to continue to grow. For nonimportable items like power and transport, whose availability is an important factor conditioning other investment decisions, there is a case for building well ahead of demand even if, for a time, this requires some subsidy. Economies from concentrating production in one firm or location must be weighed against the often intangible benefits of promoting competition and distributing development activities widely. Economies of scale may be such that the foreseeable domestic market alone would not justify investment but the domestic market, together with a realistically achievable export market, might. While no simple rules of strategy can be laid down, it is clear that the behavior of costs with scale is one of the important things for a planner to watch, and that many policy decisions will be crucially affected by this kind of information.

The relationship of economies of scale to our three requirements for take-off should be obvious. On the big push, the more rapidly the economy grows, the sooner large numbers of new kinds of economic activity become feasible. As it grows, a good many kinds of costs go down, stimulating still further growth. On balance, many kinds of interdependent and necessary activities are impractically costly at low levels of income but become efficiently possible at higher ones. On foreign trade, many of the new requirements development generates must be met, at least initially, with imports, because domestic demand is still too small to make production on an efficient scale possible. On the other hand, in some lines, rapid export expansion can provide the additional justifying market.

In summary, then, we have concluded that the take-off strategies of the developing countries require massive effort, a balance of a wide variety of activities, and a special emphasis on foreign trade, and that, in the process, planners must pay close attention to marginal savings rates, to input-output balance, to supply-demand balance, and to economies of scale. At the same time, the discus-

31

sion should have made clear the essential role to be played during this process by resource transfers, both public and private, from the developed countries, by transfers of technology and the invention of new technology through technical assistance, and by the establishment by the world community of a trading environment favorable to the expansion of underdeveloped country exports.

Monetary and Fiscal Strategy

We have said nothing up to this point about the monetary and fiscal environment in which all this physical developmental activity takes place. In developed countries, monetary and fiscal policy are important instruments of growth strategy. Most underdeveloped countries have monetary systems in which the availability of credit is subject to influence by the central bank and the treasury authorities, and virtually all of them confront the problem of managing the relation between government income and expenditure so as to yield a deficit or surplus of the desired size. Can we lay down any general rules for the strategy to be followed by the governments of underdeveloped countries in manipulating these instruments?

Financial and price-level behavior in the developing countries has revealed over the past couple of decades a wide range of patterns, from the chronic hyperinflation that has characterized a number of Latin American countries and, until recently, Indonesia, to fiscal conservatism and rather unusual price stability. While there are exceptions to this, as to virtually all generalizations about development, it is still broadly true that the most rapidly growing countries have fallen somewhere in the middle of the spectrum, with rates of inflation of a few percentage points a year, while those at the extremes both of hyperinflation on the one side and price stability on the other have, in general, done somewhat less well in growth. There are reasons to believe that some upward price pressure is hard to avoid in a rapidly growing economy, but that growth can be inhibited both by excessively restrictive monetary and fiscal policy and by policies that permit hyperinflation.

It is not hard to see why some upward price pressure is likely to be associated with vigorous growth. For reasons we have already explored, growth is likely to be accompanied by rapid structural change and the appearance of successive bottlenecks in different segments in the economy. Growth will only be vigorous if the economy is straining against these bottlenecks. In imperfect markets, where institutional forces inhibit wage and price declines in areas of relative surplus, a level of demand strong enough to keep substantial pressure on the bottleneck areas is likely to result in some inflation. This is particularly true if the bottleneck areas are an important determinant of gross product like agricultural production or imports. If monetary and fiscal policy is restrictive enough to prevent these bottlenecks from affecting key elements in the price structure, it is probably inhibiting growth. This is the element of validity in what has been termed the structural interpretation of inflation in the less developed countries. They face, in enhanced form and for somewhat different reasons, somewhat the same dilemma that has become familiar in developed countries between reasonably full employment of resources and price stability. While it is customary to argue that, for structural reasons, Keynesian deficiencies of aggregate demand are usually not the explanation for stagnation in low-income countries, and, accordingly, expansionist monetary and fiscal policies are not an appropriate cure, there are certainly cases in which these policies have been restrictive enough to inhibit growth that might otherwise have occurred.

On the other hand, when rapid price inflation is permitted to persist and to become endemic, not only will serious inequities be created but growth may well be inhibited in a variety of ways. The structure of investment and production is likely to be distorted toward residential real estate, inventories, and other easily marketable forms of capital. While inflation may increase some forms of private savings, it discourages the small saver who does not have access to the forms of investment that can give him protection from its consequences. The management of foreign exchange in such a way as to promote the expansion of exports so necessary to development, while not impossible, is rendered much more difficult by rapid inflation and is likely to be beyond the management capabilities of most developing country governments.

Thus, the goal of monetary and fiscal policy should be to keep aggregate demand growing rapidly enough to keep a constant gentle pressure on supply bottlenecks, and where there is a choice of methods for doing this, to do it in such a way as to stimulate investment and inhibit consumption. Direct action to ameliorate

33

supply bottlenecks must be an essential feature of development strategy, but an appropriate fiscal and monetary policy is a necessary supporting element. A gently rising price level—no more than a few percentage points a year at most—is very rough evidence that the degree of monetary and fiscal restraint is neither too great to limit demand unduly nor too ineffective to inhibit the gross inequities and structural distortions that chronic inflation normally brings with it. Putting the brakes on a process of price inflation to which a society has become adjusted, as have some of the Latin American economies, poses special problems of economic and political management too complex and too peculiar to the special circumstances of each particular country to be discussed here. But perhaps enough has been said to indicate the broad outline of a fiscal and monetary policy that will support growth.

A Strategy for Foreign Trade: Import Substitution and Export Expansion

We have already made clear why import requirements generally grow more rapidly than gross national product for countries immersed in the economic development process. On the other hand, the prospects for a corresponding expansion of the traditional raw-material and agricultural exports of the less developed countries to the developed world are very poor. The demand for many of these products goes up in the developed countries, if at all, much more slowly than income. It is doubtful whether Americans could drink very much more coffee no matter how much richer they were, and the development of synthetic substitutes has made the prospect for a radical expansion in the consumption of raw materials like rubber and jute very gloomy. In addition, even modest fluctuations in the world production of many of these traditional commodities produce large fluctuations in their world prices, which create great instability in the export earnings of the producing countries. These various factors make a world strategy for the management of international trade an essential part of any over-all development strategy.

Such a trade strategy can have a number of elements. In the first place, the developing countries can hold down their import requirements both by measures to inhibit the demand for imports not essential to growth and by encouraging where possible the production of domestic substitutes for some of the items that growth requires. Second, these countries can, with the help of the developed countries, stimulate an expansion and diversification of their exports and, in particular, exports of processed and manufactured items. Third, foreign exchange earnings from the more traditional commodity exports can be stabilized by a variety of commodity stabilization schemes, such as those in effect for coffee and wheat. All of these techniques, but especially the second and third, require for their success the active collaboration and co-operation of the governments of the developed countries.

The appropriate combination of commodity stabilization, import substitution, and export expansion depends on the resource potential, size, level of development, and rate of growth of the particular developing country. Both import substitution and export promotion are easier at high levels of income and rapid growth rates than for low income or slow-growing countries. Because of economies of scale and the absence of the variety of technical and managerial skills required for manufacturing operations, countries with low incomes and small markets find it particularly difficult to get new enterprises of this kind launched and operated at a level of efficiency that can be internationally competitive. Here, again, we see the virtues of the big push. For countries at the low end of the scale, heavily dependent for their export earnings on one or two tropical products or raw materials, stabilization schemes that reduce price fluctuations through the manipulation of bumper stocks, limit competitive sales in surplus years, and meet the demand from stock in years of shortage can be helpful if skillfully administered. Experience has, however, taught us a number of things about the requirements for success in these operations. First, all major producers and consumers of the commodity in question must participate in and abide by the rules of the agreement if it is not to break down. Second, it must be recognized as a device that can stabilize foreign-exchange earnings from commodity sales but cannot increase their average level over time. Because of the low income elasticity of demand for most of these products in developed countries already referred to, stabilization schemes are not a solution to the long-run problem of increasing export earnings for the developing countries. They frequently break down because of an effort to hold prices above levels that can be sustained by

35

world demand, which results in chronic excess production and the resulting collapse of the agreement. They are most promising when associated with systematic efforts by the producing countries to withdraw resources from the production of the commodity and to divert them to a more diversified range of products. They can be a useful tool for dealing with short-term fluctuations, and the international community should pursue their extension to additional commodities for this purpose, but the long-range solution to the trade problems of the developing countries must be pursued by the other two routes of import substitution and export expansion and diversification.

Here, the problem is complicated by the fact that practice in supplying a domestic market is frequently a necessary prelude to acquiring the efficiency required for international competition. Import substitution can be encouraged by high tariff protection and quantitative restrictions on imports. This is the so-called infant-industry argument for protection in developing countries. But if the level of protection is too high or the domestic market too small to achieve economies of scale, the infants may never grow up and efficiency never be achieved. The new industries in which the developing countries will ultimately turn out to have a comparative advantage are very hard to predict in advance and are much more likely to be discovered by a process of trial and error than by any systematic technique of analysis and planning so far developed. The problem confronting the trade policies of countries in the early stages of development is how to retain the tonic effect of some international competition without killing infant industries at birth and creating impossibly disruptive balance-of-payments problems.

This requires art as much as science. A number of elements of the solution requiring the cooperation of the developed countries may be sketched in. First, there must be financial transfers to the developing countries during the transitional period, when they are restructuring production, sufficient to permit them to avoid levels of import protection and regulation so high that the trial-and-error process cannot work because the errors are never discovered. The purpose of aid is not only to provide the margin of indispensable imports without which a country literally cannot grow at all but, beyond this, to furnish the extra margin that permits some testing of the efficiency of local production and the weeding out of in-

36

herently high-cost enterprises. This will not work if the management of imports is inept, but it cannot work if foreign exchange is so scarce that almost any domestic production, however inefficient, seems worthwhile.

Second, a partial substitute for competition with developed country production is competition with other underdeveloped countries for each other's markets. This, plus the economies of scale that a larger market makes possible, is the attraction of regional common-market agreements like the Central American Common Market, the Latin American Free Trade Area, and the regional agreements being considered in Africa and Asia. There has been a tendency for import substitution in some countries to concentrate on consumer goods, where the problems of economies of scale are less severe. But, over time, a growing fraction of the capital-goods requirements of the less developed countries are going to have to be supplied by those countries themselves. Regional agreements, which enlarge the market for individual producers, can greatly facilitate this process.

Third, however much trade among the developing countries can be expanded, there will also be a need for a radical expansion of exports to developed countries to finance the swelling flow of development goods that only those countries can efficiently supply. Since, as we have already seen, this expansion cannot take the form of raw materials or tropical products, measures to stimulate the export of manufactures from underdeveloped to developed countries are required. The developed countries maintain a large number of restrictions on the importation from the underdeveloped countries of processed goods and manufactures whose elimination is essential to the expansion of trade that must be part of any development strategy. In addition, there is a strong case for the temporary preferential treatment of underdeveloped country products in the tariff and quota schedule of the developed countries such as was proposed at the last meeting of the U.N. Conference on Trade and Development (UNCTAD). If, as is to be hoped, the general level of barriers to international trade is reduced over the next two or three decades, these preferences would automatically be reduced and disappear as the need for them declined. While some industries in some developed countries may suffer in this process, the experience with Japan and other rapidly developing countries confirms that the benefits to all parties of the rapid

37

expansion of trade that development makes possible far outweigh the costs to special interests that this kind of a policy involves.

The fourth requirement is that the policies of underdeveloped countries with respect to the international valuation of their currency should be realistic. There is a tendency, particularly in countries subject to strong inflationary pressures, for official exchange rates to come to reflect an over-valuation of the domestic currency in relation to the currencies of the developed countries. While the effects of this over-valuation, which stimulates imports and discourages exports, can, in theory, be largely offset by the detailed regulation of foreign trade through import tariffs, quotas, and licensing and special export subsidies and incentives, this procedure imposes a heavy drain on what is likely to be one of the scarcest resources in underdeveloped countries, namely, economic managerial and administrative competence. For this reason, it is likely both to be relatively ineffective and to divert energies from areas where this kind of competence is indispensable. Realistic exchange rates never wholly eliminate the need for careful foreign-exchange management, but they can greatly reduce the burden on such management, and anything that reduces the need for administrative regulation helps to break one of the most critical bottlenecks to growth.

In summary, then, foreign-trade policies of both underdeveloped and developed economies are a crucial element in development strategy. Commodity stabilization schemes have an important function to perform, provided they are designed with a clear eye to the limited contribution they can make to the over-all trade problem. Import substitution and export promotion strategies are required both in different mixes and with different timing, depending on the circumstances of the individual case. Measures adopted to promote both must be selected with a view to rewarding productivity increase and to penalizing persistent inefficiency. While substantial foreign aid can be a prop to wrong allocations and incorrect policies, it is a necessary handmaiden during the transitional period to valid foreign-trade strategies. Regional agreements among developing countries, reduction of developed country barriers to underdeveloped country exports, and a system of temporary preferences for less developed country manufactures all have a place in the strategy, as does realistic foreign-exchange management.

38

Illustrative Discussion of the Balance Between
Agriculture and Industry

The problem of the proper balance between efforts in agriculture and in the rest of the economy is a pervasive one that illustrates many of the dilemmas of development strategy, which we have discussed above, confronting both the governments of developing countries and those in the developed countries and in international institutions who wish to assist them. In traditional economies not yet launched on vigorous development programs, there is relatively little interconnection between the bulk of the economy devoted to subsistence agriculture and that smaller segment engaged in plantation production for export, in mineral extraction, or in commerce and the beginnings of manufacture in the limited urban communities. These economies are sometimes described as dual economies, in which the subsistence sector and the modern sector have relatively little to do with each other. As development proceeds, with the technological changes increasing the productivity of agriculture and with the appearance of many new types of commercial and industrial activity, both the input-output connections and the supply-demand connections between the agricultural and the nonagricultural sectors grow rapidly in importance.

Looking first at the input-output connections, we see that these run both ways, involving the increased dependence of newly emerging industry on agricultural inputs and the increased requirements of agriculture for inputs from industry. Many of the most promising industrial opportunities in the early stages of development, feasible then because they involve only modest economies of scale, involve the processing of agricultural commodities. These include food processing, textiles, paper, woodworking, and the like. Studies have shown that in countries that have proceeded some distance down the development path, in which nonagricultural activities have produced a rising share of gross national product, 60 to 70 per cent of the manufacturing and processing activity is based on agricultural inputs. The demand for these inputs constitutes a growing share of the total demand for the products of agriculture.

On the other hand, the new agricultural technology that lies at

39

the heart of the "green revolution," which promises such dramatic increases in agricultural yield, is based on a transformation of agriculture from a relatively self-contained process, producing its own seed and relying primarily on the nutrients and water made freely available by nature, to something very like an industrial process, using land as a matrix for production but heavily dependent on large purchased inputs of commercially produced seed, fertilizer, complex water management frequently requiring electric power, pesticides and weed inhibitors, and some new kinds of implements. Some of the processes involved in supplying these new nonagricultural inputs required by modern agriculture, such as fertilizer production and large-scale irrigation, are subject to very marked economies of scale and cannot be efficiently produced in small quantities. If farmers are to be able to buy these new inputs so necessary to increases in their productivity and incomes, they must sell a much larger fraction of their total product than is customary in subsistence agriculture.

Similar considerations underlie the growth of supply-demand interconnections. As development proceeds, the population moves out of agriculture to cities, and an increasing fraction of the labor force is involved in nonagricultural activity. This means that to feed and clothe these urban workers, an increasing fraction of agricultural output must be sold to them. This can occur only if nonagricultural incomes are rising rapidly enough to permit these people to buy larger quantities of agricultural products. At the same time, agricultural incomes must also be rising, both to permit the investment that the new agriculture requires and to finance the purchase of the increasingly urbanized standard of living that farmers come to aspire to.

This increasing interdependence between the agricultural and the nonagricultural sectors of the economy also means, of course, that there are greatly increased requirements throughout the countryside for improved facilities for transport, communications, and the like. These various kinds of balances are unlikely to be achieved if priority attention is concentrated either on industrial or on agricultural development. They are also unlikely to be achieved unless the growth of the whole economy is vigorous, that is, unless there is a big push. But a rapid expansion of production in many directions at once, in both agriculture and industry, means

40

a very high rate of investment and soaring demands for imports. With domestic demand rising rapidly, there are difficulties in the simultaneous rapid expansion of production for export. Thus, during the transition, there is an especially urgent need for foreign aid, in the form of both capital and technical assistance, with the new agricultural and industrial activity.

This problem of the balance between agriculture and industry is closely related to the problems of fiscal and monetary management. If agricultural production lags while nonagricultural incomes are rising, the excess demands for food create strong upward pressures in an important segment of the cost-of-living index. If the government attempts to deal with these inflationary pressures by the traditional technique of a restrictive monetary and fiscal policy, as happened in India during the two bad monsoon years of 1965 and 1966, the industrial growth may well be choked off and a general recession result. If, on the other hand, government attempts through an easy fiscal and monetary policy to maintain industrial vigor, the rise in the cost of living induced by agricultural shortages creates strong pressures for wage increases that stimulate the inflation still further and may well make it cumulative.

On the other hand, if the balance is pushed too far the other way, that is, if agriculture is actively promoted and industry allowed to lag, as seems to be in danger of happening in some of the green-revolution countries, another set of problems is created. Unless there is an easily available foreign market, the slackness of demand outside agriculture may cause agricultural surpluses to appear, leading to a weakening of agricultural prices and preventing the rise that would otherwise occur in agricultural income. At the same time, the industrial inputs required by the new agriculture will not be available in adequate quantity and thus, for both demand and supply reasons, the agricultural expansion may well be interrupted. Thus, while in the traditional economy these two sectors are relatively insulated from each other, in a rapidly modernizing one inadequate progress in either rapidly spreads and inhibits growth in the other. While reduced over-all growth will temporarily ease the foreign-exchange situation, it postpones to a still more distant future its ultimate solution. While this is one of the more dramatic instances of the need for balance, many other sorts of imbalances will create comparable problems.

41

How Much and What Kinds of Planning? Comments on the Role of the State

A central problem confronting planners and politicians in the developing countries is how many of the allocation decisions about resource use are to be made administratively directly by government agencies, how many are to be closely controlled by licensing and regulatory procedures, and how many may safely be left to individual private decisions in response to market forces. A case can be made intellectually for two extreme alternatives. Where markets are well organized, information is widely available, competition is vigorous, incomes are reasonably fairly distributed, and rapid changes in the environment do not interfere with gradual adjustment to emerging disequilibria, it can be shown that a reasonably free price-and-market system will provide most of the incentives for individual enterprises to meet the conditions necessary to satisfy the requirements of development. Alternatively, where knowledge is fairly complete, administrative talent that is effective and honest is abundantly available, and a sufficient quantum of analytic skills is present in government centralized planning and decision-making can theoretically produce consistent and desirable results. Unfortunately, neither of these sets of conditions obtains to any significant degree in developing countries. In consequence, neither extreme laissez-faire with maximum freedom for private decision-makers nor comprehensive regulation and control from a central administrative authority is likely to be an effective way to promote development.

The best record seems to have been turned in so far by the mixed systems. Even the classic centrally planned economies, like that of the Soviet Union, with effective political control and large disciplined and well-trained cadres of administrators, have been moving toward decentralization and increasing use of market forces. The less developed countries, with much more limited administrative resources and a much deeper tradition of the predominance of personal and caste loyalties over organizational ones, are much less well equipped to make a centrally directed administrative system function effectively.

On the other hand, even in the United States, with the most

highly organized market system man has yet devised and with a reasonably wide distribution of economic power and influence, an increasing role has been found necessary for regulation, control, and public intervention to protect the public interest. In the less developed countries, where markets are much more primitive, less sensitive, and less competitive and where private incomes and economic influence are, in general, more concentrated, the need for intervention is substantially greater. One of the paradoxes of the Third World is that, in many cases, governmental controls whose purpose is to prevent abuses of concentrated power have precisely the opposite effect. Complex licensing and regulatory procedures designed to prevent socially undesirable resource use frequently create a situation where only the large and powerful family or organization has the contacts, skills, and resources to extract what it wants from the bureaucracy or to evade its rules, while the small man can neither manipulate the system nor escape it.

Perhaps the most one can say without going into cases is to give the not very helpful advice that the mix between freedom and control should be essentially pragmatically determined. In view of the shortage of administrative and bureaucratic talent, planners should look actively for as many areas as possible in which market forces can be made to work tolerably effectively. The case for minimum regulation is less an ideological one than the urgent necessity to conserve the limited administrative resources and talents of the less developed countries for areas in which market forces either cannot work or work badly, like taxation, foreign exchange management, the management of public budgets, and the direction of enterprises that must be public because private entrepreneurs will not undertake them. Because of the rapidity of change, the interdependence of public and private activities, and the prevalence of what are called external economies in the development process, something we can call comprehensive planning, looking forward some years for all sectors of the economy, is probably called for. Plans should specify not only targets and goals but the steps required to be taken by both public and private agencies to implement them, with a clear specification of the time scheduling required for these steps. In other words, they should project the presumed evolution of the economy and of its various parts forward over a number of years, in a fashion that will permit forewarning of possible bottlenecks and suggest measures that must be taken to avoid them. Prompt and current information that will permit the monitoring of progress under plans in both public and private sectors is essential. This will reveal the areas where market forces are operating well and those where incentives need to be altered or private activities regulated because they conflict with developmental goals. We badly need a theory of the conservation of administrative talents in government that will tell us how to maximize the productivity of the very scarce administrative resources of an underdeveloped country. It is on these grounds that the choice between regulation and control on one hand and free private decision-making on the other should be made.

Resolving Conflicts of Objectives

Before concluding this discussion of development strategies, it is worth calling attention to a few of the dilemmas that confront the policy-makers of the developing world and thus, indirectly, the governments and international organizations interested in the success of the Second Development Decade, because of the variety of only partially consistent goals that development is supposed to promote. Where these dilemmas exist, their resolution depends on the preferences and values of the people of the country concerned. But the rest of the world has a legitimate interest not only in insuring that their existence is recognized but also in knowing how each country decides to handle them.

The first of these dilemmas is that between growth and equity, that is, the conflict between measures to enhance productivity and thus increase the rate of growth, on one hand, and those designed to insure an equitable distribution of the fruits of development to all sectors of the population, on the other. This conflict can take many forms. One is that a skewed distribution of income may produce higher marginal savings rates than a more equal and therefore fairer distribution. Some countries, for instance, sharply limit profits in the interests of equity and thus reduce savings that would otherwise be plowed back into enterprise. More steeply progressive income-tax rates may simply transfer private savings to government hands, while more regressive sales taxes may actually inhibit consumption and thus increase the total of available savings. This conflict may also arise in policies that deal with unemployment. In a great many underdeveloped countries, the ratio of manpower to capital is so large that no efficient combination of labor and capital that will maximize the productivity of capital and thus minimize the capital output ratio can possibly provide employment for the entire available labor force. Under these circumstances, even high rates of growth of GNP may not suffice to draw into employment the additions to the labor force created by rapid population growth, and in the absence of special measures to support rather inefficient labor intensive activities, levels of unemployment may rise, creating severe inequities. In these circumstances, planners may be confronted with a choice between uses of capital that will maximize growth and less efficient uses that, while they will slow the growth rate, will offer employment opportunities to a larger number of people. If labor intensive activities that employ very little capital and yield a significant product can be found, the sacrifice of output may be small, but the search for such activities has not been very rewarding to date.

A third form the dilemma may take occurs when the most productive way to introduce a new technology such as the new miracle varieties of wheat and rice in agriculture, for example, is to concentrate capital and other resources on the small fraction of producers who are best equipped to handle the new method, who will frequently be among the most affluent, thus increasing their affluence and leaving the large body of producers behind. The cost in productivity of trying to distribute the new technology and the resources that go with it more uniformly may be disastrously high, but the consequences for equity of a policy of concentration on the most productive minority may be very severe. Efforts should, of course, continue to be made to find ways of removing these dilemmas by inventing techniques of income equalization that will not reduce savings, labor intensive technologies that will give a high productivity to capital, and ways of introducing new methods that can benefit large rather than small groups in the population. It is, unhappily, necessary to report that efforts in these directions in the past have not been very successful.

Where the dilemma persists in the face of committed efforts to remove it, one is forced to the further unpopular conclusion that sacrifices of productivity to insure apparent equity are very likely simply to insure permanently equal misery. There is too little to redistribute in low-income countries to benefit anybody very much,

45

and the only hope for their poorer classes lies in a securely growing per capita GNP. But our whole earlier analysis emphasizes the critical importance for this result of both higher savings rates and improved productivity. To sacrifice these for equity in the short run is to kill the goose that lays the golden egg.

A second conflict of objectives related to growth vs. equity but somewhat different in character, we may call economic progress vs. social welfare. Many expenditures for purposes we think of as included in the social welfare category increase economic productivity up to a point, and to that extent they are complementary rather than competitive to growth. Thus, a good deal of expenditure in education can be justified directly in economic growth terms, improvements in health undoubtedly increase labor productivity, and there is some evidence that better housing has a similar effect. But the amounts of education, health services, and housing that are socially desirable are certainly far in excess of those that could be justified by the contributions they make to economic output. These and other social welfare activities are very costly in resource use and thus, if carried beyond the point of their maximum contribution to productivity, compete directly with growth. The connection with equity is that universal education is certainly an equalizer of opportunities for advancement, and the wide availability of health and housing services is a symbol of government's concern with the equitable treatment of all classes of its population. Here again, while the ultimate choice in cases where the conflict arises must lie with the political process of the country concerned, a warning is in order that too great a sacrifice of growth may well deprive the country of the resources required to sustain improving social welfare services.

A third type of conflict of objective revolves around the relative weight to be given to raising the incomes and improving the welfare of city-dwellers, on the one hand, and improving conditions in rural communities, on the other. Again, the large elements of complementarity here were underlined in our discussion of the balance between agriculture and industry. Since it is necessary to promote growth in both and improvements in one tend to benefit the other, the dilemma is less severe than it is sometimes believed to be. Nevertheless, there are problems. Where government has opportunities to influence the level of agricultural prices, there will be strong pressures from low-income urban groups to keep these down, while rising incomes and productivity in agriculture require that they be prevented from falling and possibly even supported at levels above equilibrium ones. There will be continuing problems of the optimal distribution between rural and urban activities of all the scarce resources crucial to growth, such as investable funds, foreign exchange, skilled manpower, and administrative time and attention. There is very likely to be a further regional problem. The rural areas of many countries are likely to be divided into regions, some of which are endowed with abundant water, productive land, and vigorous farm entrepreneurship with already relatively high incomes and the capacity to innovate, while others are backward, sluggish, and depressed. Rural productivity is likely to be advanced most rapidly by concentrating investment and other resources in both the cities and the already prosperous agricultural communities, while regional equity demands that something special be done about the backward areas.

A failure to respond to the demands and aspirations of under-developed rural areas, in addition to being inequitable, may create severe political strain, which will prevent the national system as a whole from continuing to function effectively. On the other hand, here, too, the sacrifice of productivity advance for regional equity may so reduce the growth rate that the nation's chance of ever assembling the massive resources required to develop its most un-developed regions may be permanently forgone.

Finally, there is a political dilemma whose resolution has important consequences for economic growth. We can characterize it as participation vs. control. We indicated earlier that one of the social objectives of many of the governments of developing countries is to heighten and extend participation in the modernization process by all elements in the population. Heightened participation requires improved organization and control if it is to be constructive rather than disruptive. With very limited organizational and administrative talents, the governments of underdeveloped countries may find it difficult to prevent rapidly spreading participatory activity from destroying the tenuous elements of order that the regime is struggling to impose. On the other hand, if order and system are imposed too repressively, the tender buds of participatory initiative may never flower. This is perhaps more a political than an economic problem, which deserves treatment in another kind of essay, but its management can have crucially important

47

consequences for the progress of economic growth and development. These conflicts of objectives between growth and equity, between economic progress and social welfare, between urban and rural investment, and between participation and order complicate the problems of development strategy. Problems are likely to be less severe in the context of rapid and reasonably balanced growth supported by substantial help from outside than when growth is slow or lopsided and foreign resources are inadequate.

Summary Implications for Strategy for the Second Development Decade

What lessons can we draw from this analysis about the most important ways in which development strategies for the 1970's should differ from those that have been followed in the First Development Decade? Much of what is suggested is simply a continuation and improvement of efforts already under way. One or two comments on changes of emphasis may, however, be appropriate.

In the first place, it is clear that in a great many ways a larger effort by the underdeveloped countries themselves, by developed countries assisting them, and by international agencies will reduce many of the difficulties of generating self-sustaining growth. The case for an increase in average growth rate from the 5 per cent of the 1960's to 6 or 7 per cent, and for the corresponding increase in resource transfers from developed countries from 1 per cent of national income to 1 per cent of gross national product is not simply that more is better than less but that, with a larger level of effort by all parties concerned, the prospects of generating by the end of the decade self-sustaining growth in a substantial number of countries are greatly improved.

Second, while we have explained why accelerated effort in population control is unlikely to bring quick results, there is a new awareness of the need for greatly increased attention during the 1970's on population and family-planning measures.

Third, the course of the 1960's has brought increasingly to our attention the importance of the elements of trade policy emphasized in the foregoing analysis. A good many countries that have been emphasizing import substitution are coming to realize that much greater weight must be put in the future on export promotion activities if their long-run problems of international trade balance are to be solved. This also implies much more vigorous efforts by the developed countries to assist, through their own aid and trade policies, in the diversification and expansion of export activity in the developing world.

Finally, there is a growing recognition that economic growth alone will not automatically bring with it all of the virtues of modernization, including some of its social and civic characteristics that underdeveloped countries seek, and that modernization policies must be turned more explicitly in these directions.

When all of this has been said, however, the problems perceived as central at the beginning of the 1960's are still with us. The increase in saving and investment rates, the provision of aid to cover both saving and foreign-exchange gaps, and heightened attention to the problems of increases in productivity all remain high on the strategic list. If we can weave these various concerns together more effectively, and if developing countries, developed countries, and international institutions can mobilize the will and assemble the resources to increase their collective development efforts, the higher targets that the United Nations is contemplating for the 1970's have some possibility of achievement.

A Select Bibliography

United Nations, Committee for Development Planning, *Report on the first session*. Economic and Social Council Official Records: Forty-first session, Supplement No. 14 (E/4207/Rev.1)

United Nations, Committee for Development Planning, *Report on the second session*. Economic and Social Council Official Records: Forty-third session, Supplement No. 7 (E/4362)

United Nations, Committee for Development Planning, *Report on the third session*. Economic and Social Council Official Records: Forty-fifth session (E/4515)

United Nations, Committee for Development Planning, *Report on the fourth and fifth sessions*. Economic and Social Council Official Records: Forty-seventh session (E/4682)

United Nations, *Planning and Plan Implementation*: Papers submitted to the Committee for Development Planning at its second session (Sales No.: 67.II.B.14)

United Nations, *Planning for Economic Development*. Report of the Secretary-General transmitting the study of a Group of Experts (Sales No.: 64.II.B.3)

United Nations, *Planning for Economic Development*: Volume II. *Studies of National Planning Experience* (Part 1–Private Enterprise and Mixed Economies. Part 2–Centrally Planned Economies) (Sales No.: 65.II.B.3 and 4)

United Nations, *Development Plans: Appraisal of Targets and Progress in Developing Countries* (*World Economic Survey, 1964*–Part I) (Sales No.: 65.II.C.1)

United Nations, *The Financing of Economic Development* (*World Economic Survey, 1965*–Part I) (Sales No.: 66.II.C.1)

United Nations, *Implementation of Development Plans: Problems and Experience* (*World Economic Survey, 1966*–Part One) (E/4363/Rev.1)

United Nations, *The Problems and Policies of Economic Development: An Appraisal of Recent Experience* (*World Economic Survey, 1967*–Part One) (E/4488/Rev. 1)

United Nations, *Some Issues of Development Policy in the Coming Decade* (*World Economic Survey, 1968*–Part One) (E/4687/Rev.1)

United Nations, *Economic Co-operation and Integration in Africa*: Three case studies (Sales No.: E.69.II.K.7)

United Nations, *Planning the External Sector: Techniques, Problems and Policies*. Report on the first interregional seminar on development planning (Sales No.: 67.II.B.5)

United Nations, *Planning Domestic and External Resources for Investment*. Report on the second interregional seminar on development planning (Sales No.: E.69.II.B.34)

The Development Process

W. ARTHUR LEWIS

The Lessons of Two Decades

The flood of writing about the economic problems of the less developed countries began at the end of the 1940's. What have we learned since then? The development process has turned out to differ in several respects from what was most popularly expected then. This brief essay summarizes our experience.

What we have learned is here classified under five headings, each of which becomes the title of a section. In this introduction, we summarize the main themes, thus making the introduction a summary of the whole essay.

1. *Rapid growth is possible.* It was not thought, twenty years ago, that the less developed countries could immediately start to grow as rapidly as the United States or other developed countries, but this is precisely what they have done. The target of the United Nations Development Decade—an average growth rate of 5 per cent per annum of less developed countries as a whole—has been hit. The growth of several of these countries has been no less "miraculous" than that of Germany or northern Italy. The principal reason for this has been the rapid expansion of world trade during this period.

2. *Development occurs in all directions simultaneously.* Growth runs into bottlenecks if there is not an appropriate balance between sectors, especially between industry, agriculture, and infrastructure; and between production for the home market and for exports. All sectors must expand as income grows; so the question popular twenty years ago as to which sector should have priority has been displaced by the search for appropriate balance. Less developed countries have not handled this aspect of their affairs adequately; their neglect of agriculture and of exports has produced severe balance-of-payments constraints.

3. *Success in foreign trade demands continuous adjustment.*

Less developed countries can no longer rely on their traditional exports to developed countries (tea, cocoa, coffee, rubber, and so on), the demand for which grows too slowly to support a 6 per cent growth rate of less developed countries. If they grow faster than the developed countries, there will be a widening gap between their need for imports and their potential exports to developed countries. They must cut their imports of food and light manufactures from developed countries and do more trade with each other. This requires a new network of trading relationships between the less developed countries, and a new set of institutions for financing this trade network. Developed countries would also help by opening up their markets less grudgingly to new categories of exports from the less developed countries, but the latter's trade with developed countries is no longer the exclusive focus of international discussion.

4. *Self-sustaining growth requires institutional change.* Growth responding exclusively to external demand is precarious. To attain maturity, a country must internalize its engine of growth, form its own cadre of entrepreneurs and managers, develop its own sources of savings, respond more to its own wants and its own innovations, and acquire greater economic flexibility and adaptability. This calls for changes in social structure, education, birth rates, the role of government, and so on. Rapid economic growth can take place on a peripheral basis without the great institutional changes that used to be considered its prerequisite, but self-sustaining growth is more exacting.

5. *Economic growth is of world-wide concern.* Foreign aid, almost inconceivable twenty years ago, grew rapidly between 1955 and 1961, mainly for the wrong reasons and therefore rather inefficiently from the economic standpoint. The purpose of aid is now more clearly defined as being to help countries to attain economic independence at a high rate of growth. This requires positive action on their part, as well as cooperation from the developed countries. New multilateral arrangements (Inter-American Committee on the Alliance for Progress [CIAP], consortia, and consultative groups) for monitoring the performance of aid receivers and for consultation and dialogue with aid donors improve the prospect that aid will now be used more effectively to promote self-sustaining growth. By cooperative effort, it is possible to put most less developed countries onto a high growth path that would

53

take them to economic independence by the end of this century. The political fruit would be to increase the number of countries in each continent whose peoples and governments are strongly committed to the maintenance of international order in a "poly-centric" world.

Rapid Growth Is Possible

Historically, the standard of growth of national income set by the developed countries has been about 2 per cent per head per year; this is the average rate achieved by the United States over the past 100 years, and considerably exceeds the averages of Britain or France. The figure of 2 per cent seems a small one, but such is the power of compound interest that over a century it raises output per head by a factor of 7, which is about the real difference between the standard of living of, say, Ceylon, the Philippines, and Thailand, and that of, say, Britain and France today.

Twenty years ago, hardly anyone thought it possible that the average growth rate of income in less developed countries could be 2 per cent per head in the immediate future; but this average rate has been maintained over the past fifteen years. Several of these countries have growth rates exceeding 3 per cent per head; some twenty-eight of them had rates exceeding 2 per cent per annum between 1955 and 1965; and a further seventeen had growth rates exceeding 1 per cent per annum. Underdevelopment is clearly not a vicious circle; it is an evil that we have the power to eradicate.

The list of the top twenty-eight is especially interesting because of its variety: It includes countries in every continent; of every race, religion, and creed; of the poor and the not-so-poor; of tropical climates and temperate climates. The ability to develop is not confined to any particular region or group of peoples. The list is as follows (according to the United Nations):

Africa: Gabon, Ivory Coast, Liberia, Libya, Nigeria, Sierra Leone, Tunisia, United Arab Republic, Zambia.
America: Barbados, Guatemala, Jamaica, Mexico, Nicaragua, Panama, Peru, Trinidad and Tobago, Venezuela.
Asia: Iran, Iraq, Israel, Jordan, Korea, Pakistan, Saudi Arabia, Syria, Taiwan, Thailand.

It now seems highly likely that the target of the Development Decade of the 1960's—an average growth rate of gross domestic product (GDP) of 5 per cent per annum for all less developed countries together—has been reached. And the raising of this target to 6 per cent for the 1970's no longer seems adventurous.

The secret of this achievement has been the unprecedently high rate of growth of foreign trade. The last long period of expansion of world trade, uninterrupted by wars and great depressions, was the forty years before World War I, between 1871 and 1913. During this period, the volume of world trade increased by about 3½ per cent per year. Between 1913 and 1950, the average rate of increase dropped to 2 per cent; but, since 1950, the average growth rate of world trade has been between 6 and 7 per cent per annum.

The less developed countries that have grown fastest have been those that profited most from the expansion of international trade. The Development Assistance Committee of the Organization for Economic Cooperation and Development (OECD) estimates that the correlation between growth of exports and growth of national income has been 0.7. Countries exporting oil, minerals and metals (copper, bauxite, iron ore, tin), cereals (rice, maize), or oilseeds have done best. Those concentrating on tea, coffee, or cocoa have been the least successful.

This experience is very similar to what happened between 1871 and 1913, when a great many tropical countries also made great strides in response to expanding world trade. Unfortunately, this expansion gave way to three and a half decades of depressed international trade; first, the war of 1914–18; then the 1920's, with their adverse terms of trade; then the Great Depression of the 1930's; and, finally, World War II. During this long thirty-five-year depression, the development of the tropics virtually came to a standstill.

This depression, coupled with the shortness of human memory, gave rise to the opinion, so prevalent around 1950, that rapid tropical development had never occurred and could not now occur, either because social institutions were wrong or the people not sufficiently materialistic or the natural resources inadequate, or even simply because the climate was too hot.

All these explanations have now been left high and dry by the experience of the last two decades. It is now clear that less developed countries can grow rapidly, so long as world trade is buoyant.

The average growth rate in these countries of about 5 per cent for GDP as a whole breaks down sectorally into about 7 per cent for manufacturing, 3½ per cent for agricultural exports, 2½ per cent for domestic foodstuffs, and 5 to 6 per cent for service industries. The growth of commodity production is impressive, but even more impressive is the transformation that has occurred in the infrastructure of developing countries. Incredible change has occurred in such features as the number of miles of paved roads, the number of villages with water supplies, the proportion of children attending schools, the prevalence of electricity, the number of port facilities, the death rates from malaria, smallpox, or dysentery, the number of hospital beds, or other such indicators of modernization. Both the productive capacity and the environment of living have changed beyond recognition over the past twenty years.

Continued prosperity is by no means assured. The prosperity of the underdeveloped countries is still peripheral to that of the industrial world. Their "engine of growth" is still external, whereas in a developed country, the engine of growth is internal, that is, the bulk of investment is undertaken to satisfy domestic demand, and the momentum of the economy may be maintained even if external factors are unfavorable. The transition from an external to an internal engine of growth requires structural changes that very few developing countries are making (Brazil, Mexico, and India are examples of transition), so the underdeveloped world is still nearly as vulnerable to changes in the degree of prosperity in the industrial world as it was between 1913 and 1950. We shall return to this problem in a later section.

The experience of less developed countries is diverse; not all have done well. While 30 per cent of the population lives in countries where output per head has grown by 2 per cent or more, 48 per cent of population of developing countries is in the range of 1 to 2 per cent, and 22 per cent lives in countries where output per head has risen by less than 1 per cent per annum.

The causes of poor performance are easily traced. The countries achieving less than 2 per cent per head per annum fall into three categories:

1. Tropical countries or regions with an annual rainfall of thirty inches or less. Here, the farmers are confined to low-yielding crops, and unless irrigation is feasible, they find it difficult to rise beyond subsistence production. This category includes most of the coun-

tries on the fringes of the great African deserts (although the wetter African countries are among the fastest growing). It also unfortunately includes a large part of the cultivated area of the biggest of the developing countries, India. This is the chief reason why that great country, despite enormous effort, comes rather low on the list of achievers. Though India is the most important of the less developed countries in population and in many political senses, it is not typical of others in its geographical resources or in its social institutions. Nonetheless, the Indian growth rate per head of around 1½ per cent per annum is a striking reversal of Indian history between 1920 and 1950, when output per head was almost certainly declining.

2. Countries whose governments pursue policies that stifle development. Of these policies, the most important in practice have been:

a. The maintenance of overvalued exchanges, usually resulting from inflation. This reduces the earnings of export industries, both traditional and new, and thus prevents the economy from responding to the opportunities presented by the rapid increase of world trade. This is the main reason why so few Latin American countries appear in the list of rapidly growing economies, despite the superior resources of that continent in education, skills, and capital.

b. The setting of agricultural prices at levels that discourage the farmers from investing in new seeds, fertilizers, and other modern inputs. The farmers have clearly been overtaxed in many parts of the developing world, with adverse consequences for agricultural output, for example, in Burma and eastern Nigeria. Foreign aid in the form of cheap food has had the same effect, for example, in India.

c. The adoption of restrictive licensing systems, for example, for foreign exchange, imports, or investment permits, where the licensing is managed inefficiently or corruptly. Large firms can usually manage to find their way through inefficient licensing, but the development of small and medium-size firms suffers.

d. The prohibition of private enterprise operations before the country has acquired the capacity to run efficient public substitutes, for example, in Guinea and Burma.

3. The third category includes countries whose economies have disintegrated through military operations (for example, Algeria,

or the Congo) or that have diverted large resources into military budgets.

Thus, the human factor, in the shape of bad economic policies, has played a significant role in holding down economic growth in a large number of developing countries. Many more of them could have grown by 2 per cent per head had they not handicapped themselves. These lessons are being learned. If world trade continues to grow rapidly during the next decade, twice as many less developed countries will make the successful list.

Development Occurs in All Directions Simultaneously

Growth *per se* is not enough. If growth is to continue, the various sectors of the economy—industry, agriculture, public services, and so on—must be in appropriate balance with each other; otherwise, bottlenecks will emerge that brake the rate of growth.

The development literature of the early 1950's was much concerned with the nature of this balance. Should planners concentrate on industry or on agriculture or on building up the infrastructure? This question is no longer asked.

As the national income grows, the demand for everything grows, with only minor exceptions. We require more food and agricultural raw materials as well as more manufactures and infrastructure, and neglect of any of these is perilous to the whole. The principle at work appears most clearly if one imagines that the economy is closed (that is, has no foreign trade). Suppose that income grows through an expansion of manufacturing without agricultural expansion. The price of food will rise. Wages will therefore rise, and profits will fall, this fall in profits checking further expansion. If the economy is open, food prices may remain constant, but imports will rise. This import surplus is deflationary (money used to produce manufactures is being sent abroad instead of being used to buy the manufactures produced with it); so profits fall and expansion is checked, unless the manufacturers can find export outlets for their products.

From this analysis, we get the modern theory of balanced growth, which says that, as income grows, all sectors must expand their output *pari passu* with domestic demand; except that insofar as exports can be expanded, imports may in some cases be substituted,

58

subject to the rule that total imports must not exceed exports by more than the voluntary capital inflow. The need for balance remains, but it shifts from individual sectors to foreign trade; the deficits of industries that do not keep pace with demand must be offset by equal surpluses in other industries (that is, exports must equal imports).

The development of econometric techniques over the past two decades has made a substantial contribution to the solution of problems of this kind. The combination of input-output analysis and mathematical programing makes it possible to calculate which industries should export and which should import. The drama of great "either/or" generalizations about the respective roles of industry and agriculture is thus converted into marginal adjustments of particular trades, against a background of almost universal expansion.

Less developed countries have not, in general, handled this aspect of their affairs very well. Several have neglected their agriculture; others have overexpanded some types of education and other social services. Since the supply of traded goods is adjusted to demand via foreign trade, imbalance in the commodity-producing sectors shows up in an excess of imports over exports. The general prevalence of balance-of-payments constraints is the evidence that developing countries have not been following the "laws" of balanced growth.

Agriculture has been the main victim, especially the production of food for domestic consumption. Populations in developing countries now grow by something like 60 per cent over two decades, and food consumption per head is also rising. Neglect of food production is therefore costly. Food production has, in fact, just kept ahead of population growth, but it has not been enough to cope with rising consumption per head. So, whereas before World War II developing countries were net exporters of cereals, now their net import of cereals is substantial. Even in a good year, their imports of food from the developed world come to about $4 billion dollars, a serious and unnecessary drain on their balance of payments with the developed world.

The lesson is being learned. Most of these countries are now giving extra attention to their agriculture in the form of research programs, agricultural extension, credit, fertilizer supplies, irrigation, and so on. Earlier policies of squeezing the farmer in the interest of the urban community are also being relaxed. Many countries had been keeping food prices low deliberately but are now realizing that attractive prices are an important incentive toward agricultural effort. Fortunately, the new agricultural technology—new seeds, fertilizers, pesticides, irrigation—is so productive that it is possible for the farmers to be much better off without raising food prices. Currently, the best guess seems to be that the food situation should be relatively easy over the next two decades, despite rising populations.

It used to be thought that less developed countries would have extraordinary difficulty in expanding industrial output, but, on the contrary, the difficulty has been greater in agriculture. Industry is growing faster in the developing countries than in the industrialized world. Rates of industrial growth of 8 or 10 or 12 per cent per annum are common in developing countries, whereas rates exceeding 6 per cent are unusual in developed countries.

In a country where GDP is rising by 5 per cent per annum, the demand for manufactures, for consumption and investment, rises by only 6 to 7 per cent per annum. A growth rate of output of 10 per cent can then be sustained in only one of two conditions: Either import substitution is occurring, or else exports of manufactures must be growing by more than 6 to 7 per cent. Both these conditions have held in less developed countries; import substitution has been taking place, and exports of manufactures have been growing by about 8 per cent per year.

Import substitution still has some way to go for these countries as a whole, since they still have a large import of light manufactures from developed countries. But they vary greatly in this respect. The limits of import substitution in light manufactures have already been reached in India, in Brazil, and in some other Latin American countries (especially in textiles). Some of the larger less developed countries will also continue to make headway with greater manufacture of some capital goods for domestic use.

Nevertheless, if less developed countries are to grow by 6 per cent per annum over the next decade, it seems highly probable, even after allowing for greater import substitution in both manufactures and foodstuffs, that their imports will grow at the same rate. For a while, imports may even grow faster than GDP, as the ratio of investment to GDP accelerates, since capital formation has a high import content. It follows that, even after allowing for greater foreign aid and borrowing, these countries will need a rate of growth of exports of around 6 per cent per annum, including both manufactures and agricultural commodities. (These figures include trade among the less developed countries.)

The rate of growth of exports has varied greatly from one developing country to another. This is a matter partly of natural resources and of the traditional pattern of exports. But it has largely derived from differences in trade policy. Many of these governments have deliberately neglected exports, pinning their faith instead on import substitution. Particularly lethal has been the policy of allowing domestic prices to rise, with inflation, while keeping the foreign-exchange rate constant. This not only squeezes traditional exports, for which the world market may, in any case, be sluggish, it also prevents producers from introducing new export commodities, for which world trade is booming.

An inadequate level of exports is a major constraint on growth, since the resulting shortage of foreign exchange may cut down imports of raw materials or capital goods. Some policy-makers are now saying, "Look after exports and everything else will look after itself." This is not true, since the case for fostering infant industries is as strong as ever; but it is perhaps a useful, if dangerous, antidote for countries that have gone too far in the opposite direction.

Success in Foreign Trade Demands Continuous Adjustment

So far, foreign trade has been the engine of growth of less developed countries. They have prospered because the industrial countries have prospered and have therefore had a constantly growing demand for products from developing countries. If the developed countries go into a recession, the trade and prosperity of developing countries will be severely checked. However, even if world trade continues to grow rapidly, major structural change is required in the trade of less developed countries.

The starting point of this story is that, although the trade of less developed countries has grown faster than ever before (by over 5 per cent per annum in volume), different classes of commodities have fared very differently. The big weakness has been in agriculture. Between 1955 and 1965, exports of manufactures grew by about 8 per cent per annum, of minerals, metals, and fuels by about 7 per cent per annum, and of agricultural products by about 3½ per cent per annum. More than half of the top twenty-eight countries owed their high growth rates mainly to expanding exports of minerals. In contrast, most of the countries wholly dependent on agricultural exports fall into the bottom half of the growth list.

The basic problem of agricultural trade is that the rate of growth of demand in the developed countries for the traditional tropical export crops—tea, cocoa, coffee, sugar, rubber, and fibers—is relatively low. At the same time, demand for other agricultural products has been booming. This is especially so in foodstuffs, in which developing countries themselves are mounting a large import deficit from the developed world, now running at around $4 billion a year. Thus, paradoxically, agricultural exports have grown faster from the developed countries than from the developing countries, and the prices of developed countries' exports have also been better maintained. The agricultural crisis of the developing countries is epitomized in the figures below, which show index numbers for 1965, on the basis of 1955 = 100

Index Numbers of Agricultural Exports, 1965

	Quantity	Price	Value
North America	180	109	195
Europe	154	108	170
World	155	97	151
Near East	144	91	131
Latin America	144	89	128
Africa	142	89	127
Far East	130	93	122

The table shows that Europe and North America did much better than the less developed countries in agricultural trade in quantity, price, and value. Essentially, this was because the less developed countries were exporting the wrong commodities.

The less developed countries' exports of traditional crops would be larger if the developed countries were not so restrictive. Trade is reduced by import and excise duties, by quotas, and by subsidies toward uneconomic production of competing products.

Neither are the developed countries to the fore in helping developing countries with international commodity schemes to insure more orderly marketing. Developing countries need to keep hammering away to try to get some justice for their commodity trade.

It is, however, necessary to face the fact that the development of these countries can no longer be supported wholly or mainly by selling traditional crops to developed countries. Whatever one may do, the demand of the developed countries for this particular set of commodities is not likely to grow by even as much as 4 per cent per annum over the next two decades. The less developed countries, on the other hand, want to grow by 6 per cent per annum, and need a growth rate of imports and exports of about the same magnitude. Taken as a group, therefore, they must look elsewhere.

The proposition that if developing countries want to grow faster than the developed world, they will have to trade relatively less with the developed world and relatively more with each other seems odd to those whose thinking runs in traditional channels. Actually, taking developing countries as a whole, there is no reason why they must *in the long run* depend on trade with the industrial countries. They have enough land to feed each other; they are surplus producers of most of the major agricultural raw materials, metals, and fuels; they are capable of learning the industrial skills quite quickly; and they should within the next two or three decades be in a position to finance rapid growth entirely through their own savings. So if, in the year A.D. 2000, all the countries now industrialized were to sink under the sea, this should make little difference to the potential growth rate of the countries that are now less developed.* This rupture of trade contacts would probably impair the standard of living of less developed countries by diminishing the opportunity for specialization on a world scale, but, after initial adjustments have been completed, it should make little difference to their potential rate of growth.

If this is so, developing countries should stop thinking of themselves as inevitably dependent on trade with industrial countries and should do more to build up a network of trade with one another.

They must, in the first place, become less dependent on the developed world for food; it is absurd for them to be using their land to grow unwanted commodities while at the same time having a mounting deficit of food. Not only should the less developed countries feed themselves; the developed countries now import large quantities of cereals, for feeding to livestock, that could

* The point is made for analytical purposes, to dramatize the situation; it is not a recommendation.

easily be supplied by the developing countries. With the new varieties of wheat and rice in Asia and new varieties of maize in Africa and Latin America, it ought to be possible for the developing countries to improve their balance of payments with the developed countries very considerably by importing less or by exporting more cereals to each other and to the developed countries.

One of the problems of the next ten years will be the readjustment to the pattern of world trade that will become necessary as the agricultural revolution proceeds in the developing countries. In particular, foreign aid in the form of food from developed countries will become a hindrance to development rather than a help. It will thus be desirable that foreign aid be made available without being tied to food or any other particular set of commodities.

Developing countries need not, in the second place, be so dependent on the developed countries for manufactures. In 1965, they imported from the rest of the world about $3 billion of chemicals, about $6 billion of light manufactures, and about $13 billion of metals, machinery, and transport equipment. If the less developed countries are to grow faster than the rest of the world and are therefore to have lagging exports to the rest of the world, such proportionately high dependence on imports of manufactures cannot be maintained. It is obviously not necessary to be importing $6 billion of light manufactures from the developed countries; developing countries can clearly produce more of these for themselves and for sale to each other. It is not so easy to cut imports of heavy manufactures, but two or three developing countries, notably India and Brazil, already have large capital-goods industries and are on the verge of becoming significant exporters of capital goods.

Greater trade in manufactures among the less developed countries is very much on the international agenda. Attention has focused on one institutional aspect of this development, namely, the creation of trade preferences, through regional customs unions, common markets, free-trade areas, and so on. These are making slow progress. Another important institutional aspect is that of financing trade in manufactures. Exporters of consumer goods are expected to provide short-term finance, and exporters of capital goods to provide medium and long-term finance; and most developed countries now have official institutions that facilitate the granting of the necessary credits. Those developing countries that are going to export manufactures—and already a dozen are significant exporters—will have to build up export finance facilities; but since they cannot afford to export capital to finance the purchase of capital goods, they will depend on having their sales financed by money from developed countries. Thus, regional development banks may be a useful channel, borrowing in developed capital markets money that they use to support the export credit agencies of the countries in their regions.

Finally, developing countries can export more manufactures to the developed countries themselves; this is indeed the fastest growing section of their exports. In 1965, developing countries exported $2.4 billion of manufactures (excluding metals) to the developed countries. The latter's total imports of light manufactures were in that year $23 billion, or ten times as great as their imports from the less developed countries. But, paradoxically, while the period 1955 to 1965 saw developed countries busily reducing the barriers to imports of manufactures from one another, they were equally busily raising the quotas to imports from developing countries, thus conforming to the biblical saying that from him who hath not shall be taken away even that which he hath. Even after the Kennedy Round, the tariff structure of the developed countries is such that the tariffs on the sorts of manufactures they import from developing countries are twice as high as the tariffs on the sorts imported from other developed countries. In addition, there are also numerous quotas restricting imports from developing countries.

The current situation is absurd, in that when developing countries try to export to developed countries, they are faced with barriers, whether it be agricultural commodities or manufactures—though the restrictions on manufactures are even greater than those on agricultural commodities. The less developed countries are now protesting vigorously against such treatment, and they must surely prevail. They have also asked that developed countries grant preferences in their markets to exports of developing countries over exports from developed countries; and this has already been accepted in principle by the developed countries, though no date has yet been set for action.

It is clear that the pattern of world trade must change significantly over the next two decades, as the less developed countries solve their trade problems by exporting more food and manufactures to each other and to developed countries. The latter can help

65

or hinder. They can help by reducing their barriers to imports from developing countries and by making aid and investment funds available on terms that facilitate the trade of developing countries with each other. But the onus is not all on the developed countries. Many of the less developed countries have not realized the changing nature of the opportunities in world trade and continue to bewail the weakness of traditional markets instead of seizing the new opportunities. Many have simply priced themselves out of rapidly expanding world markets by overvaluing their exchange rates. Success is impossible in world trade without continuous adjustment.

Self-Sustaining Growth Requires Institutional Change

The less developed countries grew rapidly in the forty years before World War I and again in the two decades after World War II, in each case in response to booming world trade. In the intermediate period of more than thirty years, they stagnated, because world trade stagnated.

This is not a happy situation: No country wishes its economy to be entirely dependent on world trade, to have its engine of growth exclusively in exports, so that when exports decline, the economy relapses into stagnation.

In developed countries, the engine of growth is in the home market, that is, most entrepreneurs invest first to meet domestic demand and regard their export trade as an extension added to a sound home market. The economy can therefore go on expanding on its own momentum, even though external events are unfavorable. There are limits to this situation; any economy, however large and developed, can be brought to a standstill by a persistent excess of imports over exports. In this sense, all economies depend on foreign trade to some extent and are likely to be adversely affected by a decline in exports. Yet, the differences of degree are wide enough to be qualitative. The developed country will have to adjust its imports and exports to each other, but its engine of growth is in the home market, and this gives greater independence of movements in the world economy. The underdeveloped economy with its engine of growth in exports is at the mercy of the movements of demand in industrialized countries.

We can therefore define the transition that has to be made to achieve economic maturity or self-sustaining growth. A country must grow its own entrepreneurial class, interested in serving its home market. It must save enough and tax itself enough to be capable of pushing itself along at an adequate rate of growth. It must also be sufficiently flexible to meet changing conditions of demand and supply. Thus, its agricultural system must be sufficiently modern to produce a growing supply for home demand, if not also for export, while releasing labor for the urban economy; and its education system must be capable of turning out the trained personnel required for the expanding occupations. If rapid growth of output is to translate into a rapidly rising standard of living, the birth rate must be low, since a rising population eats up capital. And if the country is not to be strangled by foolish economic policies, it must have built itself a reasonable administrative system.

Developing countries have made varying progress along this road. A few, such as Brazil and India, are well advanced in growing a domestic entrepreneurial class. Savings and tax ratios have risen sharply over the past two decades. And much progress has been made in education. But population, agriculture, and administration are still weak spots. We shall now consider each of these topics in turn.

Entrepreneurship. The quantity and quality of a country's entrepreneurial class is a function at any time of both current opportunity and history. Entrepreneurship springs up fairly rapidly when opportunities are present, even in societies which have no such tradition, as the recent experience of Pakistan testifies. At the same time, countries where market opportunities have existed for several generations have relatively more and better entrepreneurs than countries where market opportunities are just opening up.

The reason for this is that successful entrepreneurship requires not just the right genes but also the right sets of attitudes toward business behavior; and these attitudes are picked up from one's society from early adolescence onward. They include attitudes toward thrift, work, risk-bearing, managerial responsibility, the treatment of customers, the handling of personnel, the keeping of records, and so on. A youngster who grows up in an atmosphere where such matters are demonstrated and discussed continually is likely to do better in business than one who comes from a non-entrepreneurial background.

Thus, at the beginnings of economic development, a country is bound to be short of qualified domestic entrepreneurship, and the only such countries that make rapid progress are those allowing foreign entrepreneurs to come in and set the pace. This situation cannot last forever, since people dislike having their economy dominated by foreigners. Most developing countries are now in the stage of trying to domesticate their entrepreneurship.

Some easy transitions are possible. One occurs when the foreigners are racially indistinguishable from the native population, and integrate into it, as the Dutch immigrants did in England or the German immigrants in Brazil. This has not been possible in Asia or Africa. Another relatively easy transition is possible if the native culture is receptive to business mores, so that the foreigners' example is easily imitated, as in some Chinese, Indian, Japanese, or Nigerian communities. A community of native businessmen then grows fairly rapidly. The foreigners may try to prevent this, especially if they also control the government in colonial status. They may refuse to take natives into positions where they can learn business practices, or they may squeeze out native enterprises by denying them credit, suitable locations, subcontracts, or other facilities. Since immigrants tend to stick together and to support each other, foreign business communities are almost always guilty of exclusive practices in some degree.

Developing countries have wrestled mightily with this problem in the past two decades. Many politicians now in power resolved twenty years ago to get rid of foreign entrepreneurship at the earliest opportunity, but, once in power, they have tended in practice to go in the opposite direction, because the shortage of domestic entrepreneurship has been overwhelmingly obvious. They have, therefore, brought in more foreign enterprise, especially into manufacturing and mining—the very high growth rates of industrial production in less developed countries would not have been possible without foreign enterprise. Instead of banning foreign entrepreneurs, governments have tried to force them to impart their skills to the native population by requiring them to hire and train. Since secondary and university enrollments have also been increasing rapidly, there has been a considerable flow of talented young people suitable for business careers, and most large-scale foreign entrepreneurs in developing countries now take it for granted that they must recruit and train locally for responsible positions.

68

Many governments have taken a different attitude toward foreigners in small business. Some of these foreign small-business communities (such as the Chinese in Southeast Asia, the Indians in East Africa, and the Arabs in West Africa) are highly successful because they have the right set of business attitudes, which are not shared by those among whom they live. This situation can be self-perpetuating if, as is usually the case, the immigrants stick together and employ only their own. The right solution is, again, to force them to hire and train the natives of the country (just as, in 1484, an act of Richard III prohibited foreign craftsmen from taking other foreigners as apprentices). However, passions have run high in some of these cases, to the extent of the foreigners being denied the right to continue their established trades or even being run out of the country. The native population loses from this, since it then has to put up with poor service.

Direct attempts to help small business men have not come to much. In the beginning, too much emphasis was put on lending them money rather than on counseling, and much of this money was lost. Counseling is expensive and not always effective. Probably the most effective way of increasing the business class is to have a large output of youngsters from the secondary schools. To be a good businessman, one normally needs a good secondary education (unless one is endowed with remarkable genes), since one must be able to count easily, to keep records, to communicate, to absorb information, and, generally, to use the skills that are sharpened by staying in school until the age of eighteen. When the secondary output is small, most of it will be absorbed in government service of various kinds, including teaching. But when the secondary output is large, youngsters will have to accept business jobs or to start businesses of their own, and a large domestic business class will soon emerge.

Finance. A country must generate its own development finance if it is to be commercially independent and free to forge ahead even when external forces are unfavorable. The government will need something like 10 per cent of national income to spend on current civilian services, including education, health, and administration; and capital formation, public and private, will absorb another 20 per cent. Thus, personal consumption must not exceed 70 per cent of gross domestic product.

The opposite state of affairs occurs when a country has to rely mainly on foreign investment, as a result of which its principal industries are foreign-owned. Politicians inveigh against his "neo-colonialism" but seldom make the point that the only fundamental way of ending it is for the country to tax itself more and save more.

Twenty years ago, personal consumption in many developing countries was around 80 per cent of GDP. It is now nearer 75 per cent. It must fall still further to 70 per cent or less if these countries are to be able to grow rapidly while retaining financial independence. *Almost any LDC will grow rapidly if it makes 30 per cent of its GDP available for development (capital formation and public civilian expenditure), and if, at the same time, it expands its educational facilities to provide an administrative and managerial cadre.*

One may group the sources of savings into four: business savings, farm savings, household savings, and public savings. Business savings include the savings of corporations and unincorporated business. Such savings are largely reinvested in the businesses that generate them. The proportion of earnings saved is higher among businessmen than in other categories, since investing in one's business is part of the way of life of people who own and manage assets. The proportion of national income saved thus increases sharply as the business sector expands. Farmers have a high propensity to save in good years, but they have also so many bad years (through drought, flood, low prices, epidemic disease, and so on) that the savings of good years tend to be eaten up in bad years, and farm communities in developing countries tend to carry a burden of debt. Private urban households also save little. The salaried middle classes save through insurance and house purchase, but in many developing countries, they live beyond their means and contribute little to net savings.

Much stress is placed on savings campaigns and institutions, but these are unlikely to make a major impact on the volume of saving, desirable as it is that savings institutions should exist for those who can learn to use them. Private saving grows rather slowly in developing countries, and, in the absence of a long period of farm prosperity, its rate of growth is largely determined by the expansion and prosperity of the business community.

Therefore, if a developing country wishes to accelerate its savings capacity, the chief route is to increase public saving, which is the difference between government revenues and expenditures on current account, plus the net profits of public enterprises. Most developing countries have found it hard to achieve an increased public-savings ratio over the past two decades. Revenues have increased, but expenditures have increased just as fast, especially on education and public health. Another factor is the almost universal tendency of public enterprises in developing countries to make losses, whether through inefficiency, corruption, nepotism, overstaffing, or inappropriate price policies—in contrast with the socialist countries of Europe, where the profits of public enterprises and the taxes they pay are a major source of finance.

Developing countries should try to increase public saving rapidly—say from the current average of 2 to 5 or 6 per cent of GDP within the next decade—so as to reduce their economic dependence; both in the sense that they will have the resources to maintain investment, even if external winds are unfavorable, and in the sense that their resources will be owned domestically rather than in neocolonialist fashion. Besides, most developing countries desire a greater ratio of public to private sectors than was common when the Industrial Revolution began in Europe, and this is most appropriately financed through public saving. Unfortunately, progress in this sphere is slow; the minister who increases recurrent public expenditure is inevitably more popular than the minister who increases the budget surplus, even when that surplus is destined to finance important capital formation.

Agriculture. If domestic entrepreneurs use domestic finance to produce for the domestic market, the resultant increase in income puts pressure on agricultural supplies—whether of raw materials or of foodstuffs. If agriculture does not expand its output correspondingly, consumption will be met either by reducing exports or by increasing imports. Either of these alternatives puts pressure on the balance of payments. Economic growth therefore is more easily achieved when the agricultural sector is highly productive.

Economic growth is also normally accompanied by a relative decline in the agricultural population. This is partly due to the attraction of the towns; over the last twenty years, most developing countries have faced a tremendous drift from the countryside into towns.

Putting together the need for increased output with the relative decline of the agricultural labor force, economic growth normally requires an increase in agricultural output per head. The moderni-

71

zation of agriculture is at the core of the development process. Indeed, one way of measuring the degree of economic development is to ask what proportion of the labor force would have to be in agriculture to produce enough to feed the whole population. This varies from under 10 per cent in the most developed countries to over 70 per cent in the least developed countries.

The less developed countries have not done well in this department. Agricultural productivity per head has, on the average, risen by less than 1 per cent per annum, whereas what is needed for over-all 6 per cent growth is an agricultural productivity increase of at least 3 per cent per head per annum.

To raise agricultural productivity, one must have new inputs— new seeds, fertilizers, pesticides, irrigation, and so on. These tend to demand a greater labor input per acre. In countries like India or Pakistan, there is no shortage of labor. In parts of Africa, labor is fully utilized, but in others, the labor input is low only because the output from increased labor with current practices is not thought to be worth the effort. With more profitable techniques, the farmers will work harder.

Developing countries have not done as well in agriculture as they could have done if their governments had paid more attention to this sector. Most governments have now learned the lesson that agricultural modernization is at the core of economic development, and they are now willing to give higher priority to agricultural needs. In some countries, the problem is relatively simple—more money and more agricultural extension are the primary needs. In others, major institutional change is required to free the small farmer from the grasp of landlords and moneylenders whose depredations deprive him of incentive to invest more of his own time or money.

Education. Twenty years ago, the emphasis was on primary education; universal primary education was declared to be one of the rights of man and was given the highest priority. This attitude has disappeared.

On the one hand, the biggest shortage turned out to be at the secondary level. The few university-trained persons who are needed in less developed countries can, at a pinch, be imported, but one needs five to ten times as many secondary school products, and it is not feasible to import them, both because of their numbers and because transport and inducement costs would be very high in relation to salaries. Secondary school products are the steel framework of the economy—as technicians, record-keepers, supervisors, teachers, managers, and administrators. An adequate supply is vital at this level.

This shortage has dominated Africa. Asia has rather a surplus of secondary and university products. The capacity of developing countries to use such people is limited by the relatively small extent of the modern sector. If 60 per cent of the population is in small-scale agriculture, at a subsistence level, the jobs available for secondary school products aged, say eighteen, will in any year be not more than 5 to 10 per cent of those aged eighteen; and the number of jobs requiring a university training is not likely to be more than 1 per cent of the age group. When larger numbers than these are educated, the students are bound to be frustrated as they qualify, since they will have to take jobs below what they consider their training to merit. Much is made of the unsuitability of curricula and of the lack of balance between cultural and technical subjects, and this is relevant in many countries. But with the Indian numbers, students would be frustrated whatever they might study. There is no escaping the fact that there are limits to absorptive capacity in developing countries.

Africa's "educated" unemployment has been at the primary level, especially in rural areas. Partly this reflects an inevitable clash between modern schooling and subsistence agriculture with three acres and a hoe. The school inevitably lifts the youngster's horizon beyond the life lived by his father, beyond the meager income, beyond the traditional patterns of authority, and beyond the spirit-dominated world. No conceivable revision of the school curriculum could eliminate this clash, if the school retained the essentials of modernity. Change there must be; but it is the environment that must change through the modernization of agriculture.

The drift of primary school leavers from country to town that has occurred in Africa is due partly to this clash but also to widening differentials between earnings in town and country. Farm incomes have been held down by compulsory marketing schemes, while urban earnings have been forced up by trade-union action and minimum wage laws. Simultaneously, governments have concentrated on providing services in the towns (hospitals, secondary schools, water supplies, electricity, and so on), while neglecting the countryside. In such circumstances, a drift to the towns is inevitable.

It is theoretically possible to calculate how many people it would be "economic" to educate at different levels, if one could make the right assumptions, but such calculations have little political value. Education is a consumer good as well as an investment good; that is to say, education is worthwhile for its own sake (like clothes, radios, or bicycles), even if it does not increase productive capacity. In most developing countries, the demand for one kind of education or another exceeds what could be justified solely on productive grounds. Since it is hard to deny these demands, some "educated" unemployment, or at least frustration, is likely while the economy makes the transition to greater absorptive capacity.

Population. Twenty years ago, it was believed, in some circles, that population growth would prove to be an absolute block to an increase in output per head; it was even sometimes argued that the population problem must be solved before it could become profitable to devote resources to economic expansion.

Both propositions have proved to be erroneous; the output of developing countries is growing by 5 per cent on average, while population is growing by 2.5, so output per head is increasing by 2.4 per cent per annum. Output of food is growing just a little faster than population; not fast enough to raise standards of nutrition significantly but fast enough to discredit prophecies of imminent world starvation.

Population growth is a hindrance to economic development, but food is not its most serious aspect. The food situation will probably be rather easy for the next ten or twenty years, as the new varieties of rice, maize, and wheat gain wide acceptance in less developed countries, with accompanying greater use of fertilizers and pesticides. A temporary excess of food supply over food demand is not impossible, though not inevitable.

The more serious cost of population growth is that resources are used up in creating facilities for extra heads that could instead be used for raising standards for the existing population. One has to provide more schools, instead of better schools; more, instead of better, hospitals, roads, and other infrastructure. Capital that could be used to install better and more productive equipment goes instead into equipping more hands or into providing more of the same kind of infrastructure. Many developing countries

74

simply cannot cope with the drift from the countryside associated with high population growth, so urban unemployment is emerging as potentially the greatest problem of the 1970's. If population were rising by 1 per cent instead of 2.5, output per head might double in twenty years instead of thirty years. A modern economy grows rapidly because it uses its savings for improvement rather than for multiplication of facilities.

The governments of less developed countries are coming alive to this issue. One after another, they are adopting family planning programs and devoting resources to the purpose. Such programs also now figure in foreign aid. The main obstacle is not money but ignorance. It is true that many parents in developing countries are not yet ready to adopt family-planning; this is an attitude that spreads with development and especially with urbanization—a fact that emphasizes that population control comes with and after development and not before. But there are already more parents receptive to the idea than are in touch with clinics or aware of the technical possibilities; merely to reach and serve these would already make a significant difference to the birth rate, and would, as well, lay the ground for further penetration of the family-planning idea to those who are not yet prepared for it. The main problem is, therefore, to organize family-planning programs on a large scale. Beyond this, further progress in contraceptive techniques would help. The pill is too expensive for developing countries, and the interuterine device, while making good progress, falls into disfavor unless those who use it can have good aftercare treatment if they need it.

Some birth rates in less developed countries are already coming down. A drop of ten per thousand over the next fifteen years seems quite possible in some twenty or thirty developing countries.

Administration. This has proved one of the more difficult areas for less developed countries. In Asia and Africa, political independence passed political power into the hands of new political classes, most of whom set out to enjoy it. Most developed countries learned in the nineteenth century that sensible decision-making in economic affairs requires that administration be put before politics. They strengthened the quality and powers of their civil services and set up networks of committees and independent agencies insulated from party politics, to the varying extent feasible in each country's political environment. The general public has

75

caught on to this faster than one might have thought. There is now marked disillusionment with politics and politicians in developing countries. Men who, only ten years ago, were treated as near-divine have disappeared from the scene, and one military coup after another seeks to justify itself on the basis that it is cleaning up a mess made by politicians. Meanwhile, there has been a notable strengthening of economic administration as the practice has spread of creating planning agencies manned by highly trained young men devoted to the ideals of economic development.

Nearly every developing country now makes some kind of development plan for a period ranging between three and seven years. The nature, purpose, and quality of these plans has varied immensely. Many of the earlier plans were pure political window-dressing, but the political value of such exercises wears off, and this is now less common. The plans also varied in content from simple statements of intended public expenditures and public policies to highly esoteric forecasts of output in the private sector of the economy, using the latest mathematical techniques. Since these forecasts of the private sector have almost always been wrong and have had little effect on output, plans are again becoming simpler and more closely related to what the government expects to control or influence.

The governments of less developed countries are not able to control much effectively. The public sector is small, and until these governments learn to administer enterprises efficiently, extension of public enterprise seldom serves the public interest. This weakness demands urgent elimination. The governments' revenues are small and are eaten away by rapidly expanding social services. Civil services tend to be strong at the top but weak at intermediate and lower levels, so that systems of licensing are administered inefficiently and corruptly. In these circumstances, the good planner is not ambitious for the government to take on responsibilities that could just as well be left to other institutions; neither does he overload the government with tasks that are beyond its capacity.

The inescapable minimum is pretty large. Merely to provide decent public services, including health, education, and communications, is a task that taxes most of the less developed countries. Beyond this, in the economic field, the agenda is wide, even where direct operation of enterprises is not considered. Some of the fundamental matters already mentioned in this essay are difficult enough

—population policy, a balanced educational program, the modernization of agriculture, formation of public savings, development of domestic entrepreneurship, stimulating export trade—and most governments of developing countries rate rather low in most of these spheres. The sort of economic question that raises the greatest political excitement in any developing country is whether to nationalize the telephone system, or to allow private enterprise to build a steel plant. But in the context of what governments could really do for economic development, and still fail to do adequately, these are trivial questions.

Conclusion. In the language now sometimes used, the less developed countries have *grown* remarkably over the last twenty years, but their *development* is less impressive. Output has grown mainly in response to export demand, but the capacity to generate self-sustaining growth, influenced but not wholly determined by external factors, is still far off. Of course, growth is the prerequisite of development, since the emergence of domestic entrepreneurship, the rise of savings ratios, the improvement of administration, and so on, are all facilitated by growth and frustrated by stagnation. Therefore, developing countries need a further long period of expanding world trade to allow them to make the internal structural changes required for economic maturity. But they also, of course, need to understand what these changes are and to adopt conscious plans for effecting the necessary transition. This understanding does not seem to be linked to any particular political or social system—democratic, authoritarian, egalitarian, individualistic, or socialistic—since one can name examples of each kind that are succeeding economically, as well as other examples that are failing. Economic development has its own needs, which fit none of the current political stereotypes.

Economic Growth Is of Universal Concern

In 1950, the net transfer of resources from developed to developing countries through official aid and private investment was about $2 billion. Optimists hoped that this could be raised perhaps as high as $5 billion but were denounced for their boldness. In fact, the net transfer climbed swiftly in the 1950's; it reached $6.3 billion in 1956 and $9.2 billion in 1961, then declined. The 1961

77

figure was not passed until 1965; since then, growth has been slow ($12.8 billion in 1968). Official aid stood at $6.9 billion in 1968, compared with $6.1 billion in 1961, while private investment stood at $5.9 billion, compared with $3.1 billion.* To these figures, we should add an average of less than half a billion of loans from Communist states.

A considerable part of the increase in aid was inspired by political motives. The United States has given the largest amounts of aid to countries on the borders of the Soviet Union and China, and started major aid to Latin America only after the Castro revolution brought the cold war to that continent. French aid goes in largest volume to former French colonies in Africa; British aid to former members of the British Commonwealth. Not all aid is politically inspired—for example, aid from the Scandinavian countries or West Germany—but the largest donors have expected some political fruits from their contributions.

Aid so inspired gives rise to disillusionment, for two separate reasons. First, the political fruit cannot be relied upon. The results are not as negative as they are sometimes made out to be. It is true that British aid has not sufficed to prevent a greater loosening of British Commonwealth ties in Africa and Asia than had been expected. But the French have succeeded in retaining their influence in Africa. And though the Americans have not fared well politically in Latin America, their aid to countries bordering the Communist world has paid reasonable political dividends. American disillusionment over the political results of foreign aid is somewhat exaggerated.

There is more reason to be dissatisfied with the economic effects of aid given for political reasons. Aid that is given for economic purposes can be cut if the recipient government fails to pursue reasonable economic policies, but aid given for political purposes has to go on, even if it is clearly having no useful economic effects.

The most important development in the administration of aid is the independent monitoring of the performance of aid recipients, with the implication that the quantity of aid given will be related to performance. In the case of the Alliance for Progress, initiated in 1961, this is not implicit but explicit. Participating countries in

* These figures are from the Annual Reports of the Development Assistance Committee of the OECD. They include transfers to Cyprus, Greece, Gibraltar, Malta, Portugal, Spain, Turkey, and Yugoslavia.

Latin America undertook to pursue certain economic and social policies required to insure rapid growth with social justice. They have to submit their development plans for scrutiny to the Inter-American Committee on the Alliance for Progress (CIAP). Officials of CIAP write an annual report on the progress of each country, which is discussed in a multilateral meeting including any other Latin American country that wishes to be present, as well as the United States, the World Bank, and other parties giving aid to the particular country. Outside Latin America, some sixteen "consortia" or "consultative" groups have been formed for other countries. In most cases, the annual report on the country is written by the World Bank, and there is an annual dialogue between the country and those who give it aid.

This bringing together of multilateral and bilateral donors under the multilateral umbrella of a consultative group (or CIAP) for dialogue with a recipient country on its performance is potentially a considerable improvement in the administration of foreign aid. It gives donors the opportunity to do under multilateral auspices what would be very awkward bilaterally, namely, to link aid to performance. At the same time, recipients can monitor the aid performance of donors (delay, insufficient volume, unreasonable ties) and can gain the support of better donors in pressuring other donors into more adequate performance.

The second important development in aid is the more precise definition of its objectives. In the first place, aid is intended for investment, not for consumption; its purpose is to enable countries to grow faster and not merely to have their living standards subsidized. In the second place, faster growth is not by itself enough, if the fruits of faster growth are all consumed. A country is expected to move toward self-sustaining growth. In financial terms, this means that it must move toward eliminating the need for continued aid by taking the opportunity that growth of output presents to raise its savings and tax ratios relatively to national income and to reduce the gap between imports and exports. A country that receives aid but does not grow, or a country that grows but does nothing to raise its savings ratios or to improve its balance of payments, is failing to make progress toward self-sustaining growth. Aid is instead becoming a permanent crutch for such countries, and this can no longer be justified. For the time being, while foreign aid is scarce, it should concentrate on helping those who are willing to help themselves.

The Pearson Commission has considered the administration of aid and has recommended institutional changes designed to insure that aid will in the future more effectively contribute toward self-sustaining growth. The way toward this lies through firmer linking of aid with performance criteria, under multilateral auspices. However haphazardly economic aid may have been given in the past, it is clearly now within our reach to create a system that will really help the developing countries to attain economic independence.

Ten years ago, the United Nations declared the 1960's to be the Development Decade and set a target of an average rate of growth of 5 per cent per annum. This target has been attained. The United Nations is about to set a new target of 6 per cent for the 1970's. Not all developing countries can meet this, but it is clear that a great many can, if world trade continues to expand and if adequate foreign aid is forthcoming. It is not possible to calculate precisely how much foreign aid is required, but it is possible to say that the 1 per cent of gross national product (GNP) to which the developed countries committed themselves at the 1968 meeting of the United Nations Conference on Trade and Development (UNCTAD) would be adequate for this purpose. If this 1 per cent became available, the net transfer would rise from $12.9 billion in 1968 to about $22 billion in 1975, at constant prices.

Why should the rich countries make this sacrifice? The first answer is that it will do good. The case for foreign aid would be weak if it were established that the money goes down the drain, because it is stolen, or because developing countries cannot grow, or because it does nothing to help them grow faster. The last twenty years have disproved all such fears: With our new institutions and more clearly defined objectives, foreign aid can contribute significantly toward self-sustaining growth.

But why should the rich countries interest themselves in self-sustaining growth for the poor? The best answer is the moral answer; that is to say, that it is part of the higher nature of man for the rich to help the poor, for the stronger to help the weaker, for those who have useful knowledge to impart it to those who need it, and for those who have useful resources to share them with those who could use them. This belief is common to all the nations of mankind; it is part of the moral essence of human nature.

This answer will not satisfy those who, while accepting that the rich should help the poor, think that a rich country should first abolish its own poverty before turning to poverty elsewhere. This proposition was feasible in the isolated world of the eighteenth century; it is an anachronism today, when all the peoples of the world are so closely linked that each of us has a vested interest in what happens in other nations as well as in our own.

Specifically, this translates for many responsible people into an overshadowing fear that the security of the rich countries may soon be menaced by the poverty of the poor. If foreign aid were now to disappear—and it has already begun to diminish—the prospects for some developing countries would indeed be rather grave. Populations are increasing rapidly, and without the resources for family-planning and for agricultural reconstruction, some would indeed be stalked by recurrent famines in unfavorable seasons. In addition, it is feared that "the revolution of rising expectations" may lead to increasing political disorder in various parts of the underdeveloped world.

If some or all these things were to come to pass, the rich countries would find it increasingly uncomfortable, if not also dangerous, to live as an island of wealth in a sea of poverty and political turbulence.

Such things are possible, but it is not at all certain that the rich countries need fear the poor or could buy them off. The political stake in aid is rather more subtle. It derives from the fact that, in the last analysis, a country achieves political maturity only when a considerable proportion of its people is sufficiently well-educated and sufficiently independent economically to constitute a public opinion powerful enough to discourage and discipline political adventurism. Poor countries do not have this mature independent public opinion and are, therefore, highly unstable at home and unpredictable in their foreign relations. The way to make the world safer for all of us is to help to create this political maturity in as many countries as possible, as rapidly as possible, by helping to create the economic prosperity on which such maturity is founded. The world of the future will not be one of dominating power blocs; it will be a "polycentric" world whose peace is maintained by the very large number of politically mature communities, in each of the six continents, who have a mutual interest in orderly relations. This is the real political payoff of economic aid.

For this reason, we must be glad that the last two decades have demonstrated that, given help, it will be feasible for most developing countries to get their growth rates up to 6 per cent per annum. At that rate, a developing country could multiply its output per head by four in half a century and bring itself, within a century, up to or beyond the present living standards of Western Europe. Its growth could also, within a short period, become self-sustaining, at least in the financial sense. With thirty years of growth at 6 per cent, the domestic savings ratio could easily rise to 20 per cent of national income, at which level, foreign aid on concessional terms would no longer be needed.* This means that foreign aid would be self-liquidating in the sense that, with developing countries on a 6 per cent growth pattern, it could begin to taper off after a decade or so and would largely have disappeared by the year 2000, unless somewhere before that date the general consensus were to set an even faster rate of growth.

To set the less developed countries on such a path is a noble objective. It is a cooperative enterprise, unattainable unless the governments of developing countries pursue appropriate policies and the governments of developed countries make the necessary concessions in their trading policies and in the volume of aid. We have experimented and found a multilateral framework that permits all parties to consult with each other and apply needed pressures. The abolition of poverty is now a world-wide objective. It cannot be achieved in the less developed countries within a generation, but its first requisite, to put them on a high growth path of output, is within our reach if we act together. Mankind has no more rewarding task on its agenda.

---

* If such a country saved 22 per cent of additional income (a normal proportion), its domestic savings ratio would rise from, say, 12 to 20 per cent in thirty years.

A Selected Bibliography

United Nations, Committee for Development Planning, *Report on the first session*. Economic and Social Council Official Records: Forty-first session, Supplement No. 14 (E/4207/Rev.1)

United Nations, Committee for Development Planning, *Report on the second session*. Economic and Social Council Official Records: Forty-third session, Supplement No. 7 (E/4362)

United Nations, Committee for Development Planning, *Report on the third session*. Economic and Social Council Official Records: Forty-fifth session (E/4515)

United Nations, Committee for Development Planning, *Report on the fourth and fifth sessions*. Economic and Social Council Official Records: Forty-seventh session (E/4682)

United Nations, *Planning and Plan Implementation*: Papers submitted to the Committee for Development Planning at its second session (Sales No.: 67.II.B.14)

United Nations, *Planning for Economic Development*. Report of the Secretary-General transmitting the study of a Group of Experts (Sales No.: 64.II.B.3)

United Nations, *Planning for Economic Development*: Volume II. *Studies of National Planning Experience* (Part 1–Private Enterprise and Mixed Economies. Part 2–Centrally Planned Economies) (Sales No.: 65.II.B.3 and 4).

United Nations, *Development Plans: Appraisal of Targets and Progress in Developing Countries* (World Economic Survey, 1964–Part I) (Sales No.: 65.II.C.1)

United Nations, *The Financing of Economic Development* (World Economic Survey, 1965–Part I) (Sales No.: 66.II.C.1)

United Nations, *Implementation of Development Plans: Problems and Experience* (World Economic Survey, 1966–Part One) (E/4363/Rev.1)

United Nations, *The Problems and Policies of Economic Development: An Appraisal of Recent Experience* (World Economic Survey, 1967–Part One) (E/4488/Rev.1)

United Nations, *Some Issues of Development Policy in the Coming Decade* (World Economic Survey, 1968–Part One) (E/4687/Rev.1)

United Nations, *Economic Co-operation and Integration in Africa: Three case studies* (Sales No.: E.69.II.K.7)

United Nations, *Planning the External Sector: Techniques, Problems and Policies*. Report on the first interregional seminar on development planning (Sales No.: 67.II.B.5).

United Nations, *Planning Domestic and External Resources for Investment*. Report on the second interregional· seminar on development planning (Sales No.: E.69.II.B.34)

Social Dimensions of Development

PROFESSOR JOSEF PAJESTKA

The consequences brought about by the progress of civilization, coupled with the growth of population, which are reflected in changes to man's ecological environment and, more importantly, to socio-political relations on a world scale, make it more and more imperative to think clearly about the future and to make specific strategic choices. The constantly spreading awareness of this need is expressed in man's viewpoints, horizons and postulates. Nowadays, that part of the young generation which is not yet tied down to everyday practical life is becoming ever more inquisitive as regards the perspectives, sense and aim of contemporary civilization. It is to be expected that such questions and postulates will be increasingly raised in the future. The need, which until quite recently had remained somewhat intellectual, is rapidly acquiring a political dimension. *Mankind will have to think and to act in a strategically wider and more consistent manner; in other words, it will have to formulate its aims more clearly as well as the ways of achieving them.*

However, I do not propose to deal here with the general need for a strategy but with a specific requirement which has become extremely urgent for some societies. I am referring to those countries whose technical, economic and social progress is lagging. For these societies and nations, the strategic rationalization of socio-economic changes and of the development process in general, appears to be a *sine qua non* condition for the successful solution of their major problems.

Urgent need of a Strategy by Developing Nations

When considering civilization's evolutionary process on a world-wide scale, it should be remarked that this process brings about growing differences in peoples' economic and cultural conditions, that is to say, for individuals, for social groups and classes, for nations and races. Between the conditions of life and work of a man in the leading industrialized countries and those existing in countries lagging behind in development there is a gap difficult to measure. And these differences are not restricted to well-being only: affluence on the one hand; poverty and hunger on the other. They also affect fundamentally the development of man's creative abilities resulting in further increases in the disparities of living standards. Thus they concern the most essential factors which determine the fate of man and which motivate his activity. The stratification resulting from this differentiation assumes ever increasing proportions on a worldwide scale, and its manifestations and consequences in the sphere of relations among various societies and nations often become of greater significance than the consequences within a society.

As the fabric of economic and political relations—and the advance in science, techniques and culture controlled by it—produces growing differences on a worldwide scale, civilized progress simultaneously contributes to reinforcing these differences in so far as man's activity is concerned. Through education, radio, television and other mass media people are brought closer together and their appreciation of what is feasible and desirable become more akin. This must have consequences for man's behaviour and, consequently, for social and political relations. Man as well as nations are discovering contemporary civilization, merely to find soon afterwards that they are its pariahs.

Historical experience proves that the drive for equality is one of the powerful social stimuli, intensified in action. Man cannot become reconciled with growing inequalities in socio-economic conditions which are the consequence of established structures whether in respect of social groups, nations, etc. and which do not correspond to man's inner feelings of his own value. Consequently, one can expect a growing pressure and more intensive political efforts for speedier progress, from developing countries. Satisfying these demands to an extent which will be recognized by nations as a bare minimum, seems to be an indispensable condition for reaching a socio-political balance in the world and, consequently, a situation which can provide peaceful co-existence.

This is not to imply that the main purpose of countries lagging in their technical and economic progress is to ensure the elimination of existing discrepancies on a worldwide basis. Neither should the chief economic problems of the developing countries be formulated merely in terms of the elimination of existing gaps. Nations have their own traditions, their own more or less developed socio-cultural patterns, and their own urgent economic and social problems. For the future which counts for the present generation, it is neither feasible nor desirable that these countries aspire to the same type of social and economic life as that of the more highly developed countries. Their main objective is directed towards the solution of their own problems, such as the elimination of hunger, poverty, considerable social inequalities, degrading living conditions, all of which hinder the development of human creative abilities. There is no doubt, however, that the existence of important disparities on a worldwide scale results in increased pressure towards domestic progress. The witnessing of the possibilities which the scientific and technical civilization offers to some men cannot but influence one's evaluation of what is feasible or desirable in one's own country.

However, the increasing internal pressures as well as the growing aspirations which developing nations are facing at present, and which they will encounter in the future, are bound to be met by powerful counterforces. Given the structure of worldwide relations, they are opposed by polarizing forces which make those who are efficient, rich and powerful still more efficient, rich and powerful, and those who are poor, poorer still in relative terms. These polarizing forces operating in economic relations, in scientific and technical progress, as well as through political factors, are one of the important reasons for the growing discrepancies. In order to frustrate these forces, and with a view to achieving a more rapid advance in those countries lagging in development, it is necessary to apply counterforces more effective than those used until now. It is precisely for this purpose than an elaborate strategy for action is required.

In this connection, it should be noted that because of the existence of more powerful countries, highly advanced in their scientific and industrial development, the growth of the developing countries may prove to be a particularly difficult problem, far more difficult indeed than the initial growth of the former countries had been. We find here a certain analogy in the case of underdeveloped regions located within highly developed countries. The forces of concentration, of development polarization, cause these regions to succumb to a certain "underdevelopment disease" of a malignant character, resistant to treatment. Naturally, it is a curable disease, as has been shown in a number of instances, but it requires the application of particular means. A number of factors of a social, economic and political nature, account for the fact that it is much more difficult for whole countries and continents to overcome the stage of underdevelopment than it is for regions within highly developed countries. Some economists quote reasons why it is easier for whole countries to engage in the industrial process, particularly since they can take advantage of available technical achievements. However, looking at the whole picture, one finds this to be a fairly small advantage compared with other, unfavourable factors. It is necessary to apply particular methods and means for less developed countries which, by this very fact, find themselves at a particularly disadvantageous starting point for development. These methods and means have to be throughly elaborated so that the development aims which are envisaged can be achieved in spite of the very difficult circumstances created by the outside environment.

The challenge which life offers to man by placing him in a situation in which his essential endeavours and aspirations encounter dramatic obstacles and difficulties, usually arouses in him a response of increased effort and intensified activity. For rational action is essential to the efficacy of this effort; indeed such action usually conditions the effectiveness of human activity in more complex situations.

To meet the tasks required for the progress of the greater part of mankind which still finds itself at a stage of underdevelopment, *strategic rationalization* of action is indispensable:
—*on a worldwide scale,* involving all mankind, for the solution of this problem. It is a condition for maintaining world peace and it will contribute to more rapid general progress,
—*at the level of the separate developing societies,* for without it they will be unable to perform their endeavours and achieve their basic aspirations.

The difficulties of the development process connected with forces and tendencies resulting from present global structures have been indicated. Of course, problems linked to factors operating within developing societies do exist on which we still place the main emphasis. In fact, underprivileged and developing societies do not control external structures and, at best, can only counteract the negative influence or make use of the favourable aspects of these structures. On the other hand, they have, in principle, incomparably greater possibilities of influencing internal factors, of transforming domestic forces and relations. The strategic rationalization of this very activity is essential because such action is as important as it is difficult.

Development implies socio-economic change

Spectacular differences which appear nowadays in the living standards of various societies call for some interpretation. The point, however, is not to provide a historic interpretation, explaining how the present situation came about, but rather to make a *strategic diagnosis*, which will help to understand what must be done in order to modify this situation.

Undoubtedly, there is a strong and direct connection between the economic efficiency of societies and their standard of living. Thus the difference in these standards is to be accounted for by the differences in economic efficiency of individual societies. This certainly does not bring us to ignore the significance of external factors which can be very great and—at times—indeed enormous. It should however be observed that a feed-back exists between external factors and internal efficiency; greater efficiency facilitates better utilization of external factors and a more effective control of their operation. This is clearly established from the experience of most of the successfully developing countries. Thus, in the formulation of a strategic diagnosis, the postulate of internal economic efficiency and, through it, of internal developmental factors, as decisive elements in regard to economic progress and the improvement of the living standards of the population, appears to be strongly justified. Any other diagnosis can only lead to helplessness and to a reliance on the wheel of Fortune. However, it should again be emphasized that this strategic diagnosis cannot be considered as historical interpretation. Thus, it does not imply that some countries are poor because of their limited efficiency, and that they are responsible for this situation. It rather implies that without an improvement of their efficiency, they will not be able to change their fate. The role of colonialism in the exploitation of conquered nations and in hampering their development process is well known and its recognition is of essential significance for any historical interpretation; but its importance is less conse-

89

quential in so far as the strategic diagnosis is concerned. While changing their guise, colonial structures and influences have often maintained their methods of subordination and exploitation. The need to counteract these influences successfully by political means does not reject but indeed requires an increase in internal efficiency and economic power. Thus, the strategic diagnosis, placing the main emphasis on the improvement of internal economic efficiency, is of basic importance in all cases.

It must also be made clear that *economic efficiency is an integral and dynamic feature of societies.* It has nothing to do with the genetic feature of races or nations. The shared genetic heritage of the human race is the predominant element and differences between individuals of the same race or nation are incomparably bigger than those between races or nations. The social experience now available offers ample proof of this and any statements to the contrary result from prejudice devoid of any empirical bases. Economic efficiency is a social feature and, practically speaking, a high degree of efficiency can be achieved by any society. This is not to say, however, that it can be done easily and rapidly.

There are those who maintain that a limited degree of efficiency and low economic levels result from a shortage of capital and/or from a shortage of the most recent technology or, finally, from a shortage of qualified personnel. This is not the whole truth and may consequently lead to the wrong conclusions. Some of these conclusions suggest that, to solve the problems of economically underdeveloped countries, it is sufficient to import capital, new technologies and, in some cases, personnel. Carrying the reasoning further, it is also argued that import capacity is one of the main factors limiting the development of countries. The weakness of such conclusions is not that all these factors are of no significance and, in particular, that import capacity plays no essential part in the development process. The fault rests in a one-sided diagnosis, which overlooks the basic issue namely, that economic efficiency is a social feature which is determined by social relations and institutions. A full realization of this central point must precede any consideration of factors of an economic nature.

The passage from a traditional to a modern society, the movement from stagnation into development and from a lower to a higher rate of growth, as well as the maintenance of this rate— all this calls for changes in the functioning of socio-economic

90

organism. This is indeed the main issue and *the development strategy is therefore a strategy of socio-economic change*; one cannot wish for progress without wishing for change. Action implies movement.

Change is, as a rule, difficult to achieve; particularly social change, affecting established structures and social institutions which are of primary concern. To bring about change, specific socio-political forces are needed as well as reformers. There is no other method.

Change in the functioning of societies has to be adequately directed. While it is not an aim in itself, it must however serve certain socio-economic aims. Of chief importance are changes which alter man's behaviour, impart dynamism to social forces of development and improve the social efficiency of action.

Change as an inner force

Theoretically, development can be achieved through what one might call "imported development," based on massive injections of capital and technical assistance. Limited examples of this type of development are indeed available. However, the solution of the problems of most poor nations is not to be found in this direction. Calculations of the capital assistance required for such transplanted development result in amounts exceeding any realistic figures. The strategy for the Second United Nations Development Decade includes *inter alia* a target providing for net financial transfers amounting to 1% of the gross national product, at market prices, of countries economically developed, as economic assistance to developing countries. Even if the commitment were to be increased many times, the problem would still remain unresolved. Experts in the field of economic development and international economic relations, recognize the importance, however peripheral, of foreign aid in the development of less advanced countries. Thus the solutions to be sought after by these countries must be aimed primarily at internal factors and transformations.

Without denying the importance of external assistance, as well as the need for a world strategy designed to ameliorate the situa-

91

tion of developing countries, it should be emphasized, however, that in order to solve their problems these countries must, first of all, *fully assume responsibility for their modernization, relying on their own strength and concentrating on increasing their own efficiency.* Aside from the fact that this may correspond to national aspirations, it is in practice the only realistic way of approaching the problem. Experience has shown that excessive reliance on external assistance tends to reduce one's own efforts and indefinitely postpones changes which are necessary in one's own society. Concentration on internal forces and factors does not in any way diminish the desirability of outside assistance. This assistance, however, must not affect internal mobilization, or prevent necessary domestic transformations and stand in the way of a country's development strategy. Besides, experience has shown that effective utilization of external help very much depends on a country's ability to act efficiently. An increase of the internal ability to develop goes hand in hand with the competence to use outside aid reasonably and efficiently.

Furthermore, the approach which encourages reliance mainly on one's strength and efforts, which some may consider optimistic, is based on the central premise that developing countries are fully able to solve their basic economic problems. It is not the result of emotional optimism; instead it is well anchored to the historical fact that economic efficiency is itself a social feature which, as such, is acquired; it is not peculiar to only a few nations or social groups.

However, as any other ability, capacity of societies to achieve a high level of economic efficiency is a potential one. A number of factors are required to transform this capacity into a practical force likely to alter realities. Consequently, when formulating a strategy for socio-economic development, it is essential to determine the requirements for achieving this objective.

Among the preconditions for transforming this potential ability into a practical force, there is one which should be given priority. Nations and their leaders must be absolutely convinced that such a transformation can take place. Unfortunately, a feature of men as well as of societies is that they do not take advantage of their potential so long as they do not have faith in their possibilities. Consequently, an appreciation of one's own ability to solve problems is the first premise of a development strategy. This appreciation must become a powerful social force, it is indeed the only force able to win over inertia and conservatism. What is more, since the changes which are necessary for the functioning of the socio-economic mechanism are required not only at the highest echelons, this force must be widely spread. The nation as a whole must therefore possess a clear view of the potential within it and of its abilities. To generate this view is the first objective of a development strategy.

Economic analysis and the social development process

Pessimistic views as to the chances and prospect of economic progress in developing countries are often the result of certain methods of economic analysis which are dominant at present. These methods place heavy reliance on simplified econometric models with highly aggregated variables. The assumptions which they imply and which concern developmental interdependence and, per force, a development strategy, powerfully influence the understanding of economic development problems and planning methods. The simplicity of their logic make them attractive but in no way unshakable.

Let us consider, in a simplified form, one of the more typical models of economc analysis; it is a widely current one and constitutes one of the pillars on which the prevailing philosophy of economic development rests.

(a) Basic developmental interdependence:

    (i) $Y = f(C)$: national product is a function of capital

    (ii) $\dot{C} = I = g(S,M)$: capital investment is a function of savings (S) and of import capacity (M).

(b) The conclusions for the Strategy are thus as follows:

    (i) The rate of growth depends on the rate of investment, therefore the latter rate should be increased in order to accelerate growth;

    (ii) for (i) to be achieved, the rate of savings must be raised and, since it is assumed that possibilities are limited in this field, more rapid growth requires foreign aid;

(iii) for the same reason the import capacity should be increased, and this also calls for foreign aid in order to achieve a higher rate of growth.

The logic underlying this analysis would seem to be so evident as to require no further examination. However, its simplistic universality should in fact arouse doubt among the more thoughtful minds. How can it possibly provide ready-made answers to the developmental problems of any country without knowledge of the country being in any way necessary? There are many indeed who do not hesitate to propose such ready-made answers.

Let me first point out some of the implications of reasonings founded on large aggregates (e.g. national product, etc.) which make use of development models similar to the one which has just been mentioned. I have in mind the implications which I previously characterized as pessimistic. If we apply that sort of reasoning, we reach the conclusion that the major part of the population of the developing countries cannot even dream of reaching—by the end of our century, or even later—levels comparable in any degree to the present levels of the developed countries. This means that those countries are bound to be the pariahs of contemporary civilization and their men to be second class citizens of the world during a period of time so long as to have considerable historical significance. This very conclusion should at least lead to a serious reconsideration of the correctness of this entire reasoning and of the evaluations involved. Here we are facing a perspective contrary to the thesis which maintains that economic efficiency is a social feature, accessible to each society. A most discouraging perspective to say the least. If this perspective is not rejected by theoreticians, it is bound to be rejected sooner or later by nations themselves.

The weaknesses of the reasoning which lead to such pessimistic conclusions are many. First of all, they have to do with the facts. We maintain, for instance, that the per capita income of most developing countries in Asia, Africa and in some parts of Latin America, is in a proportion of 1 to 30, when compared with most developed countries. However, we know extremely little of what this difference does mean in practice; in fact, we know hardly nothing regarding its importance. It is of course obvious that a man with typical earnings in a developing country (according to estimates, the scale would approximate 30 to 40 US dollars per year) could not possibly live even for a month in the United States. Clearly, the value of income in, for instance, India and in the USA is an entirely different thing which does not allow comparison. When dealing with facts, or comparing situations, it is amazing to observe the ease with which many carry out algebraic operations on such highly problematic values which are also difficult to grasp. We should recognize the weakness of our knowledge whenever it is limited as in this particular case.

This weakness is also present when we try to evaluate those objectives which are desirable and which, aside from the factors mentioned above, are linked with various socio-economic patterns appearing nowadays and which will appear in the future, in spite of civilizing influences. It is in no way justified to insist on an increase of the bulk of produced material goods and services on a 30-fold or even 10-fold scale, in order to create conditions conducive to a physically wholesome and spiritually creative development for man (on a mass scale), and to produce an environment likely to prevent him from feeling like a pariah in our contemporary world. Much less is needed to achieve this purpose, provided social and economic management is adequate and certain principles of social justice are observed. The requirements for achieving this goal should be investigated and thoroughly considered for each and every society. This cannot be done—nor can a proper perspective be obtained—from present evaluations and prognoses regarding the national product or the national income. Neither do they provide a true understanding of existing gaps. They distort both the actual picture and the vision of a feasible and socially justified objective; they also confirm many in the economically developing countries, in their outlook of hopelessness and despair. These remarks do not deny and are not meant to deny the existence of important gaps on a world scale, nor is it the intention to minimize in the least their dramatic meaning and the menacing consequences to which they are likely to lead. But it is surely a strange fascination with figures which brings people to believe that only a 30-fold difference in the level of development is dramatic while, for example, a 5-fold or 8-fold difference are not! Can a 10% wage reduction in a single country not be called "dramatic"? The measurement and evaluation of gaps in economic levels (as well as projections for future changes) are of significance not only in the context of international political discussions. They are of

95

even greater importance where domestic policy is concerned for they are essential for the formulation of projections and the definition of policy objectives in the field of socio-economic development. Consequently, the views and methods for evaluating the gap which now enjoy a commanding influence, would seem to require a careful scrutiny.

Finally, our understanding of developmental interdependency remains weak. Statistical data often indicate a multitude of differences in incremental capital/output ratios among various developing countries. Our ability to clarify these phenomena is rather poor. Affirmations that increases in the investment ratio are either impossible or extremely difficult to achieve, are often based on an extrapolation of present tendencies. Nevertheless, we have the superb examples of Japan, of the socialist countries and of many other countries, which have raised the savings and investment ratios by relying on internal factors. To claim, as is often done, that these examples constitute quite exceptional cases, unrecurring phenomena, or the use of extraordinary means, amounts to nothing but a mental escape from the basic problem. These "exceptions" and "unrecurring phenomena" are nothing but changes in the functioning of the socio-economic system which make it possible to solve the fundamental socio-economic issues of a country.

Two conclusions can be drawn from these observations which are particularly essential here. They are formulated in a spirit of some criticism of the prevailing habits of economic thinking, since the rather simplistic and primitive approach to economic analysis is a fairly frequent hindrance to a full understanding of the development process and of the working out of a development strategy.

The first of these conclusions has to do with perspectives and the aims of development policy. As already indicated, the principal issue here concerns the attitude of mind which assumes that *nations are able to solve their problems, to reconstruct their socio-economic systems, thus achieving greater economic efficiency coupled with a matching living standard.* When they consider their aims and their possibilities, let the developing nations not overrate the suggestions that other nations have a 30-fold bigger per capita income. In my country, there is a well-known little story which shows how prosperity can be understood. Once upon a time, a poor peasant, talking to a priest, expressed his desire to reach such welfare as to be able to afford a change of underwear once or even twice a week. Reflecting further, the peasant wanted to be sure that there are people so well-off to be able to change underwear even every second or third day. But this could not, of course, be the end of his reasoning. After all, there are still richer people who change underwear daily or even a few times a day. And the richest of them all, for instance the American millionaires, surely just keep dressing and undressing. Man should not feel unhappy because he has no such prospect. *To create the basic conditions for physical health, creative work, and human dignity in a context of harmonious international relations, an increase in the present levels of national per capita income in the developing countries but a few times, would be sufficient. This sort of development is within the grasp of the majority of developing countries and could be achieved during a single generation.* The arguments to prove this contention are quite sufficient and they can be supported by historical experience. But this positive attitude as to the ability to solve one's own problems must of course be coupled with a clear understanding of targets and of socio-economic development patterns.

The other conclusion relates to a better appreciation of the character of interdependence in so far as development is concerned. The process of development does not consist of a series of algebraic relations between the increase of national income, investments, exports, imports, etc. Economic factors are powerfully influenced by social considerations; they also have weighty social consequences. Changes in the rate of expansion, in investment capacity, in the introduction of new technological processes and the like are, to a major degree, the result of modifications in the economic behaviour of man. Therefore, the development process must be viewed as a process in which progress results from changes in man's behaviour. And because it is a social phenomenon, conditioned by interhuman relations and by socio-economic institutions, the development process must be seen in a special light and certain factors must be taken into account in working out a strategy for development. Thus, such a strategy, must reckon with social development forces, social development objectives, social and institutional solutions likely to contribute to increased economic efficiency. To put it more precisely, *these social aspects must constitute the absolutely indispensable, integral element of any economic development strategy.* They are

97

particularly essential for developing countries for which significant socio-institutional changes represent the most basic factor for modernizing their economy.

General guidelines for a strategy of socio-economic change

The development strategy is always conditioned by existing structures and by factors which are both internal (economic, social, political) and external. Therefore it is pointless to try to formulate universal strategic rules which would be valid for every country. Whatever is mature or, shall we say, socially and economically feasible and desirable at some particular stage of development, may no longer be so, or may acquire different dimensions, in a future stage of development. Thus, solutions for different developmental stages in a given country cannot be universal, *a fortiori* does this apply when dealing with different countries.

I would now like to discuss certain aspects of the development strategy, placing the main emphasis on the human factor and its social conditioning. However weighty they may be, these are precisely the aspects most commonly underestimated. And they can be of wide application as general guidelines for action tending to quicken the pace of progress. Their practical use, however, always requires careful confrontation with the existing, concrete circumstances in a given country.

The following reasoning, as well as the solutions proposed in regard to a strategy, are concerned chiefly with quality rather than quantity. They provide certain guidelines for a development policy without quantitative models for developmental interdependence. Experience has shown, however, that it is precisely the qualitative concepts which are of key significance in the formulation of a development policy. We can speak of their consistency and of their socio-economic rationality, although they need not be expressed in figures. Of course, concrete programmes of action designed to implement a well-defined strategy, must be formulated in a more operational way and, to a large extent, in a quantitative way also.

Economic efficiency depends primarily on human qualities, a capacity for rational action, innovative ability, energy, etc. Not only is the contribution of each individual of concern, but the way it expresses itself in the social structure, where it acquires a new dimension and different values, is also important. This is the starting point for the multitude of undertakings related to a development strategy. We then reach rather basic conclusions which help chiefly to understand the range and type of development undertakings and to formulate the objectives of a development policy.

The distinction between economic and social objectives of development policy is widespread. Economic objectives are generally meant to include increases in the growth rate through a rise of the production potential (e.g. by way of capital investment); the expansion of exports, etc. Social aims comprise improved living standards for the widest social masses, education, health care and the like, increased employment opportunities and a more equitable distribution of income and of social opportunities. It is often argued that these objectives compete with one another and that they are mutually contradictory. Theory and practice are often based on the thesis that the implementation of social aims interferes with the achievement of a high rate of economic development.

There is no doubt that we face here a very complex and difficult problem, and that we would be ill-advised to try and formulate absolute principles of general application. Therefore, we must reject *a priori* arguments designed to show either the necessary contradiction of these objectives or their natural and total conformity with one another. Instead, we should like to demonstrate that the social objectives can be integrated with the economic ones and that both these sets of aims can be mutually supportive, resulting in a feed-back most advantageous to overall progress. This is not a purely theoretical argument; it is imbedded in reality and essential to any development strategy.

So then, improved health care, better education for the people, increased production and a wider spread of skills, knowledge and culture are not only justified social aims; they also improve physical capability, the capacities and qualifications of man, all of which are of the utmost importance whenever economic progress is concerned. Similarly, the greatest possible involvement of all those able to work, in productive activities or in any other socially useful action, is not only a social objective, it can also have significant economic effects and help to raise man's abilities.

99

A policy which promotes equal social opportunities for all individuals, has favourable economic effects, since it permits a fuller utilization of enormous human resources and talents. In general, one can say that it is by coupling skilfully the two problems *development for whom* and *development through whom* that economic and social objectives become integrated with the most favourable effect on overall socio-economic progress.

Of course, all this belongs to the realm of the potential. Its realization is a tremendous and extremely difficult task. For instance, there is no guarantee whatever than an increase in budgetary outlays for social purposes will produce any or all the economic effects already mentioned. In order actually to integrate social and economic purposes and to ensure that outlays for social undertakings are economically fruitful, the entire development policy has to be directed to this end, both in terms of the economic solutions it proposes as well as in regard to social and institutional changes.

In the light of the preceding remarks, we are able to formulate the following general conclusions:

(i) Since the human factor is of decisive importance for increasing the economic efficiency of each society, it is right that *the transformation of man—of his behaviour, and of his socio-productive features—should become the point of concentration in any development strategy* designed for developing countries.

(ii) This approach opens up the *possibility of harmonizing social and economic development objectives*; the achievement of this harmonization should be one of the main objectives of any development policy.

(iii) A development strategy oriented towards the transformation of men cannot be implemented only by increasing social outlays and by calling for change. It must assume the form of an *integrated action programme covering the whole field and all factors affecting man.* The importance and the nature of the changes required by such a programme, within existing standards of law and usage, relationships resulting from property ownership, various socio-economic institutions, the organization of social activity, training programmes, etc., will be commensurate and proportionate to the rigidity of the existing structures, relationships and traditions impeding the development process and hindering the growth of economic efficiency. The scope of these changes must also depend on the extent of the ambitions and

100

aspirations of the country. The choice of those who are able to elaborate and consequently implement such programmes of action is of course a political question which must be left open; an appropriate solution must be worked out by each of the countries determined to assume responsibility for their destiny.

These arguments and observations also have direct implications for the scope of undertakings to be covered by the development policy. They boil down to the postulate that *the scope of undertakings resulting from a development policy, which also means the range of active socio-economic changes, covers the entire economy and the entire society.* If the increase in a society's economic efficiency is indeed to be achieved by raising the activity, qualifications, ability and enterpreneurship of man, the economic effects of the development policy will depend on the extent of the changes undergone by that society and on the degree to which it acquires new socio-economic features.

Convincing as this argument may be—and it would indeed be difficult to put forward any counterargument of similar weight— the postulate is clearly contrary to the actual development policies of most developing countries. It is also contrary to the more influential patterns of economic thinking on which an understanding of the development process is based, and which is almost universally applied by developing countries in their planning.

In economic analyses, the rate of development is rather a function of investment and of import capacity than of the human factor and of human ability in raising economic efficiency. The rate of development to be achieved is very often defined as a result of algebraic operations, performed by means of a few economic variables, while the main determinant of this rate is an assumed scarcity of investment means. Man appears here chiefly as a scant "qualification factor." Consequently, the range of people covered by the development process is determined by the range of feasible capital investments. As a result, a major part of society remains beyond the compass of the development strategy.

A typical feature of a number of developing countries is their *dualistic structure.* A so-called modern sector with relatively high parameters of economic efficiency, developing on the basis of capital investment, both domestic and foreign, coexists with a so-called traditional or subsistence sector. The latter is practically beyond the range of socio-economic changes .

101

The welfare of people and their economic efficiency in the traditional sector differ hardly at all from what it was some score or even some hundred years ago. Thus, for example, it is estimated that in Africa the value added (in constant prices) per capita in the traditional sector kept growing by 0.1% on a yearly average during the period 1960-67. We find similar patterns of economic performance in the traditional sector of many countries. The differences in the level of national per capita income in various countries reflect, to a large extent, the different level of the modern sector, which is often non-indigenous, while the various social strata live in conditions which remain unchanged; differences which might appear here are mostly the result of natural conditions. The statistical data indicating a steady and quite considerable growth of per capita income of the African continent might lead to the optimistic conclusion that African countries are becoming involved in a general and dynamic process of socio-economic progress. This would be a largely misleading judgement. The majority of the population—in many cases 70% of it—remains either almost totally out of reach of the process of changes or at its poor and passive periphery. These people are to some degree affected by the results of change, and not always the positive ones, but they almost never play a part in its creation and development.

Such a situation is of significance not only in terms of the ability of wide social strata to take advantage of the positive effects of economic development. Whether the whole of society is becoming modernized and raising its economic efficiency is of similar if not greater importance. Only in such a case could we say that the maximum advance, at every level, is being achieved.

No doubt, one can express doubts as to the realism of a postulate which assumes massive change in man's behaviour as well as the involvement of all segments of society in development. But let us be quite clear, the question is not only one of changes which transform man's environment by way of large investment undertakings, thereby bringing changes to his economic efficiency. The question also has to do with all other possible changes which are available to a given society as well as with policies which have a positive influence on the activity and economic efficiency of people. I claim that this postulate is a highly realistic one. Its

102

implementation must be left to the reformers of each and every country, since they are more familiar with the conditions, possibilities and aspirations of the nation to which they belong.

The implementation of a strategy capable of imparting social dynamism through a wide range of socio-institutional transformations has certain economic implications, some of which call for consideration in this paper. In particular, one of the main objectives is to ensure consistency between the social development strategy and the basic economic solutions.

Structural policy implications

Any development policy implies certain key structural decisions which strongly affect the total development process. It is essential that these decisions should be made with due regard to social factors and their consequences of the development process previously discussed.

In this context, one of the important problems concerns the relative priority given to industrialization on one hand, and to the development of agriculture on the other. The lines of structural policy in this field are closely linked to the mutual connections between the modern sector and the traditional sector; the strategy of industrialization consists in an intensive build-up of a modern industrial sector, while agriculture remains the main field reserved to the traditional sector.

Our main thesis leads us to to the conclusion that it is necessary to give *balanced development priorities to industrialization and agricultural development*. Thus a development strategy should consist of an adequately outlined industrialization programme as well as of a programme of transformation and development in regard to traditional agriculture. At the same time, the more limited the possibilities of industrialization, the greater the need for the country's general development strategy, of reforms and improvements in the area of traditional agriculture.

The necessity of more balanced development of industry and agriculture is a general conclusion reached from the historical experience of countries which have gone through the phase of intensive industrialization. From the viewpoint of economic development interdependence, it has often been the case that in-

103

dustrial progress has been retarded by a sluggish agricultural development, leading to serious balance of payments problems and to acute market difficulties. If only for the latter reason, a more balanced development between industry and agriculture deserves greater attention. Moreover, one must also take into account that the development of agriculture:

(i) offers the benefits of transformation and advance processes to the widest possible social strata which would otherwise remain at the periphery of progress in the advantages of which they would not share. As a result, decades would be wasted away before the wider strata of society could be introduced to progress:

(ii) contributes to the gradual abolition of the considerable gap occurring between people who live from traditional agriculture and the intellectual-industrial elite; consequently, increased social vertical mobility becomes possible, reducing cultural and other differences between people, with favourable effects on industrial development;

(iii) through increases in the supply of food, makes it easier to follow policies of full employment which themselves result in other socio-economic advantages.

The argument in favour of more balanced development priorities cannot be addressed exclusively, or even mainly, to policies having to do with capital investment. It also concerns development efforts understood in their widest sense, including land tenure reforms, improvements in the distribution and marketing of agricultural products, the organization of socio-economic activities, agricultural vocational training, the development of audio-visual methods aimed at socio-productive advances in agriculture, etc. In addition, credit facilities and other forms of economic assistance are of considerable importance.

Considerable optimism has recently been generated regarding the prospects for agricultural developments in many parts of the developing world, as a result of technological breakthroughs likely to produce a "green revolution." In no way do these new possibilities reduce the need for a type of developmental activity aimed at transforming man's behaviour and at producing socio-institutional changes indispensable to reach this goal. Not even the most advanced technology can act as a substitute for increases in economic efficiency through the improvement of man's ability and the quality of social relations.

All this should not be interpreted in any way as minimizing

the prominent role of industrialization as a vehicle for structural changes and general economic progress. Besides, agricultural development cannot be assured without industrial growth. No criticism is addressed at industrial development per se, but rather at a type of industrial development which takes place without simultaneous progress in other fields and, in particular, without due regard—in the formulation of policies—to that considerable part of the population of a country which remains engaged in traditional agriculture. Along similar lines of reasoning, certain observations can be made regarding structural patterns of industrial development.

The structural problems of industry are very frequently considered in the context of a link between a country's industrial development and its foreign trade. The industrial structure is thus evaluated primarily from the viewpoint of its impact on foreign trade. The methods generally used by industry for evaluating investment projects are such as to give fundamental importance to foreign trade which sometimes receives exclusive consideration. It is not my intention here to discuss this kind of approach. Nor can one deny the considerable role played by foreign trade in the technological and economic progress of developing countries. On the other hand, it strikes me as essential that the influence of the industrial structure and of investment decisions on a country's society ought to be given at least equal weight, as the criterion of foreign trade. Personally, I believe that *the development patterns of industry and particularly its structural trends should be viewed primarily in terms of the internal economy, and indeed of the entire society,* including that portion of it which remains in the traditional sector. This should be industry's main linkage and any link with foreign trade should be subordinated to it.

There are certain conclusions to be drawn from this, chiefly in regard to the structural aspects of industrial development as well as the patterns of investment decisions which should be considered in terms of their effects:

(i)   in the field of employment and, consequently, of income;
(ii) in improving the levels of qualification of the people;
(iii) in regard to progress which might be made in other sectors, particularly agriculture;
(iv) on the patterns of consumption, etc.

From a theoretical point of view, this approach suffers from a certain weakness in that the various effects we have just spoken about are both heterogeneous in nature and hardly comparable in respect of their magnitude. But the shortcoming lies essentially in the hammering out of well-ordered formulae which would necessarily have to be based on homogeneous and quantifiable criteria. This is, by no means, a drawback when formulating policy. Are we not constantly faced with choices which we must make without necessarily having some single, homogeneous and measurable criterion? Why then should we not be able to solve this problem in a wider social framework? That we are unable to work out an easy formula in no way constitutes an insuperable obstacle.

In order to avoid dealing entirely in the abstract, it is worth pointing out that for developing countries the above criterion provides a high priority to a number of sectors, whether they relate to agriculture (fertilizers, implements and machinery); health care (pharmaceuticals, personal hygiene articles, etc.), educational and cultural needs (paper, teaching aids, books, etc.); vocational training (mechanical and electrical tools); housing (low-cost building materials, furniture, household appliances, etc.). It is worth observing that in the development planning and policies of many developing countries, industries of these types have still to be granted a high priority and the help which would allow them to grow beyond present narrow market needs, on a scale proportionate to their significance for human development. I am not suggesting, of course, that the industrial areas which I have just mentioned by way of example, could fill the needs of any industrialization programme.

We could, of course, carry our approach further and apply it to policies in the field of science and technology, as well as other areas of development policy. But I think what I have said previously makes the point sufficiently clear.

On the other hand, the stress placed on the role of social forces and of socio-institutional transformations within the development process, may require some further elaboration. By emphasizing these forces, it has not been my intention to deny the role of economic factors *sensu stricto*. A development policy cannot succeed if it ignores basic economic factors or if it is devoid of compulsory features. In any analysis of the development process, it is essential that there be a reasonable equilibrium between the social and the economic approach and that equal treatment be given to social forces as well as to economic factors in any development strategy. The socio-economic reality constitutes a whole and the development process is an integral entity. A simplified and one-sided understanding of this process hampers rational and effective action. It is all the more important, therefore, to explain this particular aspect of the development process, which is largely ignored.

Greater social justice as a goal of development strategy

The sort of strategy which has just been proposed is a strategy of engineered social change on a scale involving the whole of society. Though it is being engineered and guided, it cannot produce its effects without popular support and in the absence of active social co-participation. This type of support and co-participation requires a development policy from which the various levels of society can benefit. As previously indicated, a link is essential between the "development· through ·whom" and the "development for whom" concepts.

This simply means that social justice must preside over the distribution of the benefits resulting from a development strategy and this requires that the strategy itself must be a just one devised in the light of mankind's historical experience. Greater social justice is not only a properly recognized objective pursued by man since the dawn of history, it can also be a means of imparting additional dynamism to social development. However, this remains more of a possibility than an absolute truth, and its implementation is a proper objective of social development.

In the context of a general development strategy, social justice is indeed an indispensable condition; it is not, however, a sufficient condition for imparting dynamism to socio-economic development. Justice is not a substitute for efficiency and development dynamics. With a development policy devoid of the appropriate organizational, economical and other measures, one might have greater justice but not necessarily greater progress. We are faced here with the old and very fundamental dilemma: does greater social justice contribute to an increase in economic efficiency or does it impede it? This is, by no means, a theoretical question.

107

It is the conceptual focal point on the basis of which various strategies for socio-economic development are devised.

The present growth process of many developing countries indicates considerable and increasing differences in the living standards of various social classes, national groups, regions of the country, etc. This process leaves in its train, or in some cases even creates, large areas of stagnation, degradation, poverty and hunger; it excludes large segments of society from the development process and relegates other social groups to the periphery of progress. The differences in living and working conditions and opportunities in developing countries, clearly show greater extremes than in the highly developed capitalistic countries. The considerable gaps between the per capita income in the richer countries and in the developing countries have their exact equivalent within the latter where they naturally have immediate social and political consequences.

It is often argued that these differences are unavoidable. Supposedly, the transition from a traditional to a more sophisticated economy must be characterized by growing economic differences, particularly in the earlier stages of this transition. The reason for this is that development initially takes place in certain areas only, temporarily leaving aside some others. These areas are either those suitable for profitable crops or rich in mineral resources, or again certain sectors particularly attractive to industry. A similar argument is applied *mutatis mutandis* to certain social groups. Finally, it is claimed that sizable differences in incomes provide a powerful incentive, that great fortunes contribute to savings and, consequently, to investment. These and other arguments of a general nature are given as reasons explaining the important and growing differences now observable within developing countries.

The type of development characterized by great disparities and social injustice is undoubtedly a fact, and one which occurs on a very large scale. Facts, however, are no justification for necessity, nor do they prove that no alternative exists. Theoretical arguments, which generalize these facts, are unable to show that development based on greater justice is either impossible or that it would be less dynamic.

On the other hand, it is sometimes argued that greater social justice is such an important social objective that it is worth sacrificing, for its sake, a higher rate of economic growth. One could agree with this; in fact, an option is sometimes available between

108

the rate of growth and other important socio-economic objectives. Nevertheless, it should not be too easily taken for granted that greater social justice results, as a rule, in reduction in economic efficiency and, thereby, in a lower rate of growth. This contention has never been demonstrated through experience. In the developed capitalistic countries the economic level is, by no means, a function of economic disparities. However, this example is not necessarily relevant to developing countries. It is indeed of fundamental significance to these countries that the pauperization and degradation of important social groups become a factor which hampers development, for they are tantamount to the non-utilization and to the waste of creative energies and talents on a large scale.

For developing countries, an alternative is available through a type of development based on social justice to a far greater degree than is the case in most of these countries at present. The adoption of this alternative does not require in any way that the goal of a high rate of expansion be abandoned. On the contrary, it can bring about a speedier general advance. This paper contains a series of considerations all of which constitute arguments favouring the choice of this type of development strategy.

The question as to whom can devise and implement such a development strategy is a political problem which we shall leave aside. It is, however, obvious that such a strategy can only be carried out by forces genuinely representing the overall interests of a society.

Towards greater social justice and more dynamic social development forces

Greater social justice within the context of the development process is achieved not exclusively, or even mainly, through direct instruments of income policy but by means of the general development policy itself with its structural, economic, institutional and other components. Direct action on the distribution of incomes, e.g., through fiscal policy, can only be supplementary.

(a) *Structural lines of development*
Our approach to a development strategy, with its concomitant requirement that all levels of society be included in an active

109

development policy, with particular emphasis on the transformation of the traditional sector, insures the simultaneous implementation of the objective of greater social justice which we have set for ourselves. Consequently, this strategy, motivated by the need to render the social development forces more dynamic is at the same time justified by the goal of achieving greater social justice.

The resulting conclusions concern the structural policy of the whole economy, including industry. The structural policy of development, both in sectoral and regional terms, carries with it social aspects, and if an effort is to be made to render social development more dynamic and achieve a greater degree of justice, that policy must also be viewed from this angle. It is consequently a distorting simplification to consider the problems of the structural development of production, exclusively from a technical input/output point of view. It would be interesting to develop such a matrix of development interrelationships, the "inputs" side of which would cover different economic factors, while the "outputs" side would deal with the social effects of their various applications. These social effects would include the impact on employment, on income, on the qualifications of individuals, on health, on cultural development, etc. If we could measure all these effects and dynamically maximize them, taking into account the feedback between them and the economic factors, we would then possess an analytic instrument suitable for a strategy of socio-economic development. But even without such an analytic instrument, the social implications of various solutions relating to the structural development of production can be readily grasped, and the broad lines of action towards greater social justice can be developed.

These broad lines of action concern the equilibrium between industrial and agricultural development as well as the direction in which industry should develop. It should be emphasized that there are well-known examples of industrial development, with minimum feed-back from the other parts of the economy and, correlatively, a minimum influence on the society. Its impact on employment and income are negligible, its production links within the economy are minimal, and its influence on the population, through *products*, is non-existent. For some developing countries this type of industry is dominant. Clearly, the criterion of the impact of industry on the society of those countries was not the determining factor in setting the pattern for their development.

110

It is quite obvious that, if it is the intention to press on with one's socio-economic development, such patterns must follow directions more in line with the approach we have ourselves proposed.

In terms of the social purposes we have in mind, the chief consequences of the structural policy of industrial development reveal themselves through what we might call *"impact through product"*. But this is ignored in most cases. For instance, who could deny the very basic difference in the effect on general progress and on the implementation of principles of social justice, between the production of luxury goods and the production means in agriculture? Some examples of industrial sectors which have a definitely positive influence on man have been mentioned previously. Through increases in this type of industrial production, new products are introduced into the various levels of society, which change living conditions and working methods, raise technical skills, etc. Social objectives can thus be achieved while—at the same time—an increase takes place in the general efficiency of the country. Market mechanisms do not take such effects into account; instead, they operate in a limited and short-sighted way without being able to stimulate production adequately. The criterion of the effect of investment projects on the balance of payments is clearly out of place here and its one-sidedness becomes fully obvious. Instead, the overall priorities of the structural policy of development must be applied in order to meet the country's socio-economic goals. Their implementation requires adequate programmes and energetic and harmonized action in the field of investment, scientific and technological policy, foreign aid, etc. As a result, products adequate to the requirements of the people will become available, at levels of production which will greatly expand the market demand. There will also be cases where production can be justifiably subsidized for social reasons.

These remarks show that structural development policy is an important factor for achieving greater social justice in the development process. The various economic, organizational and institutional solutions which affect the development pattern are also of significance not only in terms of their influence on income distribution but also in a much wider social context. Viewed in this light, the investment policy should provide for an equitable distribution among the various social groups, of the advantages and opportunities accruing from development. But it is not only the impact of the products which are of importance; the level and

111

distribution of employment—both in its national and regional aspects—earnings and development opportunities are also of great consequence.

(b) *Employment policy*

A high and rapidly growing level of urban and rural unemployment is one of the major social problems in developing countries. Increased unemployment in large urban centres is a contributing factor in the pauperization of many areas, while the under-utilization of the labour force in the countryside leads to persistent socio-economic stagnation and feeds urban unemployment. These extremely serious situations are among the most spectacular phenomena of the "underdevelopment illness". Conditions which pauperize and degrade man, which—instead of raising them—reduce his value and efficiency, belong to the category of social illnesses. The non-utilisation of human resources at the levels at which it occurs is not only evidence of underdevelopment but it often deepens and aggravates this underdevelopment. Therefore, employment policy must obivously constitute a key element of the overall development strategy in developing countries.

The socio-economic arguments for the elimination of unemployment and the creation of work opportunities for all, are so strong that they hardly require any detailed justification. They include the following:

(i) In terms of *social justice,* one of the chief differences between people resides in the employment of some and the unemployment of others. Employment policy is therefore one of the main instruments for achieving a satisfactory incomes distribution policy.

(ii) In so far as individual's *qualifications and efficiency are concerned,* it is obvious that skills are more easily developed through employment. In the absence of work, these skills tend to disappear.

(iii) Considerations of an economic nature often constitute a major handicap which limits employment. It is not that employment is devoid of any positive economic effect. Indeed, the employment of labour surpluses, provided it is done sensibly, can in practice have positive effects in any society, either in terms of increases in production or in other socially beneficial ways. Unfortunately, where profit-making enterprises are concerned, the limits of economically justifiable employment are determined by the rule that marginal productivity should not be lower than the wage rate, while in public activities, these limits are determined by the financial resources of the State and by the need to maintain a sound economic equilibrium. These economic factors result in a waste of socio-economic advantages resulting from employment.

The operation of the economic factors thus creates a situation which prevents the full utilization of the human factor and which cannot be radically modified so long as the essential features of the socio-economic mechanisms are not themselves changed in some way. Our conclusions here must be clearly formulated. In the absence of fundamental changes, the situation will continue to deteriorate because of the feed-back of most negative consequences: a man who is pauperized and degraded by unemployment loses the capacity of being productively employed. The problem must be attacked frontally, radically and in a number of ways. Theory as well as economic and political efforts must be geared towards its solution.

One of the main reasons for the existence of vast unutilized human resources lies in agriculture—where outdated and feudal property relationships still exist. This is why agrarian reform should be viewed not only in terms of a more equitable land distribution, but also for the opportunities it offers for the socio-economic progress of wide segments of the rural population as well as its beneficial effects for the urban labour market. The large and menacing concentration of pauperized masses in urban areas is both the manifestation and the result of outdated property relationships in the countryside, which impede individual progress.

Modern industry is unable to provide a solution—even in the long term—to the employment problem which is now appearing in many countries. Therefore, and in addition to the indispensable social reforms, agriculture must be at the core of any dynamic development policy.

Reformers must also direct their thinking, perhaps to an even greater degree, to the urban labour market. As previously indicated, the effects on employment of the structural policy of development, can be used as an important criterion of this policy. Definite possibilities are available for applying labour intensive production techniques to a greater extent. Practical experience in this field is considerable and can still be greatly enriched. Various economic-institutional solutions aimed at fuller employment are also possible. The level of utilization of available industrial ca-

113

pacity will show the way to these possibilities. As it turns out, while countries in fact suffer from shortages of capital, the available capital is quite often underutilized.

Without minimizing the difficult nature of the economic problems connected with fuller employment, it is nonetheless fairly clear that the approach to their solution is very often inadequate and that their significance in terms of overall socio-economic progress is underestimated. A full recognition of the significance which the utilization of labour has for man's progress and for the achievement of greater social justice should be sufficient basis for adopting a *policy of employment increase as an essential part of any development strategy.*

(c) *Education policy*

The expansion of educational facilities is considered as a socially desirable objective in most developing countries. Consequently, a fairly high priority is given to education, with special attention being paid to elementary education.

Given the orientation of a development strategy aimed at the improvement of the human factor, education cannot be restricted to schools and other types of educational institutions. Man acquires knowledge, qualifications and skills, not only in school but in his practical activities as well. For instance, efforts designed to improve agricultural production and those aimed at utilizing urban labour resources belong to the realm of education. On the other hand, the usefulness of school training becomes wasted if the knowledge and skills thus acquired are lost through lack of opportunity to use and to develop them in a practical way. This means that a dynamic policy to develop education can bear fruit only if it is implemented as an integral part of the overall strategy tending towards total human development. Many examples can be given to prove that without this, educational efforts are wasted. Moreover, educated people often become frustrated which frequently leads to rather negative social consequences. Consequently, the educational development programmes are occasionally curtailed because of a failure to appreciate that—in most cases—the fault lies not in a surplus of trainees but in the absence of an active development policy, aimed at a full utilization of human resources.

The structure of education, its programme and curricula deserve, indeed require, integration in the general framework of a strategy for socio-economic development. The basic function of

114

education is to prepare the young generation for life and work in society. If the purpose of a development policy is to modernize a society and its economy, it must then find its counterpart in the school structure and in programmes and curricula. Thus our conceptual approach should be that the education system at a given moment should prefigure the sort of socio-economic environment which constitutes a country's objective for the future. In reality, the educational system often contributes instead to a perpetuation of the existing socio-economic patterns and of present economic levels. Rather than being a moving force it maintains outmoded traditions or imported patterns which, in most cases, do not meet the need for improved individual competence, for greater social dynamism and social justice.

It would be difficult to indicate here in any detail the type of educational policy which—in the light of the previous remarks—would be required. The general orientation of the strategy must, however, always be the main focus. Given this orientation, and a clear formulation of the problem, a policy-making body can, with expert advice, formulate adequate guidelines as well as the measures to be taken. It might be appropriate to indicate here, some of the guidelines in the field of educational policy, with the proviso that they should be thoroughly confronted with the given situation and with the overall development strategy.

(i) A wide extension of education facilities and a dynamic approach to educational programmes are fully justified both socially and economically. However, positive effects on economic development, depend to a large extent on the effectiveness of the general policy designed to promote human development itself. In this area, a dynamic approach implies educational programmes designed to increase elementary schooling as well as secondary and higher education, oriented towards future development needs rather than towards present requirements. The expansion of education often encounters considerable financial limitations. There is no doubt that the costs of education can be very high in certain developing countries; but this is often due to the adoption by those countries of educational patterns imported from abroad. On the other hand, there are many cases where highly efficient—and far less expensive—patterns have been used. The willingness of the people to participate in school construction can also be an added advantage.

(ii) The function of education is to provide tools to the coming generations. This requires both a social and a technical training

content, with the latter being oriented towards productive ends. As a whole, the educational system requires inter alia:
— a considerable increase of the active elements in the teaching programmes at all levels;
— the inclusion of technical training as an integral part of the programmes;
— a high priority to vocational schools, particularly in the field of agriculture.

(iii) Especially in those countries requiring overall structural modernization, adult education must be granted, whether for basic knowledge and skills or in the field of professional training.

The educational system plays a particularly important role both for the achievement of social justice and a greater degree of national integration. It is precisely through education that youth, coming from different milieux and social strata, can be given a more equal opportunity to grow, and that people from whatever social levels, tribes, races, etc., can be brought closer together. But there is more to this than the mere social aspects. A fairer distribution, through the educational system, of opportunities for human development is a prerequisite to a better utilization of talents. The exclusion of the wider masses from the possibilities offered by education, results in a tremendous wastage which itself has important economic consequences. A great potential of human strength and energy is thereby wasted which would otherwise be available to the nation. But this is unfortunately the case at present in a large number of developing countries. Here again we observe that the pursuit of social justice is, at the same time, of prime importance if long-term economic development is to be achieved.

(d) *The goal of national integration*
A policy designed to achieve more equitable development must cope with special problems linked with the pluralistic structure of the societies which exist in most of the developing countries. These societies are divided into racial, tribal, religious and other groups. And these divisions are normally accompanied by obvious economic differences which can, for instance, result from the economic prosperity of minority groups such as that of the Asians in South-East Africa, the Chinese in Malaysia, and in the slower economic pace of such groups as the Indians in certain Latin American countries. Leaving aside historical considerations, these differences tend to perpetuate themselves and are often extremely

116

difficult to overcome. They are also strengthened by sociological, institutional and other factors. Careful and consistent action at the national level is required if they are to be eliminated. Such action is desirable both from the socio-political and from the economic points of view. Economically, the importance of social integration indeed deserves special attention if successful development is to be achieved. Social integration also brings with it a more stable social equilibrium, which is extremely important for sound development. Its special significance becomes even more obvious whenever a nation has to engage in great efforts to develop itself. Therefore, as we can see, *the objective of socio-economic modernization will not be achieved by the developing countries without a high degree of national integration.*

(e) *Integrity and efficiency in the public service*
It is hardly possible to review in this paper the whole spectrum of measures and initiatives required to achieve greater social justice and to marshall all the social forces for development. But there is one indispensable condition: the type of development strategy we have in mind will not be translated into reality without a public service deeply imbued with a sense of honesty and discipline. Corruption must be eliminated. A corrupt administration is incapable either of formulating programmes which have real meaning, to devise a strategy oriented towards a greater degree of social justice, or to impart the social forces with the necessary dynamism. Even if it were the intention of such an administration to proceed along these lines, the public would not respond, given its estimation of the lack of sincerity and fairness of the policies in question in the light of the behaviour of its leaders.

Therefore, a dynamic policy aimed at socio-economic progress must first begin with the moral cleansing of the power structure and of the public service. Experience shows that there is a strong and definite correlation between the sincerity and honesty of an administration and its efficiency. As a rule, a corrupt administration is an inefficient one. This correlation is generally underestimated and formal qualifications take precedence over social and moral ones in the recruitment of public servants.

On the other hand, administrative efficiency cannot be viewed in the abstract; it must be considered in the context of the tasks facing the nation. Thus, efficiency in the performance of the basic responsibility which is the progressive socio-economic moderniza-

117

tion of a country is the first prerequisite. This requires an understanding of the needs for social transformation coupled with an earnest approach and a strong commitment to the overall interests of the society. In brief, sincerity and honesty are just as important as academic preparation, ability and efficiency.

Summary conclusions

1. Consideration of the future prospects and development objectives of the Third World should not be based on mental conceptions which merely tend to bring out the hopelessness of given situations. Other methods of approach are not only perfectly possible but entirely justified.

2. The world must urgently proceed with the implementation of a global strategy oriented towards the creation of external conditions more conducive to the socio-economic progress of the developing countries. On the other hand, in formulating their domestic policies, the developing countries must appreciate that the responsibility for their modernization essentially belongs to them and that they must rely mainly on their own forces. This view naturally stems from the belief that nations are able to solve their own problems. These two sets of requirements are in no way contradictory; they are rather complementary and each of them is addressed to two different groups. Emphasis has been placed throughout on the responsibility and obligations of the developing countries towards themselves because they are of fundamental importance. However, this in no way minimizes the essential role of a global strategy and the vital contribution it can make to the solution of the problems we are facing.

3. A narrow and quantitative appreciation of the factors which enter into the development process and their interrelationship, will always remain insufficient when it comes to formulating a development strategy. It must be supplemented by an analysis of the social factors and forces which make for development. The orientation of a strategy towards the release of these forces is an absolute necessity and can be achieved while taking into account the economic factors involved.

4. It is possible to harmonize the economic and social objectives

118

of a development policy. However, this can happen only if human development is conceived as the focal point within the overall concept of development.

5. Recognition of the human factor as the leading element of progress has particularly significant implications in so far as the scope and type of undertakings to be initiated are concerned. These must cover the whole economy and the entire society. In this connection, it is important that a variety of programmes should concentrate on the transformation of the traditional sector which has generally been relegated to the periphery without benefitting from the changes and progress which may have occurred.

6. The long term objective of a development policy should be to achieve greater social justice. A more equitable development policy produces more satisfactory economic effects, provided of course it constitutes an integral part of the overall development strategy, oriented towards the development of man and the release of social development forces.

7. Progressive social forces can be made more dynamic and greater social justice can be achieved less by means of instruments such as incomes policy than by the general development policy, and the structural, economic and institutional solutions which it proposes.

8. Structural and sectoral policies must be directed towards a better balance between industrial and agricultural development. It should also provide for a closer link between industrial development and internal transformations, chiefly oriented towards man. This requires a totally new approach in the choice of industrial investments.

9. A full understanding that the human factor is the leading element of progress has direct and extremely important implications in the area of employment policy. This is the field of greatest consequence in terms of social and economic progress and for achieving greater social justice. It therefore requires the greatest attention. A number of measures can be taken the value of which has been shown in practice, but the possibility of original initiatives should also be explored.

10. Wide-ranging and dynamic educational programmes are essential. Their economic impact can be observed only when that part of overall development strategy relating to a fuller use of human resources is carried out. The structure of the educational system, its programmes and curricula should be geared towards the

socio-economic modernization of the country. The educational system must also contribute in putting into practice principles of social justice.

11. A country's development efforts can often be made most difficult and sometimes almost impossible without national integration which implies the elimination of economic differences among various racial, religious, tribal and other groups.

12. A development strategy aimed at instilling greater dynamism into the social forces and at ensuring a greater degree of social justice will not be achieved without the most exacting moral standards on the part of the public service. Moreover, the efficiency of the administration will go hand in hand with its honesty.

13. A strategy designed to achieve socio-economic development will require a number of other changes and reforms which have not been discussed here. Political and institutional reforms are not brought about for their own sake but because of their social and economic effects. It is only through such changes and reforms— and in the light of the political and other circumstances of each country—that social and economic development will take place. Otherwise, it will not happen.

Our Moral Involvement in Development

JEAN-MARIE DOMENACH

On the first day of the student revolt which was to cause such an upheaval throughout France in May 1968, I met a young man in the Latin Quarter who had just been throwing paving stones at the police. When I asked him why he had been doing so, he answered: "Because of the underdeveloped countries." I objected that such violent action had no connection with the problem of underdevelopment, for which, besides, the Parisian police could not be held responsible.

On thinking the matter over later, I came to the conclusion that the student's anger, even if aimed at the wrong target, had nevertheless one justification: it was really directed against the indifference of the advanced societies to a situation which is the major scandal of our time: the gap between the industrialized sector of the world and the other sector, made up of the so-called "developing countries".

It is true that those nations which, until recently, were referred to as "underdeveloped" are now making progress, but their advance is slower than that of the "developed" nations. This is why the gap is widening: the proportion of the world export trade coming from the developing countries fell from 22% in 1960 to 20% in 1968; the annual growth of the *per capita* income in these countries varies between 1.5% and 2.5%, whereas in the developed countries it reaches an average of 3.6.% Simultaneously, as the Pearson Report points out, governmental aid has been diminishing, particularly since 1968: the average contribution, which represented 0.54% of the gross national output of the developed countries in 1961, is now of the order of 0.39%. And the Report notes that the reduction in foreign aid programmes has taken place in an atmosphere "heavy with disillusion and distrust".

Why should there be this *disillusionment* among a wide section of the public when, at the same time, certain warm-hearted minorities are expressing violent indignation? No doubt because the task seems long and difficult and because certain local failures have occurred here and there. But also, paradoxically enough, through the very success of the concept of development: it is suddenly discovered that the so-called developed countries have "pockets of poverty" hidden within them and that their development, as it is speeded up, increases inequalities and distortions; each social category tends to compare its situation with that of the more favoured rather than with that of the less favoured. In short, national self-centredness, reinforced within each nation by the self-centredness of the different social groups, tends to outweigh the sense of world solidarity, which was beginning to come into existence. This retreat into egotism is strengthened by an awareness of ingratitude: there had been a more or less conscious hope that the initial aid given to the underdeveloped countries would soon bring some return and that these countries, once they had begun to advance, would accept the ideas and the life-style of the industrialized nations and might even become part of their alliance; instead of which there has occurred a whole series of *coups d'état*, revolutions and conflicts, and this has led to the conclusion that a lot of money has been wasted on a poor investment.

All this suggests that whereas development demands a sustained effort the reasons for giving aid are not sufficiently thought out. Does a father question his obligations towards his son, when the son gets bad marks at school? Does a citizen question his obligations towards the state, when the state is pursuing an economic policy or a foreign policy which he considers to be mistaken? No, of course not, will be the answer, but in these cases we are dealing with indissoluble communities, held together by an essential bond which can withstand temporary vicissitudes; we are dealing, in fact, with non-prescriptive obligations. Just so, and the fundamental question to be decided is whether development, too, is to be considered as a non-prescriptive obligation within an indissoluble community, or whether it is merely the consequence of a sentimental attitude and so subject to alternations of enthusiasm and disappointment.

Unfortunately, it would seem that an important body of public opinion continues to react to these problems in a purely sentimental manner. We are increasingly overwhelmed by information from all parts of the world; through the mass media we are continually exposed to shocks, often of a very disturbing nature. A normal sensibility has difficulty in withstanding such a battering, and is either stunned or blunted: in either case, it closes in upon itself and altruism is obliterated by the welter of dramatic happenings. It is therefore urgent to establish the reasons for giving aid on a level where they can be more coherent and lasting; the interest in development must by related to our fundamental imperatives so that it remains unaffected by day-to-day events.

It must be admitted that few attempts are made to establish such a relationship. People in different quarters assert the necessity for aid, as if it were an obvious truth which flowed naturally from the basic principles of our various cultures; but the obligation is hardly ever stated in formal terms, although, as we have just noted, it is not as generally recognized as is sometimes claimed. The reason is, no doubt, that morality, being in essence traditional, is resistant to novelty and we are dealing here with a new kind of duty, or at least with a radically new expression of duties which hitherto were defined only in abstract terms. But it is also the case that, whereas we are facing a problem which demands to be solved by humanity as a whole, *there is, as yet, no universally accepted code of morality*, even though each genuine moral system claims to enunciate universal principles. The more enormous the task, the greater the need that the effort to carry it out should be rooted in the deepest human convictions. We have many different cultures, ideologies and religions and the question is: can each of them express the same obligation in its own terms? My answer is yes, because I believe—and I am going to try to prove the point—that there exists, expressed in various ways, an imperative common to all the peoples of the globe, a *world imperative* capable of answering a world challenge. I even believe that the attempt to formulate it can help to overcome disagreements and to provide the first draft of a set of moral standards that would be universally accepted, a code which is as yet latent and sporadic but is only waiting to be brought into being.

This is precisely why it is impossible to rest content with arguments about opportunism or with fashionable formulae. We should not hesitate to seek inspiration from the major attempts that have been made to evolve universal moral standards. On the basis of these initial endeavours—however far removed they may seem from the present-day situation—we shall erect a more solid structure and so discern points of convergence more clearly.

123

The Strengths and Weaknesses of the Sentimental Approach

The arguments that are often put forward in support of aid to the developing countries can be related to three traditional attitudes, which may be tabulated as follows:—

1) *The rich owe help to the poor.*
At all periods, charity has been a means of re-establishing a balance between different social conditions. The rich man, unless he lives in isolation, is faced with the painful spectacle of the hungry at his gates. He appeases his sense of guilt by distributing a fraction of his goods among them. In traditional societies, the poor are looked upon as the innocent victims of an immutable order of things; their poverty depends upon the same blind necessity as natural disasters (drought, floods or epidemics); it cannot be abolished, but only mitigated by voluntary contributions from the rich.

2) *The rich owe reparation to the poor.*
A more subtle kind of awareness sometimes leads the rich to realize that they themselves might, to some extent, be responsible for the poverty of the poor. Their feelings of pity are consequently strengthened by a sense of guilt which prompts them to restore to the poor a proportion of that wealth which, were it fairly distributed, ought to be sufficient for all needs. Thus it is, that, since the middle of the 19th century, the spectacle of social injustice has given the property-owning classes a bad conscience and has driven them to set up institutions for collective aid which are intended to reduce the effects of extreme inequality.

3) *The rich must forestall violence on the part of the poor.*
It must be recognized that an element of fear is often combined with the feeling of pity and the urge towards retribution. There is a more or less conscious anxiety about the violent action to which the masses might be driven through despair at their incurable poverty. This explains the sacrifices made by the well-to-do to appease the "dangerous classes", as the working population concentrated in villages used to be referred to in Europe, whenever the situation of the proletariat declined to an alarming level.
Pity, guilt and fear are undoubtedly dubious motives, but they

cannot be condemned outright: morality does not consist in eliminating base feelings and replacing them by lofty ones, because the two kinds are too closely intermingled; it consists in harnessing the greatest possible amount of human resources for the service of the good. The feelings just referred to are undoubtedly powerful, and it is undeniable that they have helped to influence a section of public opinion in favour of aid to the developing countries. Not only do governments and organizations exploit the pity inspired by underprivileged populations—and more especially by underfed children—in order to obtain financial help, there are volunteers who devote their energies and sometimes even their lives to the task of providing disinterested aid. By doing so, they feel they are making their contribution to the remedying of injustices for which their nation or their church seem to be partly responsible. For four hundred years, the West used its superiority as an argument for the domination of areas of the world which it claimed to be "civilizing". Even if we grant that the colonial balance sheet has some positive aspects, it still remains true that the colonial regimes left most countries in a serious state of cultural, social and economic backwardness. In some instances, the harm was further increased by repressive measures and colonial wars. It is therefore only to be expected that the former imperialistic nations, whose empires have by now almost entirely disappeared, should feel a certain degree of guilt with regard to their ex-colonies, as well as a desire to make reparation. The feeling ought not to be limited solely to the former colonial powers, since the industrialized countries as a whole treated the overseas territories as a means towards their own development, by exporting manufactured goods to them and taking from them not only raw material but also manpower for their economies and wars. The most terrible instance was the slave trade, for which the great Western nations were responsible and which contributed to the impoverishment of Black Africa.

The colonial era is now drawing to a close, but many of the links forged by it still exist today. Most of the areas which came under the influence of the colonial powers have more or less remained within their orbits, if not politically, at least economically and culturally. Although they are now independent, they continue to live within a cultural and technical framework which they themselves had no hand in evolving. While it is true that their own development can now be a separate aim, it continues to depend on the development of the industrialized area of the world. The terms of economic exchange are, generally speaking, unfavourable to the developing countries: the industrialized countries take raw materials from them at unstable prices which are determined by the temporary needs of these rich countries, and sell back to them manufactured goods at prices which are often higher than those obtainable in the advanced countries where competition causes dumping. The operation of the world market, in which the developing countries play only a minor part, means then that the rich nations exact an extra payment from the poor countries at both ends of the economic circuit. It is a fact, of course, that structural differences now work against those countries which depend chiefly on mining and agriculture; it is also true that the industrialized countries no longer have such an urgent need of raw materials and overseas products. Nevertheless, at an important stage in their development, the industrialized countries obtained valuable supplies from overseas at low prices, and this may be said to call for compensation. After all, many industrialized countries subsidize agriculture within their own frontiers because they realize that, after serving as the foundation of their development, it cannot be left to fend for itself.

The analysis can be carried further. The Western nations were no doubt wrong in using their cultural superiority as an argument to justify the colonization of "native" populations. The fact remains that they involved these populations in a common undertaking which bears the stamp of historical rationality and technological progress. All the nations in the world are now, whether they like it or not, undergoing a process of change, and they see their development as taking place according to a form of progress, the concepts and instruments of which have been furnished by Western culture. This being so, the industrialized countries can hardly deny their responsibility towards those for whom they have made it possible, and even obligatory, to follow in their footsteps. Western thought, if it is to remain consistent with itself, must accept the consequences of that universality which it has constantly invoked as a principle. Having propagated the operational rationality of technology, it must accept not only its triumphs—man's growing mastery over nature—but also the terrifying consequences of a process which finally destroys what it tries to conquer and separates what it is trying to bring together.

126

The good will which assumes responsibility for faults committed and endeavours to correct them is, of course, not to be despised. But it is inadequate and unreliable. The conscience cannot go on feeling remorse for very long; it seeks to eliminate the sensation by turning against those who remind it of its guilt; when it thinks it has undergone sufficient penitence, it becomes irritated at not finding its former adversary in a similar virtuous mood. Soon, the accused turns into an accuser and criticizes the underdeveloped country and former colony for not being able to make proper use of its independence. Compassion, too, which makes it possible to arouse mass interest and prompts admirable individual vocations, is subject to dangerous vagaries: people weary of feeling pity, especially for the populations of distant continents, and they become unconsciously hardened to the phenomenon of poverty.

On the other hand, the developing nations reject an attitude which they find humiliating. They do not wish to become objects of pity, after being objects of conquest.

And lastly, is it necessary to emphasize once more that fear is never a wise counsellor? A man who is afraid can easily become violent; a crowd in the grip of fear can soon become savage. History demonstrates that the fear of uprisings on the part of the oppressed has more often led to brutal repression than to fair and generous settlements. We cannot count on fear, and as for pity and guilt, they are—as we have seen—useful up to a point. It would be wrong to condemn them, but it would also be wrong to hope that any lasting and arduous commitment can be founded on fluctuating emotions. By its extent and the demands it makes, the obligation to give aid goes far beyond the traditional requirements of charity or the twinges of conscience of the rich. It is a primary concern of the citizens of the prosperous countries in view of the crying needs of the underdeveloped countries. At the same time, the poor now know that their fate no longer depends on some inexorable destiny, but that they are free to take it into their own hands. The obligation to give aid arises from the division of the world into advanced and backward countries, but it must not continue to be governed by that division: it must be rooted in a higher duty, a shared duty—the ensuring of world development.

Development, A Positive Requirement for Peace between Nations

What do we mean by a moral duty? However such a duty may be expressed, it rests in the first instance on the feeling that every human life is worthy of special consideration and that every man has a right to be respected as such. Sympathy or love are of a different order: they are directed towards particular individuals whom they single out. To love the whole of mankind is an impossibility. But moral duty relates potentially to the entire human race, and even when it concerns only a single individual, it is relevant to humanity through that individual. Immanuel Kant established the foundations of all morality when he formulated his practical imperative: "Act in such a way as to treat mankind, whether in your own person or in that of others, never simply as a means but always at the same time as an end".

This prescription has no meaning unless man is considered as an autonomous being endowed with reason and freedom. Man can be an "end" (a goal) for himself, precisely because he has no end (is unlimited), but is capable of self-determination and self-improvement. This power to choose or this freedom of the will (*libre arbitre* in the Cartesian vocabulary) is the human element in each individual. This is the common source of morality and law: the former is the basis of the freedom shared by all men, while the latter aims at defending the various ways in which that freedom is expressed.

This imperative was sensed and proclaimed, long before it was put forward as a guide to action. For hundreds of years, men found various pretexts—religious, cultural, social, etc.—for not applying it to other communities, which they persisted in considering as inferior and therefore unworthy of being treated with respect. But the democratic ideas of the 18th and 19th centuries have gradually affected the whole earth and spread the claim for liberty and equality to subject or dormant societies. Simultaneously, by supplying the means for the satisfaction of mass needs, technical progress set a great hope in motion. The idea of happiness infused its revolutionary force into democratic, and then socialist, theories concerning the liberation of classes, nations and races. It thus became clear that the proclamation of the rights of man would remain an abstraction as long as it was not accompanied by decent living conditions: a hungry person is theoretically free, but in practice he remains a slave. The various forms of Hegelianism, as well as Marxism, emphasized this indispensable interconnection: "the truth of the intention is in the action" (Hegel); a morality which is not put into practice remains a mere alibi for "sensitive souls". This is why the fundamental rights of man and of communities have been supplemented by a growing mass of economic and social rights: the right to work, to receive medical attention, to enjoy security, and so on. Within the industrial countries this process has been under way for the last hundred years. It now tends to spill over in all directions so as to affect the whole world.

This brings us to a major question: is this internal justice that the citizens of a given state provide for each other also valid as between states? It is understandable that men should feel themselves to be committed with regard to a community to which they are bound by their work and by a common destiny embracing a shared past and a hoped-for future. But what duty have they towards men of other communities belonging to different states with different histories? By virtue of what principle can they be persuaded that it is their duty to agree to certain sacrifices on behalf of the underdeveloped territories, even when they are conscious of belonging to privileged communities?

To say that each individual has the same duties towards everyone, according to the practical imperative, is an inadequate answer. It is true that the imperative has a universal value. But we have also seen that, for it to come into operation and acquire genuine moral weight, certain concrete requirements have to be fulfilled and, in the absence of a world state, these can be supplied only by the national states: freedom, equality and security depend upon a legislative system circumscribed by, and functioning within, the national framework. Moreover, in the developing countries, the state, more often than not, is jealous of its independence and would find it intolerable that other states should impose the conditions necessary for a complete and coherent application of the universal moral imperative. We thus find ourselves confronted with a problem of international morality and law—and an apparently insoluble one, since each state remains sole judge in its own case.

This is the problem Kant dealt with in his essay *Towards Perpetual Peace*. Considering the setting up of a world state (*Völkerstaat*) to be still a utopian dream, he proposed, on the basis of the individual autonomy of the different states, that they should conclude amongst themselves a sort of "social contract" on the international level, a permanent alliance by virtue of which each national will would unite freely with all the rest to lay the foundations of a general interchange. This would lead to the creation of a right to world citizenship (*Weltbürgerliches Recht*), which is not an immediate right but rather the preliminary condition to be fulfilled before each state, and consequently each citizen, can enjoy a happy, free and peaceful existence, instead of being subject to arbitrary decisions, barbarism and the permanent threat of war.

This is a still more fruitful prospect now than it was in the 18th century, provided it is developed and extended. At that time, it rested on traditional political foundations, of a limited and almost unalterable kind. The problem then was, how to ensure peace between states which had no real need of each other in order to survive and who evolved their policies within the framework of traditional diplomacy. Now, however, it is clear that nations cannot participate in international law except in certain economic and social conditions, involving on the one hand the utilization of their resources and on the other an increase in the volume of trade. Consequently, the establishment of peace no longer means simply creating the political conditions in which states can conclude trade agreements; it entails setting up the structures and providing the means which will allow all states—and in the first instance the most backward—to intensify the utilization of their resources with the help of other states. Peace is no longer, then, a negative demand that there should be no war, but a positive demand resulting from the harmonization of the ambitions of the various states, each of which is pursuing its development in its own way. Peace will depend less and less on diplomatic groupings and more and more on dynamic associations aiming at mutual development.

In this respect, international society will undergo the same process as that which has already transformed national communities: with the growing complexity of international life, functions have become specialized and the different professional categories are knit together in a system in which each element is in close dependence on all the rest. When carried to its logical conclusion, this interweaving of functions reaches such a high degree of perfection and fragility that the possibility of its disruption appears as the most appalling catastrophe. Is it not legitimate to suppose that this process, which has consolidated industrial unity, will gradually establish, as between states, such a variety of networks of relationships that agreement about development will come to seem to them a vital necessity, so deep-rooted and valuable that no rivalry or conflict would justify its destruction?

In short, what Kant outlined for the traditional world of his day can be taken up again and strengthened within the framework of an economic and technological expansion which demands more than peaceful international trade: it supposes the rational use of world resources for the betterment of both individuals and nations. Therefore, development is both the principle and the object of aid: it binds states together in an agreement which can no longer be simply a pact of non-aggression, but must be one of mutual assistance; and it is precisely because development expresses the determination of all states to assert and strengthen their independence that their individual liberties can, and must, be harmonized with each other, since they are all striving fundamentally towards the same end.

In our time, international law can have no basis or practical application except in relationship to the mutual desire for development. If the inequalities between nations were to increase any further, trade between the industrialized countries and the developing countries would become impossible and, as a result, all international relationships would be jeopardized. Since international law would have lost its concrete basis, each nation would revert to its own selfish interests; a state of war, at least in a latent form, would be created, and a new barbarism would replace the efforts that are being made to establish a legal code, rules of free coexistence and circulation of people and goods. A world order within the context of classical diplomacy is no longer imaginable; it supposes progress on the part of each and all nations. Conversely, the security of each state no longer depends simply on a peaceful balance of power, or the respect by each of the rights of others: it implies a positive relationship and mutual assistance.

To help other peoples to develop is to help them to establish their rights to membership of the world community, without which states can have no lasting and peaceful existence; it is to help them to become really independent entities, that is, capable

131

of entering into agreements with other states which will further world peace and common progress. When the world was more or less stable, certain societies could be left to hibernate because they existed, to all intents and purposes, outside history. Now that all parts of the world are undergoing a process of change, if one of them stagnates, the consequences produced may be dangerous for all. The only alternative to generalized development would be world hegemony on the part of one power, or competition for such hegemony and therefore a return to the colonizing of peoples who have only recently won their freedom, and perhaps of others, too, who have never been colonized.

This is why it is possible to say that to help others is, in the last resort, to help ourselves, insofar as we belong to the international community and share in the peace and in the interchange it makes possible. One point must be clarified, however. Many people think that development aid must be paid back quickly and directly; they become indignant when the aid-receiving countries fail to show gratitude and refuse to enter into the alliances proposed to them, and even have an aggressive attitude towards the donor countries. There is no guarantee that a nation supplying financial and technical aid to another will necessarily and immediately obtain that country's political support. The benefit must not be expected on the level of a bilateral return but within the framework of a lasting, general improvement, because development helps to establish the foundations of a society of nations capable of preventing war and increases exchanges of all kinds. This society, which depends upon the free consent of states, has already begun to set up international institutions which are a guarantee of, and should more and more become a stimulus for, genuinely reciprocal relationships between the aid-giving and the aid-receiving nations. It is true, of course, that as long as there is no world government, development aid will remain more or less dependent on the immediate concerns and the short-term selfish interests of states. But already the need for, and the demands of, development exceed the limitations and the possibilities of each state and tend to involve them in a practical association, the institutional consequences of which, although still vague, are inevitable. However weak the development-promoting institutions may yet be, it must be admitted that they speak the only authentic world language across frontiers of power and ideology and represent the only irrefutable beginnings of an oecumenical association.

The world may seem to have never been more divided than it is today, when almost every nationality demands to have its state. But this fragmentation itself opens the way to progressive unification, because the very impulse behind national demands—the urge to promote a particular national personality and to make full use of all its resources—gives all states a goal of self-transcendence which, if properly understood, does not set them against each other. Admittedly, imperialism remains a strong temptation and rivalry is common. Yet it is reasonable to hope that the world is reaching a turning-point beyond which favourable mutations can occur: as soon as each nation sees its welfare as being dependent on the expanding of its own resources, there is a way out of the vicious circle of shortages, which meant that one nation's gain was inevitably another nation's loss, and that conquest, plunder and slavery brought quicker returns than work. Mechanization offers the suffering masses a more reassuring prospect than manual labour at a low level of productivity or chronic unemployment; and the actual process of development can appear as thrilling as war for adventurous temperaments. From now on a nation's "living-space" can no longer be measured in square kilometers; it extends towards the future, like the galaxies, in four dimensions, the fourth being the dimension of culture. For this reason, it is possible to state, as Pope Paul VI has done, that development is now the name of peace: not only because development reduces inequalities which might provoke conflicts, but above all because it can replace the search for a precarious balance of power by a dynamic process which demands the cooperation of the greatest possible number of people if it is to succeed, and which holds no threats for anyone.

It may be objected that what I am suggesting is a policy based on a relative estimate, and not a moral compulsion depending on an absolute obligation. My answer is that development is not a policy, but a preliminary condition for any international policy, in the same way as it is now a condition for the establishment of international law. The problem is how to ensure the survival of mankind, not only on the elementary level of feeding and looking after populations in the mass, but on that higher level which intellectual and technological progress has now made a necessity of life: this involves the elimination of illiteracy, education, mechanization, urbanization, improvement in communications, etc. As we have seen, the very essence of morality is to take human nature as a thing in itself, to respect that potentiality and duty to be a man which is inherent in every individual. Man exists within humanity, but this does not mean that the individual should be sacrificed to a multifarious entity. What is involved is a very concrete obligation. As Auguste Comte emphasized, the radical distinction between human society and animal societies lies in the fact that the former includes not only all living individuals but also the totality of the dead and of those yet to be born. The link between them is progress, something which is beyond animal societies. Thanks to the work and achievements of previous generations, those now living enjoy a better life: they can and must prepare a still better life for the generations yet to come. The 19th century used the word progress but we have the richer term: development.

Development is not, then, an aim that our societies are free to adopt or reject; it is their very substance and the link between past, present and future generations. If rightly understood, it is not just one particular social duty amongst others, nor even the primary duty: development is the condition of all social life and therefore an inherent requirement of every obligation. Individuals and nations can only be united with each other if they first exist. And, as we have just seen, individual existences and the existence of human societies are a function of progress, in other words of the expansion of human potentialities and of a corresponding increase in material goods. To reject development as a primary obligation would be to reject the humanization of man and therefore to deny the very possibility of a moral system.

Development—An Imperative of Human Solidarity

A moral system cannot be adequately founded on reason alone; it must also be based in human consciences and on material realities. Morality, too, has a history; being specifically human, it too, has undergone progress. It does not prescribe the same obligations in the 20th century as it did in the Middle Ages.

It is not enough to assert that the essence of morality is to respect the humanity of man; it is also necessary to state clearly what duties are prescribed by morality here and now. In other words, there can be no morality without practical application, whether one believes in the Gospel which preaches charity in action, or in Marx who maintains that the truth of an attitude appears only on the level of *praxis*.

Progress in morality has always meant the extending of obligations to broader and bigger human groupings. There was a time when justice was only mandatory between members of the same tribe or caste: slaves or barbarians were lesser breeds beyond the law. But gradually the nation superseded the *gens* and the city-state and established itself as the modern area of moral reciprocity. Then international groupings came into being on the basis of class, ideological or cultural solidarities. However, although the moral obligation may be directed towards humanity as a whole and gradually work its way through, it has never been able to embrace humanity as a single, coherent subject. Some thinkers—Hegel and Bergson in particular—have denounced the kind of abstract love of humanity which dissolves into vague sentiments and empty words, using them as an alibi for the individual's practical duty towards his "neighbour" and his own community. Actually, it is convenient "to love humanity"—a remote, anonymous mass—while neglecting or ill-treating the people around us. As we have seen, sentiments, even fine ones, do not constitute a morality. As for love, it picks out one or several individuals and cannot, by its very nature, be addressed to mankind in the mass. This being so, how can we speak of the moral obligation of development, when development concerns humanity as a whole, without regard to race, nationality and culture? Admittedly, each of us may be moved by what we hear about happenings in distant countries; but even if my emotions are aroused and I experience pity, how, in all conscience, can I feel an *obligation* towards peoples whose histories and cultures are often foreign to me?

To answer this question, we must consider the second direction in which morality has been progressing over the centuries. At the same time as the area of obligation has been extended, the nature of the obligation has been made more profound and more complex. Graeco-Roman civilization evolved the concept of the "person", which was linked however for a long time with the part played by the individual within the *gens* or the city-state. The major religions, by establishing a personal relationship with God, gave greater depth to the concept of the independent conscience

135

and virtually extended it to the whole of mankind. A creature for whom God cares is a unique, incomparable being of infinite value. To the negative commandments ("thou shalt not steal", "thou shalt not kill", etc.) were added further injunctions which turn the other person—however foreign and despised he may be —into an individual who should be recognized as such, and also loved and helped. "Love your enemies", Christ said, quoting the example of the Good Samaritan, and the Prophet Mohammed declared: ". . . whosoever saveth the life of one, it shall be as if he had saved the lives of all mankind". Although the movements towards political and social emancipation which later affected the whole world have often been opposed to religion, it would be truer to say that they have secularized its precepts rather than contradicted them; they have asserted that man, being born free and responsible for his own fate, has a right to happiness on this earth. The democratic revolution proclaimed his legal dignity: the socialist revolution his social and economic dignity. "Socialism is the Gospel in action", as Charles Blanqui said. And the religions have come to ratify the progress they themselves inspired in the first place; they now recognize that the liberation and full self-expression of the individual on this earth, far from working against his salvation, may be its starting-point.

There is, then, a world consensus of opinion on this point: each man has a right to live, and this right implies minimum conditions of security and dignity for the realization of his potentiality of freedom and happiness. From now on, man must be considered no longer as a completed creature, limited by his nature, but as a creature in process of realization. The assertion made by the theoreticians of progress in the 18th and 19th centuries that the nature of man is to improve and grow nobler is now restated by all doctrines and all religions in their different vocabularies. For Marxists, the problem is how to reinstate a "generic being" who has been alienated; for Existentialists, how to invent a form of freedom which will constantly overcome all limitations; for Christians how to enable God's creatures to cooperate in creation, by realizing all their capacities. As Pope Paul VI has said:

"In the design of God, every man is called upon to develop and fulfill himself for every life is a vocation. . . . Endowed with intelligence and freedom, he is responsible for his fulfilment as he is for his salvation. . . . Just as the whole of creation is ordained to its Creator, so spiritual beings should of their own accord orientate their lives to God, the first truth and the supreme good. Thus it is that human fulfilment constitutes, as it were, a summary of our duties. . . ." [1]

Dr. W. A. Visser't Hooft, honorary president of the World Council of Churches, has expressed himself in similar terms: "By putting the question: 'Adam, where art thou?' God bestows upon man the dignity of a creature who can, and must, take his own decisions about his relationship with God and other men. . . . Since man's vocation is one of emancipation, development will be valid if it brings liberation but not if it reinforces bondage or replaces one form of bondage by another".[2]

Thus development is not to be considered as an external activity, as one of the various tasks to be undertaken by societies, but as a necessity bound up with the essence of man, his freedom and (in the case of believers) with his spiritual vocation. Development as a duty occurs, then, at the point of convergence between duties towards oneself, towards others and towards God. It cannot be limited to the establishment of certain cultural, social and economic conditions: it expresses the creature's urge towards growth, that vital and spiritual impulse which drives man forward and which—as the believer is convinced—has God as its principle and its aim. This being so, it is justifiable to see development not merely as a particular duty arising from certain moral precepts, but as *the* moral attitude *par excellence*: ". . . human fulfillment constitutes, as it were, a summary of our duties", as Paul VI has written.[3] Thus, by way of contemporary theology, we return to the statement we had arrived at previously by a different process of reasoning: morality is concerned with humanity as a whole and its fundamental imperative, that each man should be treated not as an instrument but as an end, has as its corollary the development of the whole of man and of all men. To treat man as an end is to want him to become more human and to provide him with the means of doing so.

Providing the means involves, in the first place, seeing that natural resources are used for the benefit of mankind. Man does not live by work and inventiveness alone: he also exists in symbiosis with nature, from which he obtains food, energy and manu-

---

[1] *Populorum Progressio*, §§ 15 and 16.
[2] "Quel développement et pour quel homme?" The 13th General Assembly of the Protestant Association of France, Grenoble, Nov. 1969.
[3] *Populorum Progressio*, § 16.

factured products. The development of man and society supposes the development of wealth. Since the beginning of history, wealth has been unevenly distributed. Minorities have enjoyed possessions and privileges greatly superior to those at the disposal of the majority. All moral systems have denounced this injustice and have set against it the duty to share out the goods of the world among all the inhabitants. Brahmanism preaches: "It is in the nature of food to be shared out; not to give some to others is 'to kill its essence', to destroy it for oneself and for other people".[1] In the Gospel, the miracle of the multiplication of the loaves symbolizes the state of plenty that God invites men to achieve so that an adequate supply of material goods frees them from the limitations of shortage and allows them to turn their attention towards spiritual values. On this point, the morality of the Fathers of the Church was stricter than that of modern times: it proscribed hoarding and usury. Through the agency of Saint Thomas, it recommended that private belongings should be used "as if they were held in common". According to the Bible, it was "the whole earth" which was given to all men. Paul VI comments: ". . . each man has therefore the right to find in the world what is necessary, for himself . . ."[2] This right precedes the right of ownership or of free exchange. Men own the earth in a form of stewardship; all appropriation is provisional and subject to the general good.

For believers, then, it is a sin to exploit creation for the benefit of individual or collective selfishness: to do so is to move away from God. The Koran expresses this clearly:

"Wealth and sons are allurements / Of the life of this world: / But the things that endure, / Good Deeds, are best / In the sight of thy Lord, / As rewards. . . ." (XLVI)

For the benefit of non-believers, it is enough to recall that the duty to respect mankind cannot be limited to a section of humanity, nor even to the generation now alive: mankind is also made up of the dead and of those yet to be born. This imposes a duty to ensure a fruitful use of the achievements of previous generations, as well as the preparation of a habitable dwelling-place for future generations. Just as we have no right to hoard, we have no right to destroy; but we have the duty to bequeath the basis of a better life to our descendents. It is therefore criminal to

[1] Marcel Mauss: *Essai sur le don.*
[2] *Populorum Progressio.* § 22.

monopolize wealth which could provide for the upkeep of other people; and it is criminal to waste wealth which may then be lacking for those who come after us. This is a still graver misdemeanour when it affects means of production which might increase output and consumption:—technological information, reserves of energy, manufacturing facilities and transport, capital for equipment, etc. The economy depends less and less on the sharing out of existing riches and more and more on the production of manufactured goods. This is why individual or national selfishness has much more serious consequences than formerly: not only does it deprive other men or other nations of essential goods, it also halts their expansion. Too many people continue to look upon the earth as if it were an estate with clearly marked boundaries or a stock of materials: it is assumed that everything taken by one set of people must make the others correspondingly poorer; hence a fierce determination to protect one's property and to reserve it for one's own exclusive advantage. This residual peasant mentality is out of keeping with an industrial economy capable of distributing a great deal to a great many people without impoverishing anyone. But the citizens of the industrialized nations are increasingly coming to envisage the establishment of solidarity in terms of a dynamic and generalized growth in wealth. Development aid implies the extension to the world as a whole of this act of faith in the capacity of technology to multiply wealth and in the benefits that accrue from opening up markets and ensuring the circulation of goods, men and ideas.

It should not be supposed, however, that this broader awareness is easy to achieve. National self-centredness and the persistence of prejudices surviving from the still recent era of competitive trade are hard to overcome. The existence of currencies and the behaviour they promote are inimical to a generous and dynamic conception of economic progress. Most people still consider that economic exchange should be carried out according to strict principles of "give and take": each item should be paid for at the correct price . . . But what is the price? The so-called "laws of the market" express unfair relationships between economies on very different levels, with the result that the weak are necessarily subject to the requirements of the strong. It is well known how much the developing nations are handicapped by the fluctuation in the prices of raw materials. This unfair situation, although it works to the advantage of the advanced nations in the short term, is likely to do them harm in the long run. For a considerable time, the colonial powers were convinced that their colonies were a source of wealth until the moment came when they realized that it was in their interest to establish new relationships with nations who, by becoming independent, were entering upon a cycle of development in which increasing needs would intensify exchanges. Within the context of world expansion, it becomes possible to set up international economic relationships which go beyond the framework of strict accountancy and to create a form of solidarity at once more disinterested and more fruitful. This is not mere idealism. It is a return to the human basis of economic activity which has been artificially cut off from its real meaning. As anthropologists have shown, primitive economy was—and still is in certain tribes—an exchange of goods conveying a message. This is why gifts were an essential part of such an economy; the aim was not to obtain some equivalent return but to establish a lasting bond between two individuals or two groups: the receiver found himself involved with the donor in an association within which, peace being the rule, friendly exchanges were possible. The receiver in his turn had to make a gift so as not to be subject to the magic power of the donor. This gave rise to a society in which economy was not divorced from the transmission of signs and in which spirituality and materialism intermingled. "Everything passed to and fro as if there were constant exchange of some spiritual matter, including both objects and men, between classes and individuals, arranged according to rank, sex and generations".[1]

It is a fact, of course, that industrial economy has gone beyond the stage of potlatch; it is too complex and extensive to be based on the exchange of gifts. Moreover, it would be dangerous for the richer countries to involve the poorer, by means of gifts, in the subtle and embarrassing bonds of one-way generosity. It is, then, not so much a question of increasing aid and gifts as of humanizing international economic exchanges in such a way as to transcend arithmetical accountancy and to initiate infinitely broader and more differentiated exchanges than those normally practised; thanks to such a humanization, goods will gradually lose their quantitative, monetary importance to become signs of creative activity and invitations to social intercourse, knowledge and a more varied and stimulating life. Development requires,

[1] Marcel Mauss: *Essai sur le don.*

then, more open and generous attitudes than those which made for success under competitive capitalism.

It should not be forgotten that altruism can prove stronger than selfishness, provided it can be stimulated and directed. Many people have carried it to the point of laying down their lives. It is the sole basis of innumerable religious and secular organisations. Experience shows, of course, that it is often easier to sacrifice one's life than one's possessions. Yet parents—that is, the vast majority of men and women—normally make some material sacrifices for their children. The desire to give is a fundamental human need and it is natural that it should extend beyond the limits of the family. An economic system which provides it with no outlet is only using part of the available human resources; and this, no doubt, is one of the great causes of frustration at the present time; it is noticeable, by contrast, from the keenness with which people contribute to major charity campaigns: it is as if they were rediscovering a lost sense of community, or a sort of fraternal enjoyment, by giving each other proof of the fact that they are capable of shaking off their ordinary selfishness and transcending their average natures. No doubt, the desire for gain and the competitive spirit are very strong. But why should economic dynamism be based solely on interested motives when it is man as a whole, with his equally strong altruistic urges, who should be appealed to? As John Stuart Mill suggested, this could be the means of bringing about great changes which would make technical inventions the common property of the human race.[1] This would be the first step towards a gift economy which would transcend the profit-making motive. A gift economy, in the words of François Perroux "is not an economy which admits gift-making in a subordinate role; it is an economy the vital institutions of which oblige everyone to act through disinterested motives, thus restoring to such motives their specifically economic effectiveness".[2]

When understood in this way, gift-making is not the same thing as charity; charity is an alibi to which the rich have recourse in order to forget the poor. Gift-making is the unrequited transmission of knowledge, services and goods to help the development of the underprivileged nations. Some countries have already begun to operate such a transmission on a small scale under the name of

[1] John Stuart Mill: *Principles of Political Economy*.
[2] François Perroux: *L'économie du XXe siècle*.

141

aid or cooperation. However, they usually try to justify it by arguments based on interest, almost as if they were ashamed of it: what we are giving, they say, will bring returns in the form of political or strategic support, contracts for the development of resources, requests for equipment, etc. But what is given has no relationship, expressible in figures, with what might be supplied in return. Helping a community to educate itself, to make use of technology or to cure an endemic disease is not the sort of service which can be paid for according to any scale of values. These things are really free services, and only if they are seen in this disinterested light can they be given their meaning and full effectiveness and will they be carried on by devoted experts with the support of public opinion which, when suitably informed, is capable of taking an interest in something other than immediate profits. No mathematical calculation can prove that it is in the interests of a nation to give: no form of accountancy can show that giving is a paying operation. But on the other hand, we know only too well how harmful competitive capitalism has been, and still is, for countries that it has ruined; and it must be recognized that the analyses of classical political economy have little relevance to the new structures of the developing economies. What we are concerned with, then, is a wager about an unforeseeable yet necessary future: the development of all parts of the world so that mankind as a whole may share the same way of life. As François Perroux has said: "It is a question of giving preference to the common endeavour over strict calculations of equivalence",—a kind of folly, perhaps, but a more reasonable folly than the sinister future that can be forecast on the basis of present statistics and policies.

Technology has placed mankind in a new situation. Its initial effects—proletarianization, colonization and mechanized warfare—were disastrous, and it is still wreaking havoc; the pauperization of certain classes and areas is being intensified. But, as Heidegger has pointed out, technology involves human freedom in an extraordinary adventure, in which salvation can be glimpsed in the very jaws of danger: "When we open our minds properly to the essence of technology, we find ourselves in an unhoped-for way caught up in a liberating urge." Technology, by doing violence to nature, eventually obliges man to transcend himself and to recognize a cosmic finality lying beyond the useful or the instrumental. The mobilization of the worker, which was confused for a time with that of the soldier, now seeks an outlet in the transformation of the world into a habitable dwelling-place. The mind can only grasp the essence of technology if it thinks of something other than technology; it must reflect on authenticity and the community; technological progress calls for a decisive choice as regards the aims of life. The outstanding thinkers sensed this at the very beginning of the industrial era. Henri de Saint-Simon said that the task of industry should be "to give all members of society the greatest latitude for the development of their faculties". What at that time was a national aim now tends to become a world aim. The workers have gradually obliged the state to whittle away privileges and to exploit wealth for the benefit of the greatest number. The common good is no longer identified with the interests of a minority, it embraces the cultural development, freedom and betterment of everyone. This is now a world-wide tendency. Men realize that there exist ways of changing life, of freeing it from want and compulsion so that it becomes an opportunity for all; they are ready for "the great scientific, poetic and moral operation, which will displace the earthly paradise, transferring it from the past to the future".[1]

The utilization of science and technology to transform and unify the earth for the benefit of all its inhabitants, which a hundred and fifty years ago seemed to be the dream of a few idealists, now appears as a reasonable proposition. The linking up of the seas, the fertilization of the deserts, the transformation of climates, the deflection of human energy away from warfare towards great development undertakings are utopian ideas which are now turning into realities. In spite of differences in social levels and standards of living, we now see the beginnings of a consensus of world opinion: men, wherever they may be, want to live a human life. The citizens of the advanced nations refuse to stop at the stage they have now reached: they demand an ever higher standard of comfort, leisure and autonomy. But the claiming of national independence and the cultural awakening in the Third World signify, in a more collective style, the same desire for progress and liberation. Happiness is a new idea in the world, even though its demands may be spread out over many different levels. However, it is now a moot question whether there is not going to be a rift between the sophisticated claims of those who

[1] Henri de Saint-Simon: _Opinions_ 1825.

possess more than the bare necessities and the basic claims of those whose daily problem is how to stay alive. A morality for development must remind the privileged that the human race is now threatened with an incurable split which will only be avoided by according priority to cooperative development, *i.e.* to the sharing out of resources so that the majority are not left hopelessly behind.

"Have more to be more": Paul VI's formula does not mean that man's progress is to be measured by the acquisition of material goods but that economic development is the indispensable basis for human development. That is why the duty to develop is not the result of a relative level of needs and possibilities, as if one had to develop so as not to be outdistanced or to catch up with the more advanced, etc. It is founded on the obligation, spontaneously recognized by every man, that he should realize his human possibilities.

". . . . Our task in the Twentieth Century—the task of all men—is so to develop and share the riches of the world together that all men may benefit and come to their full human stature. . . ." [1]

The creation of man by man is the only project which corresponds in importance to the knowledge and technological devices now at our disposal. It transcends both individuals and nations. It prompts us to get rid of our competitive economy in order to establish a global economy, which will gradually come to include things that cannot yet be expressed in numerical terms: relations between individuals and between nations, the quality of living and the progress of culture, happiness and freedom—a world economy in which states will subordinate their competitiveness to a common objective . . . Is this a utopian ideal? In part, no doubt: as long as states exist, there is no hope of putting an end to the rivalry between them. But it must also be realized that there are strong arguments working in favour of the utopian ideal. The means at the disposal of technology are now so powerful that they will lead to ruinous struggles if they are not directed towards common development. The advanced industry, nuclear industry in particular, can be geared indifferently to production for war or peace. This is sufficient indication of the fact that mankind cannot delay the choice between universal annihilation or universal salvation.

[1] The Conference on World Co-operation for Development, Beirut, 21–27 April, 1968.

Development can be seen, then, as a universal obligation. This does not by any means signify that all nations or all cultures should conform to a single model. There can, properly speaking, be no *development* except on the basis peculiar to each community. In some instances, colonialism set up structures and disseminated knowledge and customs favourable to technical progress, but it always did so in terms of assimilation, or at least subordination. *Development* is to be distinguished from *progress* precisely in that it is the exploitation of the potential values peculiar to each people. The encouragement of development is not to be confused with the spread of progress; it supposes an act of faith in the ability of all communities to use the instruments of progress to their advantage; no culture or national mentality is doomed to perish or stagnate because of its particular nature. But this conviction does not mean that what is called industrial civilization—and it, in fact, the Western response to technological progress—is the obligatory norm for all development. This point needs to be emphasized because it marks the difference between the genuine ambition of development and certain sly attempts to re-establish colonialism under the guise of assistance or cooperation. To be in favour of the development of other nations is not the same as wanting them to imitate or resemble us; it is to put at their disposal the means they ask for to ensure their own progress. Solidarity is not synonymous with conformity. Mankind is made up of communities with different histories, languages and cultures. Either we are in favour of encouraging these differences or, more or less consciously, we want the whole world to be reduced to the model which is dominant at the moment. To opt for development is to opt for the first alternative, which is stimulating though risky.

The risk incurred is inseparable from the process of strengthening someone else's personality: it is the risk inherent in education, parenthood and love, the risk of competition or even conflict—in short, the risk of freedom. But without it, there would be no moral life, since morality is in the first place our relationship with other people; in fact, there would be no life at all: human peculiarities would tend to an undistinguished banality. The temptation to create identical individuals is characteristic of any group wanting to protect itself; it leads to monotony, unchangeability and often to deadly forms of hysteria. It is the road to death. To wish for development, on the contrary, is to go along with life which progresses by means of differentiation. The aim of development ought to be to offer every human community the possibility of choosing its future in accordance with its genius. And this exceeds the scope of economy; it involves respect for the multiplicity of nations and cultures which go to make up mankind. The supreme task of the human race as it progresses and differentiates is to encourage the full flowering of each, as well as mutual interchange.

We see every day that the application of technology helps to destroy precious forms of originality and to cover the surface of the earth with a uniform layer of banality. This is an additional reason for ensuring that the various cultures find, or rediscover, their true expression, so as to create a total humanity made up of the sum of its differences. Only people conscious of their traditions and who have different personalities can communicate with each other, because they have something to say. During the last hundred years, a host of nations have set out in search of their cultural identities. The resulting revolts and conflicts should not blind us to the fact that the force behind these upheavals is the same as the force behind the desire for development. Every effort must be made, then, to direct this force towards life-enhancing rather than death-dealing activities. This is an immense political problem which will not be solved by abstract simplicifications or by schematic, technocratic proposals. Development, which is a universal problem, will only acquire strength and value if it is rooted in every nation now moved by the desire to be itself.

The challenge of development is formulated for each people in its own language and calls upon each to start or re-start its history —and in the first place, those who are on the threshold of industrialization. But it would be a mistake to think that they alone are concerned. The call to exist resounds like an echo and a summons even for those nations who think of themselves as advanced. It warns them of the danger threatening communities which shut themselves off inside their selfishness and pride; it offers them the possibility of a word communion, the outlines of which are now vaguely discernible on the horizon.

Helping Oneself While Helping Others

As has been shown, development benefits all nations without any one of them being able to count on a particular advantage.

Development aid will produce its good effects through the progress of mankind. Now, for the first time, mankind can be spoken of as a whole; for the first time, the human race is in a position to conceive of a common endeavour and to carry it out. Development, I repeat, transcends the aims of each people or state taken individually. It is the consequence of an act of faith in the new solidarity of mankind.

It would be a mistake to believe that the obligation concerns the industrialized countries only indirectly and that development, for them, is no more than a luxury activity to which they are called upon to devote their surplus production. Actually, for the advanced countries, development is an immediate and essential task. It is so in the first place because it constitutes a challenge in respect of their own principles. The Pearson Report puts the point quite clearly:

"If the rich countries try to make it so, if they concentrate on the elimination of poverty and backwardness at home and ignore them abroad, what would happen to the principles by which they seek to live? Could the moral and social foundations of their own societies remain firm and steady if they washed their hands of the plight of others?" [1]

We are concerned here with the essence of that society which invented advanced industrialization: it has never thought of itself as a particular civilization limited to one nation or one area; even during the colonial era, it claimed to be exporting universal values and forms of behaviour. It was a civilization responsible for many mistakes and crimes, but it must be credited with a kind of greatness: it always looked upon itself as being potentially a world civilization. "Men are born, and remain, free and equal in rights" are the first words of the French Declaration of the Rights of Man. It was a civilization which enunciated the precepts of freedom, reason and happiness for the whole of mankind, even though it hardly carried them out, and sometimes even suppressed them. But the contradiction itself in the end proved fruitful: sometimes with the industrialized West and often in opposition to it, the colonial peoples and backward countries have, in their turn, asked for freedom, equality and cultural and economic progress. In doing so, they have borrowed ideas, methods and sometimes even languages, from the West. And above all, they have adopted the dynamic conception of history, which is at the root of the constant progress in science and technology.

[1] *Partners in Development*, p. 8.

In this way, the universalism which lay behind the conquests of the West has often turned against it. But however fierce the resulting conflicts in the past or in the present, the conception of an indefinite expansion of freedom and happiness is now dominant the world over. Even when it is rejected politically, development as a model is now, to a greater or lesser extent, a national aim of every country achieving self-consciousness and freedom. And the phenomena of industrialization, urbanization and democratization which transformed first Europe and then North Africa are now spreading to almost every country in the world. The rationalization of administration and technological efficiency are imperatives now common to almost all the countries in the world, although circumstances differ from one to another. The developing countries are in a hurry to accomplish in a few decades what it took Europe centuries to achieve. The find themselves faced simultaneously with all the demands of progress and with a host of needs and claims which have been accumulating among their underprivileged populations, who, moreover, are now aware of the standard of living in the industrialized countries. Hence, a great deal of commotion and unrest which the inhabitants of the industrialized countries, instead of waxing indignant, should see as being the inevitable consequences of a model that they themselves have propagated to the best of their ability. The demands that are now made of them, often in a harsh and impatient manner, are in fact their own demands. If they are to be consistent, the advanced countries must accept responsibility for the principles by which they have lived and which they continue to evoke. Furthermore, they would be denying themselves in rejecting their own image; they would be discredited, through having propagated on all sides desires and dreams that they then refused to satisfy. The inhabitants of the industrialized countries must be logical with themselves: the advantages they are proud of and the life-style they have spread abroad arouse awareness and create needs in the remotest parts of the world and cannot fail to stimulate an immense appetite for progress and welfare. They are therefore faced with the choice either of helping to satisfy this appetite or of retreating into their own personal comfort and shutting themselves up inside their luxurious habitations, as the Roman patricians did at the time of the decadence.

My own position is clear; I refuse to accept the idea that the world of the future should take the form of a ghetto of the rich surrounded by shanty-towns. This would mean the stillbirth of the world community and a cleavage in humanity leading to appalling disasters. And let us be quite frank about it: it would be tantamount to a condemnation of the West, precisely at the moment when the seed sown by the West is about to germinate. The West itself would be blighted by such a denial.

It is an illusion to suppose that a civilization can survive for long if it is shut in upon itself. All civilizations have borrowed from abroad and have depended on exchanges. If one part of the world retreated into wealthy isolation, while others stagnated in poverty, there would no longer be any fruitful communication and soon not even a common language. We would become strangers to each other, mere objects of curiosity, envy or hostility, mutilated creatures incapable of change. The backward peoples would look to the advanced countries for nothing more than recipes for success, while the latter would consider the former as a romantic reserve, suitable for tourism, holidays and anthropology. The world would then lapse into a state far inferior to the one which existed at the beginning of the modern period, since at that time, although countries were culturally distinct, their standards of living were more or less the same.

A society living in isolation is doomed to spiritual death. We ought to be put on our guard by certain symptoms which have already appeared in the industrialized countries. First, there is a feeling of being "shut in", which is particularly prevalent among students. "We are caught in a trap", they say. "Whatever we do, we are conditioned to want what this particular society wants for us; there is nothing left to invent or discover; life can be summed up as a process of increasing production in order to increase consumption . . ." It is a fact that the mass media, and publicity generally, put forward obsessive models all aimed at stimulating consumption or at creating new needs when the existing ones have been satisfied. The huge production-consumption machine, the functioning of which is increasingly rationalized, demands that we obey its numerous directives and instructions. And the greater the accumulation of goods and messages, the more our power of choice seems to dwindle; the richer the possibilities of life, the more uncertain becomes the meaning of life. Nowadays, we hardly dare invoke those values, such as democracy, the improvement of people's minds by education or progress through science, which the 19th century believed in with religious fervour. A whole section of our culture reflects the image of a human being unable to communicate, degraded although living in comfort, mechanized by organization and even losing awareness of his own personality in the mass of individuals and objects. Preceding generations, who grew up in want, dreamed of abundance. Abundance is now in process of being achieved, but many young people, when asked to accept the disciplines of production so that they may share in the advantages of general consumption, ask: "Where are the aims? Where is the element of adventure?" and sometimes, in disgust, they turn away from the groaning board.

It is, as yet, beyond anyone's powers to give a general interpretation of the wave of protest which has set a large part of the intellectual youth of the advanced countries against the established order. But it is certain that one of the causes is the fact that young people are shocked by the contrast between high-minded declarations and cynical policies. If they sometimes appear to reject democracy, this is no doubt because they had taken it seriously and, having the beginnings of a world conscience, they cannot tolerate waste in one quarter of what is vitally needed in another, when for them liberty, equality and fraternity cut across all frontiers. The armaments race, the continuance of under-development and racialism, the division of the world between rich and poor, all this gnaws at the consciences of the industrialized countries, and the anger of the young generation is a symptom of the bad conscience of a civilization. The fact that the young people's indignation is rarely expressed in moral terms and takes the form of a violent world revolt is probably to be explained by the frequency with which previous generations uttered humanistic proclamations to cover up selfish attitudes and national imperialism. At the present time, to speak about morality—and more particularly about the moral obligation of development aid —is to be suspected of an abuse of confidence. However, neither romanticism nor violence can supply an answer to the following question, which is a moral rather than a political one: are the industrialized countries going to try to make their behaviour agree with their principles, or will they continue to act like those early capitalists who paid their workers starvation wages and then eased their consciences by sending their wives to give bread to the poor?

The thought of the Parisian student, whom I quoted at the beginning of this study, comes back to me again now that I have almost reached my conclusion. This is no accident, since justice starts from anger. Indignation, even when wrongly directed, is better than resignation. On the one hand, we see a huge production machine intent on increasing the quantity of superfluous goods, since they are the most profitable; on the other, great masses of people suffering from hunger and disease. No economic or political reason can justify the continuance of such a scandalous situation. Already many devoted people are trying to remedy it; the experience of those nations which have set up assistance and cooperation services shows that there is no lack of excellent volunteers. But the problem is much more than simply one of providing an outlet for youthful generosity: it is a question of opening up a system, at present limited by its own feed-back, and turning it in the direction of world development. Modern societies suffer less from an excess of wealth and organization than they do from the lack of any aim transcending the production-consumption cycle. There is lunar exploration, of course, but it has yielded no more than disappointing pebbles, whereas the earth is inhabited by men. However, the earth, seen from the moon, appears for the first time as a single entity and, in spite of its divisions, as being more than ever the place where man must accomplish his destiny.

Development aid should not be looked upon as a remedy for the ills caused by luxury. It is something quite different and more important: it helps us to rediscover a need peculiar to our societies, a need which has been concealed by the mobilization of the forces of production and the frenzy of consumption. The cleavage that technological progress has created in the world also exists, on the national level, inside each industrialized country. Masses of people have been uprooted and segregated; "depressed" areas have reverted to non-productivity. Within the wealthy countries, "pockets of poverty" have come to light. If it were simply a matter of a temporary discrepancy, no irreparable harm would be done; but, as all research shows, there is a growing gap between the majority enjoying the fruits of progress and those marginal sections whose backwardness is intensified. The progress achieved is undeniable: for the first time in history, whole populations have been shielded against hunger, cold and epidemics. But progress is not without its drawbacks: the improvements in medicine which save the lives of premature babies increase the numbers of the weak and infirm. Among the growing mass of social misfits in an

151

ever worsening condition we must also count a proportion of the elderly. Everything which provides a livelihood and a better living standard for the majority can have an adverse effect on a minority, and this minority presents the industrialized countries with their most difficult problem. The nations which considered themselves as being advanced are thus beginning to discover that underdevelopment is their concern too. This is a dangerous discovery if it diverts aid for the exclusive benefit of under-privileged national minorities. On the other hand, it can be valuable if it leads to an understanding of the causal link between internal and external underdevelopment.

The segregation and imbalance observable in the industrialized countries arise from the mad lust for profit and the unbridled industrialization in the growth stage of capitalism, which was also the time when the great empires established their dominion over so many peoples. The advanced countries have sacrificed a great deal in the cause of technological and economic competition; they have prided themselves on their productive capacities. Now they are beginning to realize the price that must be paid for this. Millions of individuals have been uprooted; the heedless exploitation of nature is exhausting resources and creating ugliness; pollution is becoming a major problem in large cities. While consumer goods become more plentiful, vital necessities such as air, water and the natural environment begin to be in short supply. Man is suddenly discovering with dismay that he is in the process of killing the earth. This worries him and so he sets about protecting trees and animals because of a vague realization that his vocation is to lead a human life, which is something transcending mere technical performance or material welfare. Happiness consists in living in harmony with oneself and the world. Powerful campaigns have been mounted to arouse public opinion in defence of threatened animal species, with the result that the massacring of baby seals has been stopped. This is a good thing, but it remains to be seen whether there is the same will to save the human race. The problem is identical in the case of human babies who are dying for lack of milk: is the earth to be abandoned to unbridled exploitation and the competitiveness of the economic powers, or is it to be organized for the benefit of all its inhabitants? No country can give a separate answer to this question, because it concerns the survival of the whole world. Whether it relates to the underprivileged sections of the industrialized countries or to the backward nations, development is a single, indivisible issue.

And, in discussing the dangers of "neo-colonialism", it must be understood that the threat exists not only in the former colonial territories but also in the industrialized countries, where technocracy looks upon ever-increasing production and consumption as an iron law, at the expense of the quality of life and balanced human relationships.

The activism characteristic of the industrial societies drives some of their members into a kind of internal emigration. Through a strange paradox, the hippies imitate the way of life and the frugality of the backward peoples at the very time when the latter are trying to become part of the technological society. Must we conclude, then, that development is an evil, since it destroys local peculiarities and primitivism, and that development aid is a snare and a delusion since it exports the disciplines and neuroses from which the advanced countries are suffering? This is a very difficult question to which we have to try to give an answer valid for both sides, since the ills of the wealthy nations cannot be cured by importing the folklore of the poor countries, any more than one can ensure the happiness of backward societies by sending them motorcars. Development is a decision which sets a given people on the road to progress, but the aim is not the accumulation of objects or even the raising of living standards but the greatest possible fulfilment of the greatest number of men. It is not a matter of dressing up in other people's clothes and imitating their way of living but of using the instrument of technology to achieve an honourable style of existence. It is not a matter of escaping from one's society and one's history, but rather of creating a society capable of inventing a history.

There are already many signs that the industrialized nations are becoming conscious of an imbalance which jeopardizes their future. They are trying to rationalize their economies, control population growth, humanize the increase in the different social categories and fight the harmful effects of pollution. These initial measures may herald the beginning of a new era, provided the different nations are resolved to renounce selfish interests and to work together to fight the dangers threatening one and all. If the industrialized countries think of development as a higher aim transcending their particular interests, it can help them to cure the ills with which they are afflicted. It is a fact that their rhythm of life is much too hurried and that the time has come for a return to restfulness, communion, friendship and qualitative living. But this is impossible within the framework of national economies devoted to competitiveness and financial rivalry. It must first be realized that life on earth should be restored and encouraged— life as a universal essence being lived on the earth regarded as a single entity. If this is achieved, world development can act as a context for, and a peaceful influence on, the various national developments; it can regulate the growth of the industrialized nations and can provide them with the oecumencial aim in which they are lacking. It can begin to humanize growth and make it less aggressive and insistent by directing it towards wider and more meaningful objectives than the indefinite acceleration of individual consumption. Frenzied economic competition and the arms race can only be mitigated if nations cooperate in an effort which transcends them all and unites them against a common enemy. (The backward countries are more affected by physiological ills, the advanced countries by psychological ones. If men realized that these two kinds of evil are as closely interlinked as are the body and the mind, competition for profit and prestige would give way to cooperation, and we would be helped by the help given to others.)

This is, admittedly, a utopian view. But such utopianism is necessary today, since it alone can counterbalance the stockpiling of the weapons of death. It is a utopianism which demands that the peoples in the vanguard of progress restore the term to its original meaning and by rediscovering the road to universality rediscover the truth of their objective by translating it into a revolution in mentality and structures. "Until nations begin to practice full development together, they will remain unaware of what they are, of what they possess and of what they can achieve".[1] The world has so far been fumbling towards international cooperation. The testing time of recognition is upon us.

The many initial attempts at world collaboration already in existence show that mankind aspires to unification. No people can now exist outside the history common to all. As Charles Péguy sensed: "No part of the human race is any longer held in reserve". Mankind is now advancing along a single front and facing the same risk. Will it recognize its common destiny in

[1] François Perroux: *Le pain et la parole.*

154

time? Individual men and individual nations can only achieve their peculiar vocations if they all accept development as a task which transcends and unites them. The exploitation of world resources and the fulfilment of the human race now represent the same single task; and development aid, our collective duty towards others, is identical with our duty towards ourselves.

Bibliography

Auguste Comte: *Oeuvres.*

Martin Heidegger: "La question de la technique", French trans-
lation in *Essais et Conférences,* Gallimard,
N.R.F., Paris.
Immanuel Kant: *Grundlegen Zur Metaphysik der Sitten.*
Zum Ewigen Frieden.

J.-L. Lebret: *Suicide ou survie de l'Occident,* Les Editions Ou-
vriéres, Paris, 1958.

Marcel Mauss: "Essai sur le don" in *Sociologie et anthropologie,*
P.U.F., Paris.

Paul VI: *Populorum Progressio.*

François Perroux: *L'Economie du XXe siécle,* P.U.F., Paris 1961.
Industrie et création collective, P.U.F., Paris,
1964.
Le pain et la parole, Editions du Cerf, Foi et
Vie, Paris, 1969.

Henri de Saint-Simon: *Le système industriel, Opinions* in *Oeuvres,*
Edition Anthropos, Paris.

The Export Stake of Industrial Countries in The Third World

DAVID WIGHTMAN

Recent Trends

One of the remarkable features of world trade in the past twenty years is the way in which trade among rich countries has shot ahead of that of others. The exchange of manufactures among industrial countries has become, in the current jargon, the most dynamic sector of world trade. The explanation, in general terms, is simple enough—the unprecedently rapid expansion of these economies; the increasing diversity of their consumer demands at higher levels of income; their thrusting technical progress and the stream of new products flowing from it; the progressive relaxation and removal of their trade and payments restrictions.

By the end of the sixties the industrial market economies were themselves absorbing about three quarters of their own exports. To an increasing extent, their export performance and prospects has come to depend on trade among themselves. Not surprisingly, their interest in trade barriers and market opportunities tends to be somewhat self-centred. These countries very largely determine the character and outcome of trade negotiations within the G.A.T.T. They are responsible for the currency crises that have buffetted the international monetary system in recent years and for the makeshift arrangements that have so far kept it afloat. Yet, understandably absorbing as these preoccupations are, they should not obscure the fact that a sizeable chunk of their export business is still with the less developed regions of the world.

In 1969 the exports of industrial market economies to the third world amounted to over $37 billion, a level 125 per cent higher than in the mid-fifties. Including the Soviet Union and Eastern Europe the total rises to around $40 billion, a level 137 per cent higher than in the mid-fifties. This is a scale of business to be taken seriously; indeed, in the obsessive struggle for export markets, which carries with it more than an echo of an earlier mercantilist age, no industrial country can afford to treat it otherwise. It is only because trade among themselves has grown so much faster that the markets of the Third World have slipped in relative importance. In the mid-fifties these markets absorbed about one quarter of their exports; by the end of the sixties the proportion had fallen to under one fifth. The proportion is not the same for all industrial countries or for all the main categories of their exports. From the array of figures presented in the statistical Appendix to this paper a more detailed picture can be drawn. Its main features are as follows:

(1) The Third World is a more important export market for Japan, the United States and the United Kingdom than for other industrial countries. In 1969 it accounted for 18 per cent of the total exports of all industrial countries, including the Soviet Union and Eastern Europe, but for over 40 per cent of Japanese, 30 per cent of U.S. and 24 per cent of British exports. By contrast, the E.E.C. countries and the Soviet Union sold between one seventh and one eighth of their exports to these markets.

(2) Since the mid-fifties the share of Third World markets in the total export trade of the major industrial suppliers, especially Western Europe and Japan, has fallen steadily. Only in the case of Australia, New Zealand, the Soviet Union and Eastern Europe, which between them account for less than ten per cent of all exports from industrial countries to the Third World, has the proportion risen. It remained constant in the case of Canada up until the mid-sixties, but has fallen a little since.

(3) Within the Third World, Latin America and Asia are more important regional markets for industrial countries than Africa and the Middle East. In 1969 the two former regions accounted for about 60 per cent of the exports of industrial countries to the Third World. The concentration on Latin America is particularly marked in the case of U.S. exports. Not surprisingly, Japanese, Australian and New Zealand exports to the Third World are heavily concentrated on Asia and the E.E.C. is the largest single industrial supplier of Africa. The regional distribution of exports from other industrial countries to the Third World is more diversified, though the relatively low U.K. share of the Latin American market is worth remarking.

158

(4) Of the $40 billion of exports from industrial countries to the Third World in 1969, the U.S. accounted for 28 per cent, the E.E.C. for a quarter, Japan for 17 per cent and the U.K. for 10 per cent. The share of both the U.S. and E.E.C. has fallen since the mid-fifties, but not so abruptly as that of the U.K. Japan, on the other hand, more than doubled its share. The Australian and New Zealand share also rose, and that of Canada remained unchanged. The exports of the Soviet Union and Eastern Europe rose rapidly in the sixties but are still well under ten per cent of the exports of developed market economies to the Third World. To a considerable extent the export gains of Japan, the Soviet Union and Eastern Europe simply reflect the low level of their exports to Third World markets in the mid-fifties.

(5) The relative export strength of industrial countries in different Third World regions shows some interesting variations. Thus the U.S. share in the Latin American market has sharply declined since the mid-fifties and to a smaller extent in the Middle East and Asia as well, but it improved a little in Africa. The U.K. share fell most heavily in Asia, followed by Africa and the Middle East, but its relatively small share in the Latin American market has not changed much. Africa and Asia account for the overall decline in the E.E.C. share of the Third World market, for in Latin America and the Middle East it has remained pretty steady. In all Third World regions, and especially in Asia, Japan increased its share of their imports from industrial countries mainly, it seems, at the expense of Western Europe. This was to be expected once Japanese recovery got under way in the 1950s. The share of the Soviet Union and Eastern Europe at the end of the sixties ranged from 4½ per cent in Asia to 8½ per cent in Latin America and Africa and nearly 12 per cent in the Middle East.

(6) Machinery and transport equipment is the largest and fastest growing category of goods exported from industrial countries to the Third World. In 1955 it accounted for one third of this export business and by 1969 for 43 per cent. In the case of the U.K. the proportion in 1969 was almost one half. The category "Other Manufactures", which consists mainly of consumer goods, made up over one quarter of the total in 1955, but declined in relative importance to a little more than one fifth of the total in 1969. Roughly speaking, machinery and transport

equipment, and chemical products account for well over one half the total exports from industrial countries to the Third World, manufactured consumer goods for one fifth and the category food, beverages and tobacco for nearly one eighth.

(7) Exports of machinery and transport equipment from industrial countries to Third World markets doubled during the sixties. In 1969 23 per cent of their exports of machinery and transport equipment was sold in these markets compared with 18 per cent of all their exports. Less developed countries accounted for 46 per cent of the export trade of Japan in these goods and for about 27 per cent of that of the U.S. and U.K.

(8) Latin America and Asia each account for around 30 per cent, and Africa for one fifth, of the exports of machinery and transport equipment from industrial countries to Third World regions. But since the mid-fifties the Latin American market has become relatively less important and the Asian market relatively more so. The same is true for iron and steel products, though here the share of Africa has increased more markedly than that of Asia. Exports of chemical products are even more heavily concentrated on Latin America and Asia. The Third World market for other manufactures from industrial countries, mainly consumer goods, is geographically more diversified, except that the Asian share has increased and the Middle East buys much less than any of the other regions. On the other hand, the Middle East market for these goods has grown noticeably faster since the mid-fifties than Latin America or Africa. As might be expected in view of its acute food problems, Asia is much the largest Third World market for food, beverages and tobacco exports from industrial countries, though the proportion going to Latin America and Africa, about one fifth, is still appreciable.

(9) Over 80 per cent of the machinery and transport equipment exported from industrial countries in the Third World is supplied by the U.S., E.E.C., Japan and the U.K. The U.S. and E.E.C. each account for over one quarter of the total, the U.K. for 12 per cent and Japan for 17 per cent. Compared with the position in the mid-fifties, the U.S. share has fallen sharply and this seems to be the main reason for the earlier mentioned decline in its overall share of the Latin American market. The U.K. share has also declined a great deal, whereas the E.E.C. has on the whole held its position rather better. By contrast, the Japanese share of machinery and transport equipment exports to the Third

World has greatly increased since the mid-fifties and so, to a much lesser extent, has that of the Soviet Union and Eastern Europe. The same trend is apparent in the exports of consumer goods to less developed countries, though here the U.S. and U.K. have held their share better than in the case of capital goods.

(10) The major industrial suppliers' share of exports of chemical products to the Third World is much the same as for machinery and transport equipment, except that E.E.C., with over a third of the business, is a comparatively more important source, and Japan, with a 12 per cent share, a comparatively less important one. The share of both E.E.C. and Japan in these exports has risen since 1955 while that of the U.K., and to a smaller extent the U.S., has declined.

(11) Japan has also impressively strengthened its share of the Third World market for iron and steel products from industrial countries and now accounts for over one third of these exports. The E.E.C. share of this market has fared rather worse than that of the U.S. or U.K.

12) In the other major category of exports, food, beverages and tobacco, the U.S., with 40 per cent of the business, is the dominating supplier of Third World markets. In fact, this is the one major export category in which the U.S. increased its share of these markets up until recently, a reflection, of course, of the enormous flow of American food aid to less developed countries since the mid-fifties.

Perhaps the most striking, and certainly the most portentous feature of the industrial countries' export stake in Third World markets is the increasing extent to which it rests on the sale of capital investment goods, such as machinery, transport equipment, chemical and iron and steel products. This is by far the largest and fastest growing part of the business. By the end of the sixties the sale of these products accounted for 60 per cent of their total exports to the Third World. An industrial supplier's share of this business will largely determine its overall share of this market. The U.S. spoils the argument a little; since the mid-fifties, its share in Third World country imports of capital goods has fallen noticeably more than its share in their total imports from industrial countries. This is mainly because food, beverages and tobacco, and agricultural raw materials have formed a growing proportion of U.S. exports to these countries. By the end of the sixties these primary products accounted for about one fifth of its total exports to the Third World.

161

In the case of Japan it is pretty clear that its increasingly strong export position in less developed regions owes a good deal to its rising share of their imports of capital investment goods. By 1969 its share of Third World imports of capital goods from industrial countries had risen to 19 per cent, compared with about 12 per cent for the U.K., 27 per cent for the U.S. and 30 per cent for E.E.C.

The development programmes of Third World countries explain, of course, the more rapid growth in their demand for capital investment goods than for other kinds of exports from industrial countries; indeed, their rate of development crucially depends upon the import of a growing volume of these goods. The relation between the level and rate of their economic development on the one hand and their import demands on the other thus provides the starting point for an examination of their potential demand for goods very largely supplied by industrial countries.

Future Prospects

Poor countries are poor customers. If that simple truth needs any underlining the following table should serve the purpose well enough. (Table I) Two points stand out clearly.

The first is the huge disparity between rich and poor countries in their purchases of internationally traded goods. Thus in 1968-1969 Western Europe's purchases per head of population were nine times larger than those of Latin America, more than thirteen times larger than those of Africa and more than twenty-four times larger than those of South and South East Asia. The disparity is almost as great between Australia/New Zealand and Third World regions and still very large when the comparison is made with North America. Japan shows it up in another way. In 1958-1959 its purchases per head of population were no greater than Latin America's; by 1968-1969 they were over three times larger than those of Latin America.

On the whole the level of per capita imports in Third World regions reflects the level of per capita income. The Middle East comes out top mainly because of Israel, where the level of per capita imports is as high as in Western Europe, and of some of the major petroleum-producing countries. Kuwait, for instance, appears to have the highest level of per capita income and imports in the world.

162

TABLE I: Value of Imports Per Capita in U.S. Dollars

Country	Average 1958/59	Average 1963/64	Average 1968/69	Annual Average Growth of Imports per Capita 1958/59 — 1968/69
E.E.C.[1]	144	242	373	9.0
E.F.T.A.[2]	216	308	416	6.2
North America[3]	112	126	224	6.5
Australia/New Zealand	221	269	327	3.7
Japan	36	77	138	13.0
Latin America[4]	39	35	43	0.9
Central American[5] Common Market	47	59	74	4.2
Africa[6]	24	26	29	1.8
South and S.E. Asia[7]	11	13	16	3.4
Middle East[8]	59	70	99	4.8

SOURCE: U.N. Statistics.

NOTES:

[1] Belgium/Luxembourg, France, West Germany, Italy, Netherlands.

[2] Austria, Denmark, Norway, Portugal, Sweden, Switzerland, United Kingdom.

[3] Canada, United States.

[4] Argentina, Bolivia, Brazil, Chile, Columbia, Ecuador, Mexico, Paraquay, Peru, Uraquay, Venezuela.

[5] Costa Rica, El Salvador, Guatemala, Honduras, Nicaragua.

[6] Excludes South Africa and Southern Rhodesia.

[7] Includes South Korea and China: Taiwan.

[8] Aden, Cyprus, Iran, Iraq, Israel, Jordan, Kuwait, Lebanon, Saudi Arabia, Syria, Yemen.

The second main point the table makes is that the disparity in the level of per capita imports between rich and poor countries has been growing wider. Industrial countries have increased their purchases of internationally traded goods at a much faster rate than Third World regions. This is simply a reflection of the well-advertised fact that rich countries are growing richer rather more rapidly than poor countries are overcoming their poverty.

There is another point worth noticing however. Among Third World regions the member countries of the Central American Common Market show a comparatively high average level and rate of growth of per capita imports. For the proponents of regional or sub-regional economic cooperation among less developed countries, this is an encouraging trend. And it is one which

163

can be expected to boost the exports of industrial countries as well.

It is obvious then that a rising level of development in the Third World will expand the market for internationally traded goods. Indeed, its imports can be expected to grow at a faster rate than its gross domestic product. This is because the investment goods required to sustain development usually have a higher import content than other goods.

What may be less well appreciated is that the total income of less developed countries cannot be expected to grow rapidly in the long run without a rising volume of imports. Historical examples of rapid development despite an unchanged level of imports are few in number and even in these cases the process did not last for long. Increasing output requires increasing inputs. For less developed countries with little or no industrial base and lacking perhaps essential raw materials and fuel resources, some portion of these inputs have to be supplied from abroad. Above all, they must import capital equipment. This means that their rate of investment is crucially dependent on their capacity to import. Unless their foreign exchange resources grow sufficiently fast to pay for a growing volume of imports the process of domestic capital accumulation and diversification could slow down. Alternatively, the burden of adjustment to a slow growth of imports could fall on personal consumption and government expenditure. Worse still, the competing claims of investment, personal consumption and government expenditure could simply lead to inflation and a worsening of the balance of payments.

If an unchanging capacity to import has to accommodate more investment, more welfare expenditure, more personal expenditure, more public works and so forth, something is bound to take off—usually the printing press. The development of any Third World country whose import of goods and services per head of population stagnates or declines over a long period is thus sure to run into trouble—just as an individual family would suffer if its purchases did not rise while those of the neighbours did. And the trouble could have political repercussions. If the total volume of resources are too small and growing only slowly, a stagnating capacity to import will severely strain the ability of the political system to allocate available supplies in an orderly and acceptable way among competing social groups and claims.

This association between imports and development in Third

164

World Countries is born out by recent experience as the following table indicates:

TABLE II

Categories according to real product growth	Number of Countries	Percentage of total population	Growth Rates 1960-68	
			Total real product	Imports
High—6% or more	22	11	8.1	10.5
Medium—4% to 5.9%	33	30	5.0	4.8
Low—under 4%	30	59	2.9	0.7

SOURCE: U.N.C.T.A.D. Review of International Trade and Development 1970.

The figures show a close parallel between rates of growth of gross domestic product and imports. Low rates of increase in imports have been closely associated with low rates of increase in total output. Another point to notice is that imports have grown at a faster rate than total real product in the case of high growth countries.

Lumping together Third World countries under average figures can sometimes produce misleading results however, and so to test the conclusions further a sample list of high and low growth countries has been made in Table III. Petroleum producing countries have been deliberately excluded because this particular resource puts them in an exceptionally favoured position. Countries were selected from all Third World regions and have been ranked according to their per capita growth of G.D.P in the period 1960-1965, the first half of the First U.N. Development Decade. During this period the average per capita growth rate of all Third World countries was two per cent. Countries in the top half of the table grew much faster than this and those in the bottom half at somewhat slower rates. In general the results bear out the earlier conclusion:

(i) The highest and lowest economic growth rates are closely associated with the highest and lowest rates of growth in per capita imports.

(ii) In the majority of cases rates of growth in per capita real product and in per capita imports rise and fall together. An acceleration in the former rate is associated with an acceleration in the latter rate and conversely.

165

TABLE III: Comparative Growth Rates and Levels of Per Capita Output and Imports: Selected Third World Countries.

Country	Annual Average Growth Rates[1]				Gross Domestic Product per Capita[4] U.S. $	Imports of Goods and Services per Capita U.S. $ Av.
	GDP[2] per Capita %		Import of Goods[3] & Services per Capita %			
	1951/59	1960/65	1951/59	1960/65	1965	1965/66
	(1)	(2)	(3)	(4)	(5)	(6)
Jordan	5.9	6.0	10.2	3.4	198[5]	97
China (Taiwan)	4.7[6]	6.0	1.9	9.5	200	51
Israel	5.6	5.6	0.2	9.6	1,204	442
Panama	1.5	4.7[7]	2.6	7.6	474	203
Nicaragua	2.6	4.6	8.4	11.3	325	119
Syria	0.0[8]	4.6	2.6	0.1	162	52
Thailand	3.8[9]	4.2	3.9	6.7	113	28
Pakistan	0.5	3.8[10]	—0.7	13.9	95	10
Peru	2.3	3.7	4.1	12.1	238	76
Malaysia	—0.3[11]	3.7	1.1[12]	3.5[12]	280[13]	126[14]
Guatemala	0.8	1.7	4.3	4.9	298	58
Brazil	2.7	1.5	0.5	—7.0	232	18
Paraguay	0.4	1.4	4.1	3.1	200	36
Burma	4.4	1.3	6.0	—1.4	60	10
Honduras	0.7	1.3	3.8	6.9	207	65
Equador	1.8	1.3	6.6	3.8	200	39
India	1.5	1.2	4.1	4.8	92	7
Columbia	1.6	1.2	—0.6	0.9	267	42
Ceylon	0.9	1.1	3.3	—3.5	137	39
Uganda	1.8[15]	1.1	3.2[12]	5.7[12]	83	27
Kenya	2.5	1.0	4.6[12]	3.5[12]	86	37

SOURCE: World Bank estimates, except Col. 5, which are U.N.C.T.A.D. estimates.

NOTES:

[1] The average period growth rates are the compounded rates of growth between initial and terminal years, the initial year being always one year earlier than the period described; e.g., for 1960-1965 the years employed are 1959 and 1965. Since data for 1949 are not generally available for most countries, 1950 had to be taken as the initial year for the earlier period. As a result, the average period growth rates cover nine years only; i.e., 1951-1959.

[2] Gross Domestic Product at constant market prices. Where such estimates were not available, values at constant factor cost have been used.

166

(iii) In the majority of cases per capita imports grew at a faster rate than per capita real product during both the 1950s and the first half of the 1960s.

(iv) With few exceptions the level of per capita imports closely follows the level of per capita real product.

The relevance of these conclusions to the Western industrial countries' potential export stake in the Third World becomes clearer when it is remembered that the latter depends on the former for well over 70 per cent of its commodity imports, a proportion that has not changed much over the past ten years. If the Soviet Union and Eastern Europe are included among industrial countries, the proportion rises to well over 75 per cent. A sharply rising volume of purchases from industrial countries is therefore both a predictable result and an essential condition of higher levels and rates of development in the Third World.

As was apparent from the earlier analysis of the structure of exports from industrial countries to the Third World, the composition of this rising demand can be expected to continue to favour capital investment goods and intermediate products such as chemicals, lubricants, fuels and other essential raw materials, rather than manufactured consumer goods. Table IV shows how much the pattern had changed by the mid-sixties. The picture will not have altered much since then.

The share of capital goods and intermediate goods in total imports is highest for Latin America and lowest for Africa. It has been increasing in all three regions though here again Africa

---

[3] Nominal growth rates based on current values in U.S. dollars. Imports of Goods and Services in Columns 3, 4 and 6 are defined to exclude factor and transfer payments to and from abroad. "Investment Income" has been used as an approximation of factor payments.

[4] Gross Domestic Product at factor cost.

[5] 1964.

[6] 1952-1959.

[7] 1961-1965 at factor cost.

[8] 1954-1959.

[9] 1952-1959.

[10] 1961-1965.

[11] 1956-1959.

[12] Goods only.

[13] West Malaysia only.

[14] Malaysia, Sabah and Sarawak.

[15] 1955-1959.

TABLE IV: COMPOSITION OF IMPORTS OF THIRD WORLD COUNTRIES (Percentages)

	Average Share of Imports		
	1953-1955	1956-1960	1961-1965
All Developing Countries	100.0	100.0	100.0
A. Consumer Goods	42.7	39.1	38.2
1. Foodstuffs	17.8	16.6	16.9
2. Other Consumer Goods	24.9	22.5	21.3
B. Intermediate Goods	31.5	31.7	30.3
C. Capital Goods	25.8	29.2	31.5
Africa[1]	100.0	100.0	100.0
A. Consumer Goods	46.5	46.3	44.6
1. Foodstuffs	17.8	17.5	18.1
2. Other Consumer Goods	28.7	28.8	26.5
B. Intermediate Goods	24.1	24.3	24.6
C. Capital Goods	29.4	29.4	30.8
Asia[2]	100.0	100.0	100.0
A. Consumer Goods	45.8	42.5	40.7
1. Foodstuffs	20.4	19.9	19.0
2. Other Consumer Goods	25.4	22.6	21.1
B. Intermediate Goods	38.8	34.3	31.6
C. Capital Goods	19.4	23.2	27.7
Latin America[3]	100.0	100.0	100.0
A. Consumer Goods	33.8	29.4	28.8
1. Foodstuffs	14.4	11.7	12.0
2. Other Consumer Goods	19.4	17.7	16.8
B. Intermediate Goods	33.1	34.0	32.6
C. Capital Goods	33.1	36.6	38.6

SOURCE: U.N.C.T.A.D. *Trade Prospects and Capital Needs of Developing Countries.* 1968.

NOTES:

[1] Excluding South Africa.

[2] South and S.E. Asia and Western Asia (Middle East).

[3] Latin American Republics, Jamaica, Guyana, Trinidad and Tobago.

shows the lowest increase. Conversely, the share of consumer goods, other than foodstuffs, has declined in all Third World regions and particularly in Asia. The scope for further shifts from consumer goods to "development goods" would appear therefore to be greatest for Africa and lowest for Latin America. Another interesting pointer is that this shift in import structure has been

168

more pronounced for high growth than for low growth countries. The trend is not without its risks however. For one thing the increasing weight of capital goods and intermediate products in the import structures of Third World countries makes them more vulnerable to any fall off in their foreign exchange receipts. It becomes more difficult for them in this situation to reduce their import expenditures without jeopardising their current levels of investment and future development. It makes, in short, for greater rigidity in their external accounts.

Some indication of the potential growth in the Third World's demand for the exports of industrial countries is provided by two recent United Nations studies. The first, by the U.N.C.T.A.D. Secretariat, attempts to assess the trade prospects and capital needs of Third World countries in the mid-seventies on two alternative assumptions about the average annual rate of growth of their domestic product between 1963 and 1975. The "low" assumption postulates a growth rate of 5.2 per cent (4.9 per cent excluding the Middle East petroleum exporting countries). This represents some improvement in the historical trend and broadly corresponds to the First U.N. Development Decade target. The "high" assumption postulates a growth rate of 6.1 per cent (5.9 per cent excluding the Middle East petroleum exporting countries). This is moderately, but not greatly, higher than the historical trend and corresponds to the average annual growth target for the Second U.N. Development Decade of the 1970s.

On the "low" growth assumption Third World imports are projected to increase by 5.3 per cent per annum and by 6.7 per cent on the "high" growth assumption. This implies that its commodity import requirements in 1960 prices would increase from $32 billion in 1963 to $60 billion in 1975 on the "low" assumption and to $70 billion on the "high" one.[1]

On the basis of these estimates and assuming their share in Third World imports remains the same, the industrial countries would increase their exports to this market by between $25-30 billion. Or put differently, the generalisation to the Third World of rates of growth already recorded by a number of less developed

[1] For further details see: *Trade Prospects and Capital Needs of Developing Countries*, 1968 Study prepared by the U.N.C.T.A.D. Secretariat. TD/34/Rev.1.

countries in the 1960s[1] would by 1975 more than double the 1963 level of exports from industrial countries to these markets.

The second study to note is by the U.N. Centre for Development Planning, Projections and Policies. This postulates growth targets for Third World countries by 1980 which imply that their average annual rate of growth would rise from 4.5 per cent in 1960-1965 to between 6.2 and 6.9 per cent in 1975-1980. The implied rise in the average annual growth rate of per capita G.D.P. is from 2.0 per cent in 1960-1965 to between 3.5 and 4.1 per cent in 1975-1980. Quite a few Third World countries had achieved these higher rates in the sixties.[2] If the achievement could be generalised throughout the Third World in the 1970s, its average level of per capita income would rise to around $240-250, an increase of $100 above the 1965 level. This would still leave average income per head in the Third World far below the present day levels of even the lowest income countries among the developed member countries of the world economy. A lesser aim can hardly be contemplated if the development of the Third World is to be taken at all seriously. In fact, the minimum average annual growth target for the Second U.N. Development Decade is 6 per cent, or about 3.5 per cent per capita, with the possibility that a higher rate can be set for the second half of the 1970s.

On the assumption that Third World countries achieve an average growth rate of 6.5-7 per cent by 1980 and that they significantly improve the productivity of investment, the U.N. Study postulates a rise in their import requirements at 1960 prices from about $40 billion in 1965 to $107-113 billion by 1980.[3] If the industrial countries maintain their shares of these imports, their exports of goods and services to Third World countries would amount to around $80-85 billion by 1980, or more than two and one half times above the level of 1965. This is the scale of the extra export business they would gain from a generalisation to the Third World as a whole of the rate of development which quite a few less developed countries achieved in the 1960s.

[1] See Table II above.
[2] Loc. cit.
[3] For further details see: Developing Countries in the Nineteen Seventies: Preliminary Estimates for Some Key Elements of a Framework for International Development Strategy. 1968. Doc. E/AC.54/L.29/Rev.1.

All such projections are of course purely hypothetical, and not forecasts. They are intended to illuminate the policy options open in the present. And they do lend a dimension to the export prospects which industrial countries can expect to enjoy from accelerated development in the Third World.

But the prospects, however impressive on paper, will not materialize if less developed countries cannot finance the postulated growth of imports. Any realistic development strategy in the Third World has to face up to this problem. And since it raises a host of questions for the trade and aid policies of industrial countries as well, it cannot be ignored by them either.

The Financing Problem

The bulk of the Third World's foreign exchange receipts come from its own commodity export earnings. These earnings pay for 97 per cent of its commodity imports; excluding the Middle East, a major petroleum exporting region, reduces the proportion to just under 90 per cent. The extent to which commodity imports are financed out of export earnings varies, of course, between different parts of the Third World as the following figures indicate. It is the lowest in South and South East Asia and highest in the oil producing Middle East. It is very notice-

RATIO OF EXPORTS TO IMPORTS

THIRD WORLD	Average 1958/59	Average 1968/69
THIRD WORLD	92	97
LATIN AMERICA	100	100
Excluding Venezuela	87	88
AFRICA	79	117
SOUTH & S.E. ASIA	82	72
MIDDLE EAST	137	145
THIRD WORLD Excluding Middle East	90	89

able, too, how the exclusion of Venezuela, another big oil exporter, lowers the ratio for Latin America. On the whole it is lowest for the countries with the lowest average level of per capita income. Throughout the sixties the ratio rose in Africa

171

and the Middle East, remained steady in Latin America and fell in South and South East Asia.

The ratio of export earnings to commodity imports is not, of course, a true reflection of the ability of Third World countries to pay their own way in the world. For to their commodity import bills must be added payments for services, the profits and dividends on their private capital borrowing and the amortization and interest payments on their public capital borrowing. When these items are thrown into the balance, the Third World's export earnings are found to cover only about three quarters of its total foreign exchange outlays. This is clearly too low a proportion to offer much hope that most of these countries will be able in the foreseeable future to pay their own way in the world.

In recent years commodity imports have accounted for around three quarters of the total foreign exchange outlays of the non-oil producing countries of the Third World. As already argued, it is difficult to cut this import bill without jeopardising current levels of investment and future development. Many less developed countries have tried to save foreign exchange by a concentrated emphasis on the substitution of domestic manufactures for imports, but this has generally proved to be a somewhat costly and inefficient process. In any case, the foreign exchange saving is invariably less than expected because of the continuing need for imports of capital investment goods and intermediate products. As cereals account for about 5 per cent of the Third World's imports, a more rapid expansion of domestic food production would seem to offer a more promising way to save foreign exchange. But even here the potential saving may be offset by a larger import bill for the fertilizers, pesticides and other inputs needed to improve agricultural productivity.

Another claim on the foreign exchange resources of Third World countries which is arousing much concern, is their mounting burden of service payments on external debt. A later section of this paper will show why some easement here is plainly desirable. In the long run, however, the only sure way of improving their overall payments position is through a substantial boost in their export earnings. It is the volume and price of their exports which very largely governs their capacity to finance imports.

Acres of print have been devoted to the export problems and

prospects of Third World countries. Innumerable international meetings have talked the subject into the ground. Nothing less than the whole international economic order has been challenged on its behalf. A few simple facts will help to explain why.

Third World exports have increased less rapidly than the exports of industrial countries and below the average for world trade as a whole. From 1950 to 1968 Third World exports grew at an average annual rate of 4.7 per cent; the western industrial countries' exports grew at 8.7 per cent and world trade at 7.9 per cent.

As a result of these trends, the Third World's share of world trade declined from over 31 per cent in 1950 to 18 per cent in 1969 (or from one quarter to less than one eighth if the major oil exporting countries are excluded). Over the same period the western industrial countries' share rose from 61 per cent to 71 per cent.

World trade in foodstuffs and raw materials has been growing much more slowly than world trade in manufactures, chemicals and fuels. The fact that about 45 per cent of the Third World's exports in the late sixties still consisted of food and raw materials goes a long way, therefore, to explain its declining share of world trade. True, the demand for high quality foodstuffs (protein and vitamin rich foods and fruit) has remained buoyant; but these items do not bulk large in the Third World's food exports, which depend more on a sluggish World demand for items such as tea, coffee, sugar, oils and fats.

Third World petroleum exports have expanded rapidly and by the late sixties they accounted for one third of its total export earnings. But only a relatively few countries produce oil and share in these earnings.

Third World exports of manufactured goods have also risen rapidly, and by 1969 they contributed 22 per cent of its total export earnings. But without unwrought non-ferrous metals (copper, lead, zinc and tin) the proportion falls to 15 per cent. So small a proportion is not surprising when it is remembered that the Third World's share of world manufacturing production is under 5 per cent. Excluding petroleum products and unwrought non-ferrous metals, its manufactured exports consist mainly of low cost, relatively labour intensive goods such as textiles, clothing and wood, food and leather products. Textiles, clothing, leather and footwear together make up nearly 40 per cent of

173

the total. Again, as in the case of oil exports, only a limited number of Third World countries share in these earnings. Seven countries (Argentina, Brazil, India, Mexico, Pakistan, South Korea and Taiwan) accounted in 1969 for 40 per cent of the total and Hong Kong alone for another 25 per cent.

To a large extent then, the export record of Third World countries reflects the commodity composition of their exports. Even Nature's lottery explains a great deal. If they are lucky enough to discover oil and minerals, they have no serious foreign exchange problem. But if they are unlucky enough to depend on jute, coffee, tea and similar products their export earning capacity is severely limited.

The earning capacity of many of them was squeezed still further after the mid-fifties by a downward drift in world prices of primary products relative to world prices of manufactured goods. In other words the purchasing power of their exports grew even more slowly than the value and volume of their exports. In short, the terms of trade moved against them.

Just how serious this squeeze has been may be judged from a calculation the U.N.C.T.A.D. Secretariat has made of the additional foreign exchange they would have earned and saved during the sixties if they had been able to sell their exports and buy their imports at the average 1953-57 world prices instead of at the prices then ruling. For the period 1961-67 the estimate comes to nearly $2½ billion a year on the average. The point may be made another way. During 1961-66 their average annual loss of foreign exchange on this calculation amounted to over 40 per cent of the official development assistance they received from western donor countries.[1]

In the second half of the sixties, it is fair to add, the Third World's terms of trade remained pretty constant. But with powerful inflationary pressures at work in industrial countries and the demand for many of its products in its most important markets remaining sluggish, the outlook for the seventies is less reassuring.

In most Third World countries exports account for a major portion of their total output as well as for the bulk of their foreign exchange receipts. A good export performance can, there-

[1] See: U.N.C.T.A.D.: Handbook of International Trade and Development Statistics 1969. Table 5.5.

fore, be expected to exert a powerful shove behind their whole development effort. In fact, there is an observable tendency for countries with above average growth rates to show above average rates of growth in export earnings. It is this relationship which explains the earlier noted association between rates of growth of imports and total output. Hence, it is not surprising that petroleum and mineral exporting countries should figure so prominently among the star growth performers of the Third World.[1] More important for those not so well favoured with natural resources are the outstanding growth records of countries like South Korea and Taiwan which have diversified their economies and export structures through a rapid expansion of manufactures. The achievement of the minimum growth targets of the Second U.N. Development Decade greatly depends on the ability of most Third World countries to achieve a better export performance than in the sixties.

The poor or indifferent export performance of Third World countries is sometimes due to failures on the supply side. Recent examples that come to mind are Argentine meat, Bolivian tin, Chilean copper and Burmese rice. Inflation and overvalued exchange rates are common to many less developed countries and keep their prices above world market levels. There is doubtless room, too, for more determined efforts to lower real costs of production and to develop export promotion activities. But failings on the supply side are far from the whole story. Their exports have faced, and still face, formidable difficulties on the demand side.

Although the Third World's exports to Eastern Europe and the U.S.S.R. have risen rapidly since the fifties, they account for less than 5 per cent of its total exports and for only around 6 per cent of the value of its exports to western industrial countries. These latter markets absorb well over 70 per cent of the Third World's exports, a proportion that has not changed much in the past ten years. It is in these markets, therefore, that the difficulties facing Third World exports have largely risen. Three sets of causes can be identified.

[1] Though the relatively poor growth record of Algeria, Nigeria, Cameroons, Guyana and the Democratic Republic of the Congo indicates that petroleum and mineral resources are not in themselves a sufficient condition of rapid development.

First, the demand of industrial countries for Third World exports of basic foodstuffs and raw materials has been growing only sluggishly. As these societies grow richer, they spend a smaller proportion of their income on basic foodstuffs and even on manufactures, and a larger proportion on services. But an increasing expenditure on services does not call for a proportionate rise in the demand for commodity imports. Hence their demand for basic foodstuffs and raw materials from the Third World is singularly unresponsive to rising incomes or declining prices.

Secondly, the growth in the industrial countries' demand for Third World exports has also been restrained by the countermanding thrust of technical progress. The output of their big growth industries such as chemicals and durable consumer goods tends to have a lower import content than more slowly growing industries like textiles and clothing. Raw material inputs per unit of output have been declining. One simple example is the way bulk handling techniques have reduced the demand for cotton and jute bags. The most obvious trend though, has been the substitution of synthetic products for natural products. Between 1954 and 1966 the world's consumption of synthetic rubber rose from 38 per cent to 62 per cent of its total rubber consumption. Man-made fibres have made equally striking inroads into the market for natural fibres such as cotton, wool and jute. The demand for wood and some metals has been affected by plastics.

Thirdly, the exports of Third World countries have to surmount various commercial policy obstacles in western industrial countries. There is a clear tendency for the tariff structures of these countries to be biased against low cost, relatively labour intensive manufactures and processed foods and raw materials. This restricts the import of light consumer goods from Third World countries and discourages them from processing their natural resources. In the case of textiles and clothing, which accounted in the late sixties for about one third of U.S. and U.K. imports of manufactures from Third World countries and for about one quarter of those of E.E.C., it is quotas more than tariffs that are the real barrier. By means of quota restrictions, the western industrial countries have put a brake on the expansion of Third World textile exports in the interests of their own domestic textile industries.

176

Agricultural protection in western industrial markets takes a wide variety of forms: quotas, tariffs, subsidies and support prices. Much of it, of course, is directed against temperate-zone foodstuffs of interest to only a few Third World countries. But it also covers products of wider interest to them like sugar, vegetable oils and oilseeds. The protection of relatively high cost domestically produced beet sugar against cheaper cane sugar from developing countries is a good case in point. Furthermore, western industrial countries, particularly E.E.C., impose fiscal duties on beverage crops and bananas which also limit consumer demand.

When it comes to judging the export outlook for Third World countries the trends of the recent past are a fair guide to the expectations of the near future. Technological progress, the continuous expansion of synthetic materials and the shifting patterns of consumption in industrial countries, will almost certainly continue to have a dampening effect on their demand for many Third World products. The outlook for agricultural raw materials like rubber, jute and hard fibres is particularly bleak. It is not much better for basic foodstuffs. So long as the present international distribution of income persists, Third World exports of basic foodstuffs are likely to expand only very slowly.

Exports of petroleum products and manufactured goods, on the other hand, face a much brighter prospect and should continue to expand rapidly. This means that countries in a position to expand these particular exports will gain the lion's share of the total increase in Third World export earnings. But, as already pointed out, the vast majority of Third World countries depend on earnings originating in agriculture. Their capacity to finance imports out of export earnings will remain severely limited.

Giving a quantitative dimension to these prospects is a hazardous exercise, but for purposes of illustration the United Nations study mentioned earlier,[1] provides some useful guidance. On the assumption that the annual average growth rate of industrial countries in the 1970s would be 4.7 per cent, which is moderately higher than their average growth rate from 1955 to 1965, and that Third World countries would reach an average rate of 6.5 to 7 per cent by the end of the 1970s, the U.N. study postulates a rise in Third World exports of goods and services from

[1] See footnote[3] p. 14.

$42 billion in 1965 to $112 billion in 1980. This compares with the earlier noted postulated rise in its import requirements to $107-113 billion in 1980.

The apparent balance between the two calculations is highly misleading, however, because a number of Third World countries, the oil exporters especially, are expected to have a hefty trade surplus, which means that the remainder will run a hefty trade defecit. The U.N. Secretariat estimates that about 20 countries, accounting for between a fifth and a quarter of the Third World's total gross domestic product, would have a foreign exchange surplus of $13-14 billion by 1980. But about 50 countries, accounting for the bulk of the Third World's total output and population, would have a foreign exchange gap of $27-30 billion. A deficit of that order would be four to five times larger than this group of countries ran in 1965. Moreover, it takes no account of the rising burden of debt service payments they face.

It has to be emphasised again that all such calculations are hypothetical. There is ample room for argument over the figures. On one point, however, professional judgements are agreed. A faster rate of development will widen the foreign exchange gap of most Third World countries. Obviously these countries must strive harder to expand their export earnings and to improve the productivity of their resources. There is scope, too, for reducing their import bill for services by developing their own shipping, insurance and banking services.

But what are the implications also for industrial countries?

Some Policy Imperatives for Industrial Countries

A more rapid development of Third World countries will clearly benefit the exports of industrial countries very considerably. In this prospect both groups of countries share a common economic interest. What for their part, then, should the industrial countries do to bring it about? The obstacle they can best help to remove is the foreign exchange bottleneck on the development of the Third World countries. Three broad imperatives suggest themselves.

In the first place, it is important that the industrial economies themselves should expand at a brisk and steady pace. The better their growth performance the higher their demand for the exports of Third World countries. For instance, the econo-

178

mies of Japan and E.E.C. have recently been expanding faster than those of Britain and the United States—and so have their imports from Third World countries. A high rate of growth should also make industrial countries more willing and able to adopt liberal trade and aid policies.

In the second place, rich countries ought not to erect trade barriers against imports from poor countries.

Generally speaking, Third World countries can be expected to have a clear cost advantage over industrial countries in manufacturing production which is relatively lavish in the use of labour, particularly unskilled labour, and relatively sparing in the use of capital. Textiles and clothing are obvious examples. But in light consumer goods generally, they are usually able to compete in world markets at a comparatively early stage of their industrialization. Today it may be mainly textiles, clothing, footwear and wood products; tomorrow it could be mainly metal products, cutlery, ceramics, glassware, bicycles, motor cycles and other relatively labour intensive products.

Yet it is precisely against this kind of product that the tariff policies of industrial countries are notably biased. Such obstacles lower the ceiling of international demand for the exports of Third World countries and so aggravate their foreign exchange difficulties. To offer them financial aid in compensation is, in effect, to give a disguised subsidy to the domestic industries being protected. To extol the virtues of self-help to them, while restricting their opportunities for earning a living from the world economy, is to dress an injury in the rags of hypocrisy. No wonder poor countries complain that the international trading system is rigged against them.

More to the point still, these barriers are not in the national economic interest of industrial countries either; dismantling them would not be a charitable gesture on their part, but an act of economic self-advancement. It would speed up the shift of resources out of slow growing industries, where labour productivity is well below the national average, into faster growing industries, where labour productivity is well above the national average. It would thereby enable them to concentrate still further on sophisticated, capital intensive goods which both embody and give an impetus to advanced technology. And it is precisely on these goods that the bulk of the Third World's additional foreign exchange earnings would be spent. In this way both trading

179

partners—the less developed countries and the industrial countries—would achieve a more efficient use of resources.

The classic case of adjustment to this process is the British textile industry. On the eve of World War I nearly two-thirds of cotton textile goods entering international trade came from Lancashire. In the mid-sixties Britain had a sizeable trade deficit in cotton goods. Imports supplied 16 per cent of its domestic consumption in 1951, but 30 per cent in 1967. Over the same period the labour force in the Lancashire textile industry declined by 60 per cent. But through a regional diversification into metal using, chemicals and other manufacturing industries, alternative employment opportunities were no less quickly made available.

Textile imports from Third World countries are, in any case, not the only, or most important reason, for the loss of textile jobs in western industrial countries. The International Labour Organisation[1] has roughly estimated the loss due to imports in the first half of the U.N. Development Decade at a mere 0.04 per cent of their total manufacturing employment. As a proportion of total employment in textiles, the loss works out at 0.7 per cent in North America, 0.5 per cent in E.E.C. and 0.3 per cent in E.F.T.A. (excluding Switzerland). The loss of clothing jobs, which can be attributed to imports from Third World countries in the same period, works out at 0.05 per cent of total manufacturing employment in North America, 0.6 per cent in E.E.C. and 0.1 per cent in E.F.T.A. As a proportion of employment in clothing the corresponding figures are 0.8 per cent, 1.2 per cent and 1.9 per cent. This is hardly evidence of shattering disruption. More importantly, the I.L.O. estimates that in all cases the jobs lost through imports have been only a small fraction of the jobs lost through increased labour productivity.

Obstacles to international trade, whatever their source, constrict the opportunities for a more efficient use of the world's resources. Poor countries suffer the effects more than rich countries because they are less able to adjust to them.

Why then do industrial countries maintain restrictions against imports from Third World countries? The short answer is that

[1] I.L.O. *Some Labour Implications of Increased Participation of Developing Countries in Trade in Manufactures and Semi-Manufactures*, U.N., Doc. TD/46/Rev.1.

the sectional interests being protected are politically persuasive and the remnant of thoughtful citizenry is not. The overall benefits of cheaper imports are difficult to quantify and can only be indicated in general terms; whereas the competition they provide is felt in a real way. But curbing this competition at the behest of sectional interests inflicts an economic loss on the rest of the community.

From time to time western governments have subscribed, usually with qualifications, to general declarations about the desirability of reducing or eliminating tariff and non-tariff barriers against imports from Third World countries. Undertakings to this effect were included, for example, in an International Development Strategy for the Second U.N. Development Decade, which the U.N. General Assembly adopted in October 1970. Of more immediate and practical significance, however, are the preferential tariff concessions they have offered on manufactured and semi-manufactured imports from Third World countries under the System of Non-Reciprocal, Non-Discriminatory Generalised Preferences, G.S.P. for short, which was agreed to that same month in U.N.C.T.A.D. On the face of it, the Third World appears to have made a major breakthrough here. But on closer inspection the impression does not look quite so overwhelming.

The first point to note is that G.S.P. is not, as its title implies, one general scheme. The western governments took the view that increased imports from the Third World, as a result of preferential tariff treatment, would be a burden on their domestic industry and economies, a form of 'aid', in effect, which should be equitably shared among them. But they failed to agree on how to do this within a single common scheme, which is not surprising since the alleged burden is hard to define, much less to measure. Third World countries were presented instead with an assortment of individual schemes from Austria, Canada, the E.E.C., Ireland, Japan, New Zealand, the Nordic countries (Denmark, Finland, Norway and Sweden), Switzerland, the U.K. and the U.S.

This obsession with burden sharing meant that the concessions the western governments offered tended to be influenced by what the most protective minded among them was prepared to offer. The U.K., for example, withdrew textiles from its initial proposals when it saw that they were not included in the offers

181

of Austria, Canada, Japan and the U.S. and were subject to quantitative import ceilings in the E.E.C. scheme. Footwear is another item excluded from some schemes. A sizeable proportion of the Third World's manufactured exports will thus continue to face quantitative restrictions in the markets of industrial countries. On the rest, the concessions offered provide for duty free entry or for tariff cuts that give a preferential margin over the existing most-favoured nation duty. The E.E.C., Austria and Japan have, in addition, set quantitative ceilings on the amounts of preferentially treated goods they are prepared to import.

Almost all the individual schemes also proposed to grant preferences on selected lists of processed agricultural products and a number of them include some primary products. Imports from the Third World on the E.E.C. list of these products amounted in 1968 to over $30 million. The U.S. list covers imports to the value of $114 million in 1967 and the Japanese list for imports to the value of $36 million in 1969. The U.K. list covers imports to the value of over $29 million in 1967 from developing non-Commonwealth countries. The U.K., U.S. and the Nordic countries will grant duty free entry to all but a few of the products in their lists, while the other schemes provide for varying degrees of tariff cuts. For the E.E.C. list the preferential margin offered is pretty small. As a guide to the scope of these offers, the western industrial countries' imports of processed food, drink and tobacco products from the Third World amounted in 1969 to one billion dollars.[1]

The full title given to G.S.P. suggests that the offers made under it do not discriminate between different Third World countries. This is not, in fact, the case. The E.E.C. scheme, for example, carefully preserves the unrestricted duty free entry status its Associated African States enjoy in the European Common Market. It does not, in other words, wipe out this advantage over other Third World suppliers. The industrial countries can also safeguard existing preferences by offering concessions on products of little or no interest to the countries already receiving preferences. Again, the E.E.C. and Austrian schemes intend to help smaller and economically weaker suppliers by applying country quota ceilings on imports from the bigger and

[1] U.N.C.T.A.D. *Trade in Manufactures from Developing Countries: 1970 Review.*

182

competitively stronger ones. In principle, the offers are open to all developing countries that elect to receive them. In practice, some picking and choosing among them seems inevitable. Is it likely that the U.S., for example, will make its offers available to Cuba?

The G.S.P. agreement is neither permanent nor binding. Its initial duration is ten years and all the western governments have insisted on safeguards to ensure some control over the level of imports that may result from their tariff concessions. Most of them reserve the right unilaterally to withdraw or modify their concessions if, in their view, increased imports cause or threaten unacceptable harm to their domestic producers. The E.E.C., Austria and Japan intend to safeguard domestic interests mainly through quantitative ceilings on preferentially treated imports. All of them also reserve the right to reduce preferential margins by lowering or removing tariffs on imports from one another.

The E.E.C. and Japan propose to implement their G.S.P. schemes from July 1971. The timing in other cases depends on legislative sanction. The big question here is whether a susceptibly protectionist Congress will approve the U.S. scheme. If it does not the E.E.C., Japan and other industrial countries may well have second thoughts about their own schemes. Any abandonment of a major scheme, however, would almost certainly invite a bitter political row with Third World countries.

The political significance of G.S.P. is therefore clear. Its likely affect on the export earnings of Third World countries is much harder to gauge. Any worthwhile estimate of the probable effects of tariff changes on trade is notoriously difficult to make. All that can be hazarded here are a few guesses of a general nature.

In the short term, the bulk of the additional foreign exchange the Third World should earn through G.S.P. is likely to accrue to the relatively few Asian and Latin American countries that account for most of its manufactured exports. This additional foreign exchange will largely be spent in industrial countries. If, therefore, Asia and Latin America are the chief gainers, Japan and the U.S. are likely to be the main recipients of these additional foreign exchange expenditures, since their export share of the Asian and Latin American market is much larger than that of other industrial countries.[1]

[1] See Appendix Table II-A.

In the long run G.S.P., if maintained and improved, should encourage the setting up of new export oriented industries in Third World countries as well as the expansion of existing ones. It might even persuade large international business corporations to take advantage of relatively cheap labour in the Third World by setting up factories there to supply preferentially treated imports of components for assembly plants in industrial countries. Much depends, of course, on the efforts Third World countries themselves make to improve their export capacity.

A number of problems arising from G.S.P. remain to be settled and among them the question of reverse preferences, that is, the preferences granted to industrial countries by Third World countries, deserves a special mention. The most important examples of reverse preferences are those granted to the E.E.C. by its Associated African States. The U.S. insists on their removal and the E.E.C. say this is up to the African countries themselves. British membership of the E.E.C. could further complicate the issue. Firstly, it would bring a number of Commonwealth developing countries into associate status with the enlarged Community. Secondly, the U.K. would presumably have to adopt the E.E.C. scheme of preferences. If reverse preferences have not been abolished by then, the U.S. and Japan might make their own preference schemes available only to those Third World countries which did not grant preferences to the E.E.C. Latin America would thus become more closely linked to the U.S. market and much of Asia to the Japanese market. The prospect is all too reminiscent of the way discriminatory trade policies between the two World Wars carved up world trade into dominating spheres of influence. The foreign trade links of Third World countries would again be shaped up by the mercantilist rivalries of the industrial powers. International cooperation for development cannot advance on that basis.

Finally, a word or two about Eastern Europe and the U.S.S.R. in relation to the G.S.P. The U.S.S.R. already grants duty free entry to products from Third World countries and Czechoslovakia and Hungary, the only two countries in Eastern Europe with tariff regimes, intend to grant them tariff preferences. In addition, all the European governments have promised to take various steps within their planned foreign trade programmes to increase their imports from the Third World.

Trade makes Third World countries real partners in the whole international development effort and not simply recipients of aid. Indeed, trade not aid has become a fashionable cliché and an oversimplification. What is needed is more of both. Even the most optimistic estimates still show a huge gap between their prospective export earnings and the import requirements of more rapid development. Here then is the third broad imperative open to industrial countries: a substantially bigger aid effort.

According to the hypothetical estimates noted earlier, an accelerated development of Third World countries in the 1970s would leave about 50 of them with a foreign exchange gap of $27-30 billion in 1980. The western industrial countries have accepted a United Nations resource transfer target of 1 per cent of their gross national product. On the basis of the trends for 1960-65, the U.N. Secretariat think their gross national product in 1980 might be expected to reach about $2,100 billion which is possibly too modest. The 1 per cent target would, therefore, yield $21 billion of external financing. On certain assumptions the United Nations Secretariat thinks the expected amount from the centrally planned economy countries might be put at $5 billion, which seems rather optimistic. So the net flow of capital from both groups of countries in 1980 might amount on this reckoning to $26 billion. This is not enough to close an estimated foreign exchange gap of $27-30 billion; but it is sufficiently near to offer more than a pious hope that with determined efforts on both sides, a foreign exchange bottleneck need not be an insuperable obstacle to more rapid Third World development.

However, at this point it has to be admitted that the economic interests of industrial countries and Third World countries do not converge so obviously on aid as they do on trade. For there can be no denying that aid is a real cost to the donor countries. As the introduction to this paper pointed out, it is highly questionable and probably impossible to prove that it is to the economic advantage of richer countries to provide aid to poorer countries. Such considerations are, of course, irrelevant to the deeply felt moral case for aid which many find more worthy of respect. To invoke economic self-interest in such company is almost to perpetrate a blasphemy. Nevertheless, that is the angle of approach required here.

It is commonly necessary for industries to have to invest time and money in developing the market for their product as a

185

prelude to achieving increased sales. From this point of view "foreign aid" may similarly be regarded as the cost to industrial countries of expanding their markets in the Third World. In both cases it is a matter of weighing the short term costs of market development against the longer term gain from trade. But before the analogy is pushed too far, two important qualifications should be inserted.

First of all, the "foreign aid" must be directed to building up the export earning capacity of recipient countries. The aid, as well as the trade policies of industrial countries, have been too biased against encouraging and facilitating an export-led development process in Third World countries. The bias should be reversed. Official aid especially ought to concentrate more on promoting output which can be marketed in the donor countries as well. The credit the Soviet Union and Eastern Europe provide under their aid agreements is typically serviced and repaid through the acceptance by them of commodities in return.

Secondly, the market development cost to industrial countries is not so great as their nominal aid figures suggest. Donor governments do not mind a gloss being put on their figures so long as it makes them shine. But that should not blind their citizens to the real burden they are carrying. The next section of this paper will, therefore, examine the nature of this burden and the return benefits which donor countries derive from various kinds of aid operations.

The Burdens of Foreign Aid

If public policy could be prosecuted for misleading advertising, the label "foreign aid" would be an obvious case for the courts. For this label has been used to sell a false bill of particulars to an unsuspecting public. Much of what it purports to describe is not foreign aid at all. Take, for instance, the well-known commitment of wealthier countries to transfer to poor countries resources amounting to at least one per cent of their total output of goods and services.[1] This commitment is commonly thought

[1] The International Development Strategy for the Second U.N. Development Decade calls on the donor countries to achieve this target by 1972 or not later than 1975. Among the O.E.E.C. member countries which had not already reached it in 1969 (See Table VI) Australia, Austria, Canada and

186

to be an "aid" target. It is, in fact, a resource transfer target and private foreign investment and commercial export credit count as much towards its fulfilment as officially financed transfers. The sum total of these very different flows is not a true measure of a country's "aid effort".

Only the funds made available by governments as grants or loans on concessional terms and intended primarily to promote the development and welfare of less developed countries, can properly be called "foreign aid". That is what the Development Assistance Committee (D.A.C.) of the Organisation for European Cooperation and Development (O.E.C.D.) and the report of the Pearson Commission[1] mean by "aid". An alternative approach, which U.N. reports adopt, is to drop the label altogether and speak only of "financial flows" or "resource transfers".

The burden of "foreign aid" raises, therefore, the question of whether total financial flows are being considered or only aid in the sense defined by D.A.C. and the Pearson Commission. The quantitative importance of the distinction is brought out in Table V. The figures are presented as net flows which means that capital repayments on past lending have been subtracted from gross capital flows. From 1960 to 1969 official development assistance, or aid proper, amounted on the average to almost 60 per cent of the total flow of financial resources to less developed countries. Private lending and investment accounted for nearly all the remaining flow. The distinction between private and official flows is also reflected in the claim they make on the total output of the supplying countries. This is shown in Table VI (page 34).

In all cases the total flow of financial resources claims a rather larger proportion of the total output of donor countries than their official aid. For the group as a whole, the ratio of official aid to G.N.P. is well under half the ratio of total financial flows to G.N.P. In the majority of cases it is evident that essentially private transactions account for a larger proportion of the output transferred than officially financed transfers. But both proportions show the same downward trend in the sixties.

Two kinds of financial flow are not represented in Table V.

the U.S.A. have declined to commit themselves to its achievement by any specific date. But a target with no date attached to it is meaningless.
[1] Partners in Development, Report of the Commission on International Development, 1969.

TABLE V: FLOW OF FINANCE RESOURCES FROM INDUSTRIAL COUNTRIES[1] TO THIRD WORLD COUNTRIES[2] AND MULTILATERAL AGENCIES 1956-1969.

(Million U.S. Dollars)

Net Disbursement	1956	1957	1958	1959	1960	1961	1962
TOTAL OFFICIAL	3,260	3,856	4,387	4,311	4,965	6,143	6,034
OFFICIAL DEVELOPMENT ASSISTANCE[3]					4,703	5,198	5,521
Multilateral	n.a.	421	367	333	535	521	511
Bilateral	n.a.	3,435	4,020	3,978	4,168	4,677	5,010
OTHER OFFICIAL[4]					262	945	513
PRIVATE FLOWS	2,998	3,779	2,917	2,820	3,150	3,106	2,453
Direct Investment	2,350	2,724	1,970	1,782	1,767	1,829	1,495
Bilateral Portfolio	{ 190	{ 601	{ 733	{ 691	633	614	147
Multilateral Portfolio					204	90	239
Export Credit[5]	485	454	214	347	546	573	572
TOTAL FLOW:	6,258	7,655	7,304	7,131	8,115	9,249	8,487

SOURCES: *Partners in Development* Report of the Pearson Commission on International Development. Praeger, 1969. *Development Assistance: 1970 Review* O.E.C.D.

NOTES:

[1] Excluding U.S.S.R. and Eastern Europe.
[2] Including less developed countries of Southern Europe. Over the 1960s the flow of financial resources to these countries has averaged $0.7 billion a year.

188

TABLE V: Flow of Finance Resources from Industrial Countries[1] to Third World Countries[2] and Multilateral Agencies 1956-1969.—(Continued)

(Million U.S. Dollars)

Net Disbursement	1963	1964	1965	1966	1967	1968	1969
TOTAL OFFICIAL	6,076	5,942	6,238	6,537	7,101	7,150	7,292
OFFICIAL DEVELOPMENT ASSISTANCE[3]	5,873	6,015	5,937	6,135	6,688	6,400	6,707
Multilateral	368	387	364	341	718	682	1,007
Bilateral	5,505	5,628	5,573	5,794	5,970	5,718	5,700
OTHER OFFICIAL[4]	203	—73	302	402	413	750	585
PRIVATE FLOWS	2,557	3,200	4,182	3,810	4,208	5,963	6,280
Direct Investment	1,603	1,783	2,496	2,187	2,117	2,899	2,566
Bilateral Portfolio	327	416	687	502	796	880	1,260
Multilateral Portfolio	—33	141	248	15	306	604	414
Export Credit[5]	660	860	751	1,106	989	1,579	2,040
TOTAL FLOW:	8,632	9,142	10,420	10,348	11,310	13,113	13,572

NOTES (Continued):

[3] Funds made available by governments on concessional terms primarily to promote economic development and the welfare of less developed countries. It is this flow which the Development Assistance Committee (D.A.C.) of the Organisation for Economic Cooperation and Development (O.E.C.D.) describe as "aid". The figures under this classification are only available for 1960-69.

[4] Official export credits and net purchases by governments of bonds, loans and participations of multilateral agencies.

[5] The coverage of non-guaranteed export credit is not complete.

TABLE VI: RESOURCE FLOWS TO LESS DEVELOPED COUNTRIES[1] IN 1969 AS PER CENT OF GROSS NATIONAL PRODUCT.

	Official Development Assistance	Net Total Flow of Financial Resources
Australia	0.56	0.74
Austria	0.12	0.65
Belgium	0.51	1.12
Canada	0.34	0.50
Denmark	0.41	1.13
France	0.69	1.24
Germany	0.39	1.33
Italy	0.16	1.03
Japan	0.26	0.76
Netherlands	0.53	1.36
Norway	0.31	0.78
Sweden	0.44	0.77
United Kingdom	0.39	0.97
United States	0.33	0.49
Average, above 14 countries	0.39	0.92

SOURCE: O.E.C.D.
[1] Including less-developed countries of southern Europe.

One is the funds transferred by voluntary agencies, churches and private foundations which to the ordinary citizen are very much "aid", particularly since the funds really are "given away". The size of this flow is hard to determine, but a rough estimate puts the average for 1968-69 at between $550-600 million.[1] By comparison the level of government bilateral grants in 1968-69 averaged about $3 billion and aid from the United Nations about $300 million. The aid of voluntary agencies and private foundations thus amounted to nearly 20 per cent of the flow of government grants and twice the level of U.N. aid.

Financial transfers from the Soviet Union and Eastern Europe to Third World countries are also omitted from the table. Virtually the whole of this flow is credit at 2.5-3 per cent interest

[1] O.E.C.D., 1970 Review of Development Assistance. One difficulty in estimating this flow is to distinguish the funds which governments sometimes channel through private organisations.

and maturity of 8-12 years. The amount of resources the European communist countries annually transfer is again hard to estimate precisely, but is almost certainly well below $500 million, which means that it is probably only about 3-4 per cent of the total flow of financial resources from western industrial countries. The bulk of the credit is supplied by the Soviet Union; even so, its contribution is unlikely to amount to more than 0.2 per cent of its total output. The flow is also heavily concentrated at the receiving end. In recent years most of it has gone to U.A.R., Iran, and Algeria. The credits mostly finance the supply of complete plants for heavy engineering based industry and power projects in the publicly owned sectors of the receiving countries.

A novel feature of these bilateral credit arrangements is that repayment is accepted in the form of traditional exports such as sugar, fibres and rubber and sometimes, also, of the goods produced by the plants the credits helped to finance. This gives the loans a self-liquidating character and thereby lessens the drain of foreign exchange through debt service payments. By the same token the arrangements give a very direct boost to trade between European communist countries and Third World countries. Total trade turnover between them increased more than fourfold from the mid-fifties to the mid-sixties. Finally, it is worth recording that over and above their bilateral contracts, the European communist countries in recent years have contributed about $10 million annually to U.N. technical assistance and relief programmes.

Taken together the resources transferred to Third World countries from all other sources are unlikely to amount to as much as 10 per cent of the total flow shown in Table V. The latter figures really do represent most of the story. Following the distinction mentioned earlier, the burden of foreign aid will be considered only in relation to official development assistance. But before turning to this question, something should be said about private capital flows. These comprise commercial export credit and foreign investment and lending.

Private Flows

(a) Export Credit.

Selling goods on credit is as old as the invention of money. Commercial export credit is inseparable from normal trade and should not be confused with aid. As a means of financing the transfer of resources from wealthier to poorer countries it nevertheless counts towards the fulfilment of the one per cent target mentioned earlier. In recent years it has formed a major part of the total flow from several industrial countries, notably Denmark, Italy, Japan, Norway and Switzerland.

The average annual net flow of private export credit from D.A.C. member countries increased from $375 million in 1956-58 to over $1,200 million in 1966-68 (Table V). In 1969 the flow topped the $2 billion mark. The figures very likely underestimate the flow because the portion not officially insured is less completely recorded than government guaranteed credit. In addition, a substantial amount is actually supplied by official institutions. The net flow from both sources, private and official, reached a 1968-69 average of 18 per cent of the total transfer of financial resources from D.A.C. member countries.

Export credit is an instrument of trade promotion. The large increase in the flow to Third World countries reflects the lack of alternative means of financing their growing import demands, particularly for capital goods. Manufacturers eager for orders have been only too ready to arrange a sale on private credit terms. Short term accommodation has thus been stretched to finance long-term investment. Such transactions are presumably good business; it is less apparent that they are always in the national economic interest of the countries involved.

For one thing, favourable credit terms have to some extent become more decisive in winning orders than the price and quality of the goods themselves. The more generous the terms the more likely the order. This does not necessarily reduce the effective cost of borrowing to the buyer, because apparently favourable terms have often been offset by a substantial overpricing of the goods supplied. The Berne Union, an international association of export credit insurers, agreed in the 1950s to limit suppliers' credit insurance to 5 years for heavy capital goods and 7 years for certain kinds of aircraft and ships. But by 1967 virtually the entire net flow had a maturity of over 5 years. It is a fair indication of how keenly exporters of capital goods are now competing for Third World orders.

At the end of the sixties export credit constituted more than one quarter of the total external debt outstanding for Argentina, Peru, Korea, Rwanda, Mauretania, Niger, Ivory Coast, Ghana

192

and Chad. This points to another danger in the growing competition in export credit terms, namely, the build-up of an excessive amount of privately contracted debt in the receiving countries. In a number of cases—Argentina, Brazil, Chile, Ghana and Indonesia for example—it has been the major reason for the need to reschedule their external debts. The cost of rescheduling or of default, usually falls on official aid, that is, on the taxpayers and balance of payments of the creditor country. Even if a debt crisis is avoided, the rapid accumulation of these relatively short-term obligations can seriously complicate the foreign exchange budgeting problem of Third World countries.[1]

The ultimate responsibility for ensuring that external debt is kept under proper surveillance and control lies with the governments of receiving countries. To help them the Pearson Commission recommended the World Bank to operate an "early warning system" on the build-up of debt. Industrial countries, too, should act together to exercise more restraint. It is extraordinary that autonomous public institutions, operating in isolation from government aid agencies, can insure a large extension of suppliers' credit without regard for the capacity of the receiving country to support the added repayment burden entailed. Bodies responsible for export credit insurance could at least consult national aid agencies to ensure that purely commercial trade interests do not conflict with the policy aims of official development aid. It is difficult to see how officially insured export credit can escape proper government surveillance at the supplying end as well.

(b) Foreign Investment.

Before 1914 private foreign investment was channelled into developing countries mainly through bond issues on the international capital market. Nowadays, it very largely takes the form of direct corporate investment; the bond market plays only a minor role as a source of external finance.

The volume of foreign direct investment in less developed countries has fluctuated considerably from year to year but shows

[1] In 1968 export credits accounted for 20 per cent of the total outstanding debt of Third World countries, but for 41 per cent of their total debt service payments. See: "The Use of Commercial Credits by Developing Countries for Financing Imports of Capital Goods", I.M.F. Staff Papers, Vol. XVII. No. 1. March, 1970.

no marked long-run expansion. The average level fell from $2.3 billion in 1956-58 to $1.6 billion in 1961-63 and then rose to $2.5 billion in 1967-69 (Table V). But whereas in 1956-58 it had accounted for one-third of the total flow of resources to less developed countries, by 1967-69 the proportion had fallen to one-fifth. Even these figures exaggerate the volume of resources actually transferred; because an increasing share of private capital flow is financed from the reinvested earnings of companies already established in Third World countries. The net transfer of resources through direct investment has quite likely been declining over the past decade.

Statistics are no guide, however, to the actual or potential development impact of private foreign investment. In most cases its contribution goes beyond the provision of foreign exchange resources or the creation of new jobs and new tax-paying entities. It also embodies the transfer of modern technology including managerial and technical skills. The special quality of direct investment is that it brings all these benefits together in one package. Its big drawback for most very poor countries is that it tends to by-pass them.

Private foreign investment in the Third World is heavily concentrated in mineral exploitation, above all petroleum, and in the fast growing manufacturing sectors of countries with a relatively high average level of income such as Argentina, Brazil and Mexico. Many countries in Asia and Africa receive none at all. Political and economic insecurity, an inadequate provision of supporting facilities and services and the limited size of national markets inhibit a larger and more generalised flow.

Of the total flow of direct investment to less developed countries since the mid-fifties the United States alone accounted for around 45 per cent and Britain and France together for another 35 per cent. Germany, Italy and Japan, which began the post-war period with hardly any outstanding direct investment assets overseas, have gradually become fairly substantial exporters of private capital. Canada and Sweden are the only other significant sources. The main flows, however, are from the United States to Latin America, from Britain to developing Commonwealth countries and from France to the overseas franc area. In the mid-sixties Latin America received almost as much direct investment as official aid. By contrast, the Middle East received far more private capital than official aid, while Africa and more

194

especially Asia, received far more official aid than private capital.

According to an O.E.C.D. estimate the accumulated direct investment stake of D.A.C. member countries in the Third World at the end of 1966 amounted to about \$30 billion.[1] This was almost one-third of all their direct investment assets overseas. Net additional flows since then increased the total in 1969 to some \$37-38 billion. Over half the Third World total is located in Latin America and the Caribbean region. It must be emphasised, however, that these estimates are subject to wide margins of error.

The profitability of foreign direct investment in the Third World is not easy to determine—it varies between years, countries, industries and firms. Reliable estimates for petroleum are notoriously difficult to make. On the basis of British and American data, a rough calculation puts the average rate of return[2] in manufacturing at between 8 and 12 per cent in the mid-sixties. Average yields in mining ranged from 12 per cent to as high as 34 per cent. In petroleum, however, they were perhaps no more than 10-11 per cent. In general, petroleum was much less profitable in the mid-sixties than it had been after the Suez crisis of the fifties.

Profitability is by no means the only or even the main impulse behind foreign investment. It is no longer true that corporate investors, for instance, are simply interested in maximising profits. They are often more concerned to expand the market for a particular product and if this can only be done in the face of strong competition, the investment would be unlikely to earn big profits. But do the investing countries benefit from foreign investment?

The United States and Britain, the countries with the largest foreign investment stake in the Third World, have been very conscious in recent years of the burden of capital exports on their balance of payments. How serious a burden it is depends on the time horizon adopted. It has been found, for example, that British direct investment in less-developed countries has a more favourable initial and continuing effect on the demand for British exports than British direct investment in other industrial

[1] See *Partners in Development*, Annex II, Table 13.
[2] Net profit after tax (in host country) and interest as a percentage of capital employed.

countries.[1] Direct investment also often leads to a greater demand for all kinds of insurance and other services from the investing country. If, therefore, a steady rate of capital export is maintained for several years it would very likely earn a sufficient return flow of income to finance the annual quota of new foreign investment. The impact on the balance of payments is really a question of weighing short run costs against long term benefits.

National and international aid agencies have long been engaged in seeking out and publicising promising foreign investment opportunities in the Third World.[2] The need to encourage a bigger flow of private foreign capital on terms acceptable to both the host country and the investor has been repeatedly voiced in U.N. forums. The disenchantment with official aid has given comfort to a vague feeling that private capital would do the same job more efficiently. Private business is being more than ever exhorted to play a bigger role in the development of the Third World.

Few, if any, would deny that foreign investment has a singularly effective contribution to make. But it is an illusion to suppose that it can replace official aid within the foreseeable future. For one thing, as already mentioned, private capital tends to by-pass most of the very poor countries in the Third World. For another, official aid is very much needed for roads, schools, health facilities and other social overhead capital. The ability to attract private capital often depends on this kind of public investment. A more generous provision of official aid might even induce a more generous treatment of foreign private investment. The function and purpose of official aid and foreign investment thus support and complement one another rather than overlap.

Finally, some mention should be made of portfolio investment in the Third World. In contrast to the position before 1931 the international bond market has been a rather minor source of development finance. On a gross basis only three countries, Argentina, Israel and Mexico, were each able in the period 1964-68 to float bonds totalling more than $100 million. In gen-

[1] See, e.g. W. B. Reddaway, *Effects of U.K. Direct Investment Overseas. Final Report*, Cambridge University Press, 1968.

[2] See, e.g. *Industrialization Schemes for the African States associated with the Community*, Commission of the European Communities (E.E.C.) June, 1967.

cral, the main borrowers have been countries which enjoyed a traditional access to particular capital markets, notably New York and London. The steady rise in interest rates has made this a very expensive form of borrowing. But the basic reason for its limited scale is the poor credit standing of the vast majority of Third World countries.

The capital markets of industrial countries, especially New York, are, however, an indispensable source of funds for the World Bank and for regional banks such as the Inter-American Development Bank (I.D.B.). The World Bank alone sold far more bonds in the period 1965-70 than all the less developed countries together. In addition, the Bank has been able to sell a sizeable chunk of its own portfolio to private investors thereby acting, in effect, as an underwriter of private foreign investment. Its gross disbursements to Third World countries averaged $330 million in 1960-61 and $580 million in 1967-68, but the annual average for the 1960s as a whole is around $460 million. The Bank's own lending rate reflects the cost of its own borrowing and has, therefore, kept in step with rising interest rates in private capital markets. In 1970 its average lending rate rose to 7¼ per cent.

The geographical distribution of World Bank bonds and borrower's obligations in the middle of 1970 is set out in Table VII. The scale of its dependence on American capital is not surprising. More interesting, perhaps, is the extent to which it has directly drawn funds from strong creditor countries like Germany, Japan and Switzerland. The sizeable interest payments which Germany and the United States have received from the Bank is also worth remarking.

Official Development Assistance

By official development assistance is meant the resources made available by governments on concessional terms in order to promote the development and welfare of less developed countries. Unlike private capital flows incidental to normal trade and finance, the amount and terms of this official aid are deliberately set by public policy.

In the 1960s official development assistance accounted on the average for about 60 per cent of the total flow of financial re-

TABLE VII: International Bank for Reconstruction and Development. Estimated Geographical Distribution of I.B.R.D. Bonds and Borrowers' Obligations as of 30th June, 1970.

(Expressed in millions of United States dollars)

Country	Direct Borrowings		Estimated Holdings of Outstanding IBRD U.S. Dollar Obligations	Participation in I.B.R.D. Loans		Interest Received on I.B.R.D. Bonds and Loans
	Gross	Net[1]		Gross	Net	
Australia	—	—	19.1	20.8	—	N.A.[2]
Austria	15.0	10.0	22.5	15.2	9.2	N.A.
Belgium	10.0	—	25.0	89.8	17.8	N.A.
Canada	124.9	72.9	119.8	89.3	6.3	32.0[3]
Denmark	—	—	8.0	3.8	—	N.A.
Finland	—	—	16.0	39.9	8.5	N.A.
France	—	—	35.8	225.2	130.6	39.2[4]
Germany	2,599.0	1,235.5	208.7	26.1	12.5	234.8[5]
Italy	24.0	24.0	52.5	200.0	87.7	14.7[6]
Japan	200.0	200.0	25.0	163.7	163.2	55.7[7]
Netherlands	58.0	39.6	15.3	203.2	47.1	N.A.

Norway	—	—	42.2	20.1	—	N.A.
Portugal	—	—	2.0	—	—	N.A.
Sweden	14.5	14.5	6.2	0.2	0.2	N.A.
Switzerland	335.1	180.8	68.5	90.5	0.8	73.3[8]
United Kingdom	48.0	31.0	9.3	26.0	3.0	29.2[3]
United States	2,860.0	2,016.3	1,673.6	682.8	144.3	725.0[7]
Others	2,222.9	743.7	527.2	453.2	82.1	N.A.
Total:	8,511.4	4,568.3	2,876.7	2,349.8	713.3	

NOTES:

[1] Represents amount outstanding. In addition, the Bank has entered into agreements to sell additional bonds totalling $43,525,000. These agreements provide for delivery against payment at various dates up to and including July 8th, 1970.

[2] Not Available.

[3] Interest paid on Bonds and Loans of 6.30.67.

[4] Interest paid on Loans as of 12.31.67. Interest paid on Bonds not available.

[5] Interest paid on Bonds as of 12.31.66. Interest paid on Loans not available.

[6] Interest paid on Bonds as of 12.31.66. Interest paid on Loans not available.

[7] Interest paid on Bonds and Loans as of 6.30.68.

[8] Interest paid on Bonds and Loans of 12.31.66.

sources to less-developed countries. The proportion was higher at the beginning and lower at the end of the decade. The Pearson Commission proposed a government aid target of 0.7 per cent of G.N.P. by 1975 or in no case later than 1980. The strategy adopted for the Second U.N. Development Decade endorsed the target and urged donor countries to do their best to reach it by the middle of the decade. It will be quite an effort for most of them.

In 1969 France had virtually reached the target; but only in the case of Australia, Belgium and the Netherlands did official aid exceed even 0.5 per cent of G.N.P. (See Table VI). Not surprisingly, perhaps, Belgium and the Netherlands have accepted the target without reservations. So have Finland, Norway and Sweden. Canada and New Zealand accept the figure, but not the date, while France favoured a target between 0.6 and 0.7 per cent of G.N.P. Most of the other donor countries recognise the need for an increasing volume of government aid, but decline to commit themselves to a specific target or date.

Throughout most of the sixties the level of official development assistance rose only slowly. It increased from $4.7 billion in 1960 to $6.7 billion in 1967, fell to $6.4 billion in 1968 and then rose to $6.7 billion again in 1969 (See Table V). For the last few years the flow of resources primarily intended for development has thus virtually stagnated. Since private investment tends to by-pass them, the poorest countries have likely borne the brunt of this stagnation. Because of rising prices for the goods and technical assistance services aid provided, the flow to them in real terms may even have declined in recent years.

Over the 1960s the U.S., France and Britain accounted for nearly 80 per cent of the total flow of aid. The U.S. share alone was about 55 per cent. The combined share of these three major donors has been steadily declining, however, while that of Australia, Canada, Germany, Japan, the Netherlands and Sweden has risen. By 1967 Germany had displaced Britain as the third largest donor country after the U.S. and France and by 1969 Japan, too, had overtaken the British total (See Table VIII).

The distribution of aid has been influenced more by political and strategic considerations than by economic criteria. The main directions are from France to French speaking Africa, from Britain to less developed Commonwealth countries and from the U.S. to countries in Asia and Latin America with whom it has special links. For these donors, at least, aid is very closely an instrument of foreign policy. Only Germany among the big four donors has distributed its aid in a more general way.

Official development assistance is a label that covers many kinds of resource transfers under widely differing conditions. In distinguishing its main components the first feature to notice is that the overwhelming bulk of the flow is contributed under bilateral programmes. Over the 1960s only about 9 per cent of it was channelled through international institutions. This means that over half the total flow of financial resources to less developed countries has consisted of official bilateral aid.

The Pearson Commission rightly scotched the misconception sometimes held that all aid is "given away". In fact, the proportion provided in the forms of loans on concessional terms rose from an average of 11 per cent in 1960-61 to an average of 35 per cent in 1968-69. Over 40 per cent of all bilateral aid in 1969 consisted of loans. The correspondingly larger amortization payments which the donor countries will receive from this rising volume of loans means that, for any desired expansion in the flow of net official aid, the gross flow of aid will have to increase more rapidly still.

Another important component is technical assistance. This flow, too, expanded relatively rapidly in the 1960s and now represents over one quarter of bilateral aid. In some cases the proportion is much higher. It accounts for around half of Belgian, French and Swedish bilateral aid. Most technical assistance is provided as an outright grant. That has also been true of a great deal of food aid.

Food aid made up over 20 per cent of the average annual flow of bilateral aid in the period 1960-69. The proportion reached a peak of 27 per cent in 1964 and then declined to under 10 per cent in 1969. Over 90 per cent of all food aid came from the United States and it accounted for a substantial proportion of American bilateral aid.

Strictly speaking, the bulk of food aid has been sold for local currency. But when resources are obtained at virtually no foreign exchange cost to the recipient, they amount, in effect, to a grant-like contribution. The United States is now phasing out local currency sales of food in favour of dollar sales on soft loan terms. This change of policy and the reduced scale of food aid in recent years, largely explain the rising proportion of official bilateral aid in the form of loans and the corresponding drop in the share of grants from well over 80 per cent in 1961 to around 60 per cent in 1969.

Sometimes aid is distinguished according to whether it is intended for specific projects or for more general purposes such as balance of payments or budget support. Non-project assistance, for example, accounted in 1967 for about 47 per cent of official bilateral aid. The essential point in the present context is that the diversity of aid involves an equally wide range of different costs for the supplying countries. Although there is no simple way of calculating these costs, economists are generally agreed that the real burden they represent is much less than the face value of the aid provided. Why this is so can be indicated in general terms. But first of all, it should be said that there is more than one way of looking at the burden of aid.

The Burden of Aid

A common way of judging the burden of aid is to relate the amount provided to the donor country's total income. The arbitrary target of one per cent of G.N.P. reflects this particular approach. In truth, as mentioned earlier, it is not really an "aid" target at all. A better guide is the ratio of official development assistance to total income, though even this measure says nothing about the quality of a country's aid effort. One donor might reach a given target by simply channelling official loans into projects which directly boost its own exports. Another may fail to reach the target and yet be concentrating much more on meeting the real development priorities of recipient countries. But if no allowance is made for the quality of aid, it is fair to say that a given ratio of official development assistance to total income implies a greater burden for a less wealthy country than for a richer one. The ratios for 1969 are set out in Table VI above.

France tops the list with a 0.69 per cent ratio of official aid to G.N.P. and is followed by Australia, Netherlands and Belgium. None of these four countries rank among the four wealthiest countries in the world. The wealthiest country, the United States, managed to do less than averagely well: it ranks tenth in the table. Nor does the trend in aid follow closely the rise in total income. The ratio of official aid to G.N.P. for the United States, France and Britain, which together accounted for nearly

80 per cent of the average annual flow of aid over the 1960s, was steadily declining in this period.

Since official development assistance involves some cost to the budgets of donor governments, the amount they provide per head of population is a rough measure of the burden it places on their taxpayers. The relevant figures are presented in Table VIII.

Over the 1960s the average "taxpayer cost" of official aid for the countries listed rose from around $9 per head to $11 per head. France topped the list in 1969 at over $19 per head, followed by Sweden and the U.S. at over $15 per head, Australia at over $14 and Belgium at over $12 per head. The trend for much of the sixties, however, was downwards for France, the United States and Belgium and upwards for Australia and Sweden. Within the last few years it has risen also in Canada, Denmark, the Netherlands and Germany. If donor countries are ranked according to "taxpayer cost" there was a marked fall in the sixties in the relative position of Britain and a marked rise in that of Denmark and Sweden.

Another way of looking at the taxpayer burden is to take the share of aid in the total expenditures of donor governments. These governments typically spend around 30 per cent of the national income. Since their aid averages under 0.4 per cent of G.N.P. it follows that it accounts on the average for less than 1.5 per cent of their total expenditures.

The Pearson Commission recommended an official aid target of 0.70 per cent of G.N.P. by 1975 and thought its achievement could well raise the net flow of aid in that year to around $16 billion. Assuming that the population of the donor countries (listed in Table VIII) grows by 1 per cent a year the Person estimate would raise the average "taxpayer cost" of aid from around $11 per head in the late sixties to about $25 per head in 1975. The annual average increase from 1968 to 1975 works out at about $2 per head or, say, U.S. 2 cents a week.

However even these calculations exaggerate the possible "taxpayer cost" of official development assistance. For what they leave out of account is the flow of income the donor governments receive from their official loans. This aspect of the picture will be looked at later.

The burden of aid that most exercises donor countries, however, is its foreign exchange cost to the balance of payments. It

TABLE VIII: NET FLOW OF OFFICIAL DEVELOPMENT ASSISTANCE TO LESS-DEVELOPED COUNTRIES[1] AND MULTILATERAL AGENCIES 1960-69.

(U.S. Dollars)

	1960		1961		1962		1963		1964	
	Total $ millions	Per Capita $	Total $ millions	Per Capita $	Total $ millions	Per Capita $	Total $ millions	Per Capita $	Total $ millions	Per Capita $
Australia	58.9	5.73	70.7	6.70	73.8	6.87	95.9	8.76	100.0	8.95
Austria	0.1	0.014	2.9	0.41	7.0	0.98	2.1	0.29	11.8	1.64
Belgium	100.9	11.02	92.1	10.03	69.8	7.57	79.7	8.58	71.3	7.60
Canada	75.2	4.20	60.6	3.29	34.5	1.85	64.6	3.41	77.9	4.04
Denmark	5.3	1.16	8.1	1.76	7.5	1.61	8.7	1.86	10.1	2.14
France	847.3	18.55	942.9	20.43	975.9	20.77	851.7	17.81	828.2	17.14
Germany	237.4	4.46	330.0	6.11	398.3	7.30	392.8	7.08	460.4	8.20
Italy	76.6	1.54	59.6	1.19	80.1	1.59	70.3	1.38	47.6	0.93
Japan	105.1	1.13	107.8	1.15	85.3	0.90	137.6	1.43	115.8	1.19
Netherlands	35.3	3.07	55.9	4.80	65.0	5.51	37.8	3.16	49.2	4.06
Norway	5.2	1.45	6.8	1.88	7.3	2.00	9.9	2.70	9.6	2.60
Sweden	6.7	0.90	8.4	1.12	18.5	2.45	22.9	3.01	32.8	4.28
Switzerland	3.5	0.65	7.9	1.44	4.9	0.87	6.2	1.07	9.2	1.57
United Kingdom	406.8	7.77*	456.8	8.65	421.0	7.89	414.5	7.72	493.3	9.13
United States	2,702.1	14.95	2,943.4	16.02	3,231.5	17.31	3,626.6	19.15	3,636.3	18.92
	4,664.4	8.45	5,153.9	9.22	5,480.4	9.68	5,821.3	10.16	5,953.5	10.26

SOURCE: O.E.C.D. and U.N. Statistics.
NOTES:
[1] Including less-developed countries in Southern Europe.

TABLE VIII: NET FLOW OF OFFICIAL DEVELOPMENT ASSISTANCE TO LESS-DEVELOPED COUNTRIES[1] AND MULTILATERAL AGENCIES 1960-69.—(Continued)

(U.S. Dollars)

	1965		1966		1967		1968		1969	
	Total $ millions	Per Capita $	Total $ millions	Per Capita $	Total $ millions	Per Capita $	Total $ millions	Per Capita $	Total $ millions	Per Capita $
Australia	118.6	10.41	126.1	10.87	157.3	13.31	159.8	13.28	174.6	14.19
Austria	31.5	4.34	31.4	4.30	26.0	3.55	22.8	3.10	15.5	2.10
Belgium	101.6	10.74	76.1	7.99	88.8	9.27	88.0	9.14	116.1	12.03
Canada	96.5	4.92	187.1	9.33	197.9	9.68	174.7	8.41	245.2	11.62
Denmark	13.0	2.73	21.1	4.40	25.9	5.35	28.7	5.89	54.3	11.10
France	752.2	15.42	748.8	15.14	825.5	16.66	873.9	17.50	965.3	19.18
Germany	430.5	7.57	439.7	7.65	528.1	9.15	553.3	9.53	595.0	10.13
Italy	60.0	1.16	78.4	1.50	154.7	2.95	146.0	2.71	129.6	2.43
Japan	243.7	2.49	283.3	2.87	384.3	3.85	356.2	3.52	435.6	4.25
Netherlands	69.6	5.66	93.9	7.54	113.5	9.01	123.3	9.68	143.1	11.11
Norway	11.3	3.04	14.1	3.76	14.5	3.83	26.6	6.98	29.5	7.66
Sweden	38.1	4.93	56.9	7.29	59.9	7.61	71.4	9.02	120.8	15.16
Switzerland	11.8	1.98	13.0	2.16	13.0	2.14	24.2	3.93	29.5	4.73
United Kingdom	472.0	8.69	486.0	8.89	485.0	8.82	413.0	7.47	431.3	7.76
United States	3,465.0	17.80	3,459.0	17.56	3,567.0	17.91	3,303.0	16.41	3,163.0	15.56
	5,915.4	10.09	6,110.9	10.31	6,641.4	11.10	6,364.9	10.52	6,648.0	10.90

SOURCE: O.E.C.D. and U.N. Statistics.
NOTES:
[1] Including less-developed countries in Southern Europe.

has troubled particularly those countries such as. the United States and Britain, which have been struggling to correct a serious and persistent deficit in their external accounts. Their main worry has been to prevent any further drain on their gold and foreign exchange reserves as a result of their own aid efforts. This could occur if the recipients of their aid spent it in another supplying country which then added the funds to its foreign exchange reserves instead of respending them. Donor countries with balance of payments deficits have, therefore, been loathe to see their aid being used to finance exports from other countries. Hence the practice of aid tying, whereby a particular donor requires its own aid to be spent on its own goods and services. Put simply, the practice proclaims a willingness to provide aid in the form of goods and services, but not in the form of freely spendable cash.

The United States set the pace in aid tying in an effort to reduce the balance of payments drain on its gold reserves. Other donors followed suit but not always for the same reason. To some extent tying has been used to promote exports or to prevent the pre-emption of export markets by the tying practices of rivals. Ensuring the national interest in this way makes it easier, so the argument runs, to justify foreign aid to an aid weary public. Export promotion is all part of "the common aid effort". As a result, by 1969 only about 18 per cent of gross bilateral aid disbursements were not contractually tied. In the case of the United States the proportion was more like 5 per cent. This compares with 2 per cent for Japan, between 25 and 30 per cent for Britain and France and over 40 per cent for Germany. Trade follows aid is a truer aphorism than trade follows a flag.

Much has been said and written about the disadvantages of tied aid for the recipient countries. It compels them to buy goods and services at prices often substantially above the cheapest source of supply. If the transfer is financed with a loan their debt service payments will be correspondingly inflated. Moreover, the debtors have to repay in convertible foreign exchange. Imports at uncompetitive prices may harm their own potential export competitiveness. Tying may also mean that they are importing the wrong sort of technology.

For these reasons tying is thought to reduce the real value

of aid by at least 20 per cent.[1] It amounts, in effect, to a "cut in aid".

On the other hand, it is easy to exaggerate the cost of tying to recipient countries. The calculation is usually based on a comparison between the price of tied aid goods and their market value. But non-tied aid has not always been spent on the cheapest available supplies. There are now perhaps four or five industrial countries capable of supplying a wide range of equipment. Even if each of them tie their aid, it should still be possible for recipient countries to shop around for the best buys. There is no supplier's market. In other words, the recipients could reduce the cost of tying by improving their own purchasing arrangements, knowledge and skills. Possibly they need the international equivalent of a national consumers' advisory service. That is something competitive suppliers should welcome. But is it so obviously in the interests of donors to tie their aid at all?

The burden of aid on the balance of payments of donor countries is not measured by its nominal value. For one thing, some resource transfers involve little or no foreign exchange expenditure. Aid in kind falls under this heading. Take, for instance, food aid which has formed a sizeable portion of the official development assistance of Australia, Canada and the United States. In real terms, farm surpluses cost these countries very little and at one time in the United States, at least, it was cheaper to ship them as aid than to store them. In the period 1960-66 government financed transfers of agricultural products from the United States accounted for over one quarter of its total agricultural exports. Food aid has undoubtedly benefitted the farm sectors of the surplus producing countries and all those interests with a stake in farm prosperity.

A large proportion of technical assistance is provided at no foreign exchange cost to the donor countries. The salaries of experts and teachers serving overseas are paid in their own country or partly remitted home. The bulk of aid-financed students and trainees receive their instruction in the donor country rather than in their own country or elsewhere. The Pearson Commission reckon that each $100 spent on technical assistance probably

[1] E.g. by the Pearson Commission.

represents only $20 in foreign currency. The significance of the estimate lies in the fact that 23 per cent of government aid at the end of the sixties consisted of technical assistance. It is often said, moreover, that experts and trainees become "salesmen" for the goods and services of the donor country which trained them. Looked at in this way, technical assistance may be likened to 'advertising expenditure".

Food aid and bilateral technical assistance are by their very nature tied to the source of supply. Other forms of aid are tied by deliberate policy. The practice does not, however, reduce the donor's balance of payments deficit by an amount equivalent to the aid provided. Some of the exports financed by tied aid would occur anyway, particularly if the recipient normally buys a sizeable proportion of its imports from the tied source of supply. The recipient simply substitutes tied aid goods for the goods it would have bought in any case, thereby freeing an equivalent amount of foreign exchange for other purposes. This means that the foreign exchange the donor hoped to save through tying is correspondingly reduced. The donor may then try to ensure that the tied aid goods are additional to those the recipient would normally purchase from it. In the process the efficiency of its aid operations will become increasingly enmeshed in red tape.

The spread of aid tying to other donors weakens still. further its advantages for any one of them. For on the debit side must now be subtracted the export orders each had expected to gain from the untied aid of the others. To this extent the policy becomes self-defeating. It lessens the impetus given to world trade by the repeated spending of the purchasing power which untied aid injects into the international economy. In the aid business, too, money, as Francis Bacon the sixteenth century English sage remarked, "is like muck, not good except it be spread".

Tying distorts the channels of world trade insofar as it encourages a shift from lower to higher cost sources of supply. It marks a return to the very bilateral trade discrimination which the industrial countries have striven throughout the post-war period to banish from their economic relations with each other.

Aid tying often represents a disguised subsidy for the competitively weaker enterprises of donor countries; the more efficient ones can hold their own in competitive bidding. United States legislation, for example, requires 50 per cent at least of all

American aid-financed goods to be carried in American flag ships. However persuasive the case for this kind of protection— and taxpayers can decide such issues for themselves—the cost of it ought not to be called "foreign aid". Tying tends to damage a donor country's reputation for competitiveness. Moreover, any policies and practices which lower the value and efficiency of aid will only prolong the recipient's dependence on aid.

Most discussions and estimates of the balance of payments cost of aid take a short run view which exaggerates the burden. On the basis of data for 1964-66 the former British Ministry of Overseas Development, for instance, reckoned that the foreign exchange cost to Britain is between 33 per cent and 42 per cent of the value of the aid it provides. The higher figure applied when British industry is working at full capacity, for then aid-financed exports are more likely to displace exports which could have been sold on commercial terms. The calculation does not, however, take account of debt service receipts or the export orders received as a result of the aid programmes of other donor countries. It indicates only the short term cost of marginal changes in the size of the British programme and not the cost of the programme as a whole. No account is taken of the potential impact on the British balance of payments of follow-up orders, the export opportunities which the expansion of the recipient's market may open up, the ability and willingness of recipients to continue debt service payments and to allow the repatriation of private capital and dividends. Without an aid programme, Britain would have to count the losses under all these headings. Hence the balance of payments cost of the programme as a whole is less as a proportion of the value of the aid provided than it is for short term marginal changes in the size of the programme.

Although it may be politically necessary for a donor country, especially if faced with a serious balance of payments deficit, to calculate the foreign exchange cost of its own aid, the problem disappears when all donors are considered together. For apart from petroleum producers, which anyway receive very little aid, Third World countries do not accumulate foreign currency reserves: they spend all the aid they receive. What the donors are fighting over is their individual share of this expenditure. The major weapon they have forged for the purpose is tied aid.

If each donor's share of total aid were approximately proportional to its share of Third World markets a general untying

209

of aid should have no adverse impact on its balance of payments. But as Table IX shows, the United States' export share is much smaller than its aid share. The ratios seem unfavorable to France also, except that the potential foreign exchange liability of French aid is considerably reduced by its heavy emphasis on technical assistance. By contrast the export share of Britain, Germany, Italy and, most notably, Japan, is rather larger than their share of official aid. These countries can expect to do well out of untied aid. But they are unlikely to untie their own aid if the United States does not follow suit.

There were hopeful signs in 1970 that some way out of the impasse may shortly be found. In March of that year the Peterson Task Force on the future of the U.S. foreign aid programme proposed that all industrial countries agree to untie their bilateral development loans.[1] The U.S. President included this recommendation in a message to Congress on foreign aid the following September. At the same time a majority of the O.E.C.D. member countries agreed in principle to devise a generalised scheme of untying for bilateral development loans. The strategy for the Second U.N. Development Decade, which the General Assembly adopted in October 1970, likewise enjoined the donor countries to reduce the extent of their tying.

Some modest gestures in this direction have already been made. United States aid, for example, can now be used to purchase goods and services from less developed countries. Other donors have also recently liberalised their tying regulations in favour of Third World suppliers. The relaxations are helpful, but cannot be dubbed a major advance. That will only come if the donors agree to allow their bilateral development loans, which contribute over 40 per cent of all bilateral aid, to be freely spent in any other donor country.

Negotiations on a generalised untying scheme are likely to prove difficult. There are big enough differences in the volume, composition and terms of bilateral aid to provide plenty of room for argument about burden sharing. Thus the donors who provide a relatively larger proportion of their aid in the form of grants might argue that the onus for untying rests mainly with those who provide a relatively larger proportion in the

[1] *U.S. Foreign Assistance in the 1970's: A New Approach*. Report to the President from the Task Force on International Development.

form of loans. There is also the risk that untying might induce some legislatures to cut back on aid, particularly if the balance of payments cost still worries them.

The whole problem is often thought to be rooted in gold reserves and international liquidity. But to invoke this argument as an excuse for limiting aid is rather like a millionaire refusing to contribute to charity because his bank balance is low. Sensible people adjust their liquidity to their spending and not the other way round. By managing their monetary systems in ways that make them feel poor, rich countries have put a brake on the flow of aid to countries that really are poor. In any case, several billion dollars a year of additional international purchasing power have recently been created through Special Drawing Rights (S.D.R.'s.) in the International Monetary Fund. The lion's share of this new international money has been distributed to rich countries free of charge, which makes it all the harder to see why they cannot now contribute a correspondingly larger amount of aid to poor countries.

In the final analysis, however, the capacity to give aid is a function of income and by this test the rich countries can certainly afford more.

Export Orders and Multilateral Financing

In the late 1950s international agencies played only a minor role in the external financing of Third World development. By 1967 they had become the channel for over $1 billion of net financing, roughly half of which was disbursed on concessional terms. At present they are responsible for about 10 per cent of the total flow of financial resources, but for more than half of all development loans.[1]

The big surge in multilateral financing came initially from the creation of new international agencies such as the European Development Fund (E.D.F.) of the E.E.C.; the Inter-American Development Bank (I.D.B.); the International Development Association (I.D.A.), an affiliate of the World Bank; and the United Nations Special Fund, which subsequently merged with the United Nations' Expanded Programme of Technical Assist-

[1] *U.S. Foreign Assistance in the 1970's: A New Approach.*

211

ance to form the United Nations Development Programme (U.N.D.P.).

With an exuberant disregard for "family planning" the channels of multilateral finance continued to multiply throughout the sixties. But until the end of the decade donor governments generally showed no greater disposition to use them. Multilateral aid accounted for much the same proportion of total aid in 1967-68 as in 1960-61. In 1969, however, the proportion contributed through international agencies suddenly rose to 15 per cent.[1] Here again, however, the overall average conceals wide differences in national policy. Smaller donors have shown a greater preference for multilateral distribution than the big donors. In 1968-69 the Scandinavians (Denmark, Norway and Sweden) contributed on average nearly 50 per cent of their official aid through international agencies. The Netherlands' proportion reached 22.5 per cent, Germany channelled 19 per cent, Britain and Japan 16 per cent, the United States 9 per cent and France 6 per cent. For a variety of historical, political and commercial considerations the big donors greatly prefer bilateral aid.

The Pearson Commission proposed that multilateral aid should form 20 per cent at least of the total flow of official development assistance by 1975. This implies that if its target of 0.70 per cent of G.N.P. for official aid is achieved, the volume of multilateral aid should rise from a little over $600 million a year in 1966-68 to over $3 billion in 1975. Such an expansion seems a quite unreal hope in the light of the strong attachment of the big donors to bilateral aid. Actually, it means that on the average only one third of the expansion recommended in the total flow of official aid would be channelled through multilateral agencies. The Pearson proposal does not imply any displacement of bilateral aid. The Peterson Task Force, the U.S. President and the strategy for the Second Development Decade have all called for a larger volume of multilateral aid. But while the donor countries collectively recognise the need to channel a larger share of their aid through international agencies, they have not committed themselves to the idea of a target.

Some donors, the United States most of all, have been con-

---

[1] This was mainly due to paid in capital subscriptions to replenish the funds of the International Development Association (I.D.A.).

cerned to reduce the foreign exchange cost of their contributions
to international agencies. Others have shown that their contribution to a particular agency is influenced by the return flow of
export orders they receive and expect from its financing activities.
The size and distribution of the orders directly obtained from the
main sources of multilateral finance is, therefore, of more than
ordinary interest. Multilateral aid, any more than aid in general,
is not, of course, supported on such a narrow foundation of
national self-interest. International organisations are instruments
for national diplomacy and enshrine the ideals their member
governments profess to share. Governments support them with
contributions for a variety of reasons and the economic benefit
they derive in return is not necessarily one of them. All the

TABLE IX: Exports and Net Flow of Official Development Assistance to Less Developed Countries.
Cumulative 1964-68.

	EXPORTS		NET FLOW OF AID		RATIO OF AID TO EXPORTS
	$ millions	Percentage share	$ millions	Percentage share	Percentage
Australia	3,398	2.4	661.8	2.1	19.4
Austria	606	0.4	123.5	0.4	20.3
Belgium	2,904	2.1	425.8	1.4	14.7
Canada	3,252	2.3	734.1	2.4	22.6
Denmark	1,232	0.9	98.8	0.3	8.0
France	13,023	9.3	4,024.6	13.0	30.9
Germany	13,608	9.7	2,412.0	7.8	17.7
Italy	6,400	4.5	486.7	1.6	7.6
Japan	20,807	14.8	1,383.3	4.5	6.6
Netherlands	3,799	2.7	449.5	1.4	11.8
Norway	833	0.6	76.1	0.2	9.1
Sweden	1,827	1.3	259.1	0.8	14.1
Switzerland	2,622	1.9	71.1	0.2	2.7
United Kingdom	17,351	12.3	2,349.3	7.6	13.5
United States	48,991	34.8	17,430.3	56.2	35.6
	140,653	100.0	30,966.1	100.0	22.0

SOURCES: O.E.C.D. *Development Assistance: 1970 Review.*
I.M.F. and I.B.R.D. *Direction of Trade 1964-68.*

same, it may be useful to dispel the impression that the cost of these contributions is a one way drain.

In the following illustrations, two types of international agency are represented. The first draw their funds mainly from private capital markets and lend them out on conventional terms. The World Bank and the Inter-American Development Bank come under this category. The second type depend upon voluntary contributions or pledges from governments and make these funds available on concessional terms, as soft loans or outright grants. The International Development Association, the U.N. Development Programme and the European Development Fund are the chosen examples in this category.

(1) *The World Bank.*

The World Bank obtains its funds from member government subscriptions, the flotation of Bank bonds in national capital markets, the sale of its own loans, the receipt of debt service payments on previous loans and the income from its own operations. In the past decade the most important single source has been its own borrowings. Since the Bank must remain solvent and retain the confidence of private investors, the terms of its own lending are necessarily geared to the cost of its own borrowing. All its loans must be guaranteed by the governments of recipient countries and it is required to pay due regard to their capacity to repay.

By the middle of 1971 the cumulative total of World Bank lending had reached over $16 billion. Third World countries borrowed roughly two thirds of the total. But within the Third World itself, the Bank's financing has been highly concentrated. Seven Latin American countries (Argentine, Brazil, Chile, Columbia, Mexico, Peru and Venezuela) and five Asian countries (India, Malaysia, Pakistan, the Philippines and Thailand) account for about 60 per cent of the Third World's total cumulative borrowing.

In the past few years Third World countries have received around three quarters of the Bank's total gross disbursements. For fiscal years 1968-1970 the average annual gross flow amounted to about $700 million. But because of debt service payments to the Bank, new subscriptions and net changes in the holdings of the Bank's obligations, the net flow was rather less.

214

TABLE X: WORLD BANK
PAID-IN SUBSCRIPTIONS AND IDENTIFIABLE ORDERS
RECEIVED.
ELEVEN MAIN SUPPLIERS: CUMULATIVE TOTALS TO
30TH JUNE, 1970.

Country of Supply	Paid-in Portion of Capital Subscription		Share of Identifiable Orders Generated by World Bank Financing[1]	
	Amount $ Million	Per cent of Total	Amount $ Million	Per cent of Total
Belgium	45.0	1.94	176	2.4
Canada	79.2	3.42	199	2.7
France	105.0	4.53	404[2]	5.5
Germany (Federal Republic)	128.0	5.53	909	12.3
Italy	66.6	2.87	482	6.5
Japan	77.2	3.33	476	6.4
Netherlands	55.0	2.37	84	1.1
Sweden	24.0	1.04	206	2.8
Switzerland[3]	—	—	225	3.0
United Kingdom	260.0	11.23	1,126	15.2
United States	635.0	27.42	2,683[4]	36.3
Total Countries Listed	1,475.0	63.7	6,970	94.2
Total	2,315.9	100.0	7,397	100.0

NOTES:

[1] By 30th June, 1970 the Bank had disbursed $10,355 million of which $2,958 million (28.6%) had gone to finance local expenditures on broad development programmes where the source of the items imported with Bank funds was not specified. The balance of $7,397 million represents disbursements for identifiable imports by Bank borrowers.

[2] Excluding $60.0 million disbursed under Bank loans to Algeria where almost all the suppliers are known to have been French.

[3] Switzerland is not a member of the World Bank Group but in recognition of its importance as a source of capital for Bank lending, borrowing countries are permitted to make purchases in Switzerland.

[4] Up to 30th June 1970, the cumulative total of the World Bank's administrative expenditures in the United States amounted to $325.0 million.

215

The export orders generated by World Bank financing are obtained through international competitive bidding. Table X shows their distribution among the industrial countries which supplied 95 per cent of the identifiable orders placed down to the middle of 1970. The United States' share alone is 36 per cent. Britain comes next with about 15 per cent and then Germany with over 12 per cent. The combined share of Britain, France, Germany and Italy, the four main European suppliers, is a little more than that of the United States.

Nearly 70 per cent of the $7.4 billion of identifiable orders received by industrial countries came from Third World countries. The traditionally close commercial ties of the United States with Latin America might be expected to put it in a favourable position to benefit from the fairly heavy concentration of Bank financing in that region. In fact, the American share of identifiable Third World orders down to the middle of 1970 was about one third, whereas the combined share of the four main European suppliers rose to well over 40 per cent. If this reflects a competitively weaker American pull in Third World markets, it would be consistent with the sharp decline, noted at the beginning of this paper, in the relative export strength of the United States in Latin America since the mid-fifties.

The export orders the United States receives are, of course, only one element in the overall effect of the Bank's operations on the American balance of payments. A large part of the Bank's administrative expenditure, for example, accrues to the United States. The cumulative total up to the middle of 1970 amounted to $325 million. Indeed, despite its immense calls on American capital, the financial operations of the Bank in 1966-70 are estimated to have contributed on the average of about $380 million a year to the American balance of payments.

(2) *The Inter-American Development Bank.*

The Inter-American Development Bank (I.D.B.) was founded in 1959 and quickly expanded into an important source of development finance for Latin America. Similar banks were organised for Africa in 1965 and for Asia in 1966. Through these new channels it was hoped to make development financing more responsive to special regional needs and concerns.

The membership of I.D.B. comprises twenty two Latin Ameri-

216

can and Caribbean countries and the United States. By the end of 1970 their subscriptions to its ordinary capital resources amounted to $2.8 billion and their contributions to its Fund for Special Operations to $2.3 billion. The ordinary capital provides loans on pretty conventional terms whereas the Fund for Special Operations can make loans on concessional terms. By mixing loans from both sources the I.D.B., like the World Bank and its affiliate, the International Development Association (I.D.A.), is able to reduce its average loan rate to borrowers. In addition the I.D.B. administers for the United States a Social Progress Trust Fund of $525 million. At the end of 1970 it was decided to increase the Bank's resources by $3.5 billion ($2 billion for the ordinary capital and $1.5 billion for the Fund for Special Operations). Its total resources of nearly $6 billion is thus being raised to some $9.5 billion. In 1963 its gross loan disbursements were only $75 million; by 1970 they reached $428 million. The flow was much less on a net basis when allowance is made for debt service payments, subscriptions and net changes in holdings of I.D.B. funded debt.

In raising funds through bond issues the I.D.B., like the World Bank, has been heavily dependent on the American capital market; however, it has managed to mobilise capital from non-member countries as well. Table XI shows the distribution of these contributions and of the export orders which suppliers in non-member countries have received from I.D.B. financed projects. In several cases the value of the orders received closely matches the amount of capital contributed. France has done notably well out of I.D.B., having received $35.6 million in orders and contributed nothing.[1]

Since 1965 the procurement of goods and services financed from the Fund for Special Operations has been tied to the contributions of member countries. As a result about 90 per cent of the outlays have been disbursed in the United States. Up until the end of 1967 procurement from the ordinary capital resources of the Bank was based on international competitive bidding and therefore untied. But under pressure from the United States, whose share in procurement was less than its share in contributions, the I.D.B. decided from the beginning of 1968 to make procurement from non-member countries con-

---

[1] Though see footnote to Table XI.

TABLE XI: INTER-AMERICAN DEVELOPMENT BANK
Contributions of Resources and Acquisitions—Non-Member Countries
December 31, 1970.

(U.S. dollars)

| | Contributions of Resources | | | | | Acquisition of goods and services |
	Bond issues and loans	Funds in administration	Parallel financing agreements	Loan participations and others	Total	
Austria	11,538,462				11,538,462	11,603,800
Belgium	6,000,000			895,536	6,895,536	4,980,100
Canada		59,406,000	14,851,000	2,526,000	76,783,000	28,854,100
Denmark						8,529,000
Finland	1,100,000			10,000,000	11,100,000	1,117,100
France[1]						35,662,400
Germany (W)	153,005,462	8,994,536		105,000	162,104,998	99,031,200
Israel	5,000,000				5,000,000	242,600
Italy	72,000,000			870,000	72,870,000	38,936,100
Japan	30,000,000			8,175,000	38,175,000	32,201,200
Netherlands	8,287,293		35,000,000	100,000	43,387,293	6,479,600
Norway	4,000,000	2,000,000			6,000,000	1,942,100

218

South Africa	2,500,000				2,500,000	234,800
Spain	12,500,000			7,500,000	20,000,000	5,400,000
Sweden	9,665,179	5,000,000			14,665,179	14,425,700
Switzerland	36,588,154			408,000	36,996,154	23,584,900
United Kingdom	22,856,810	7,250,400		1,275,000	31,382,201	29,725,100
U.N. Special Fund				3,195,000	3,195,000	
Vatican		1,007,000			1,007,000	
I.C.E.M.		1,250,000			1,250,000	
Other Europe						1,392,000
Others						595,800
Total:	375,041,351	84,907,936	49,851,000	35,049,536	544,849,823	344,937,600

[1] In February 1971 the I.D.B. placed its first public bond issue in France for an amount equivalent to $18,000,000.

ditional in an appropriate contribution from them to the resources of the Bank. In other words the amount of export orders they obtained would be related to their contributions.

(3) The International Development Association.

The International Development Association (I.D.A.) was organised in 1960 to provide loans on highly concessional terms to countries with a rather limited capacity to service loans on conventional terms. It is affiliated to the World Bank and membership of the Bank is a requirement for membership of I.D.A. Nevertheless, it was thought advisable to establish I.D.A. as a juridically separate agency so as not to risk the good standing of the Bank among private foreign investors. For not only does I.D.A. provide very cheap credit: it lends only to governments and does not insist on a government guarantee of its loans. In practice though, it really is the Bank's own soft loan window. For instance, the Bank can blend its own loans with I.D.A. credit so as to moderate the cost of borrowing from the Bank alone. Without I.D.A. and, for that matter, official aid in general, the scale of the Bank's operations in the Third World would quite possibly have declined.

I.D.A. has received some profit income from the Bank, but is otherwise entirely dependent for its funds on the voluntary subscriptions of its member governments. This means that it is a charge on their national budgets and their taxpayers. By the middle of 1970 the cumulative total of government contributions amounted to almost $3 billion, 87 per cent of which came from twelve industrial countries.

In most cases I.D.A. loans carry a 50 year maturity, a 10 year grace period before repayment begins and a three quarter per cent service charge. Only poor countries are eligible to receive them and in 1964 the test of poverty was defined to mean countries with a per capita G.N.P. of less than $300. Gross disbursements from I.D.A. reached $342 million in fiscal year 1966/67 and then, because of delays in negotiating a further replenishments from I.D.A. reached $342 million in fiscal year 1966-67 1969-70. The bulk of its lending has been to Asia; down to 1968 the Indian share alone was 48 per cent and the Pakistan share 18 per cent. The heavy concentration on these two countries aroused criticism, however, with the result that the Indian share is now fixed at about 40 per cent and the Pakistan share at about 12.5 per cent.

The contracts I.D.A. finances are won through international competitive bidding. But in 1968 it was agreed that the current American contribution would not be used to finance purchases outside the United States until 30 June 1971 at the earliest. In other words, I.D.A. would only call upon the American contribution to finance contracts won by American suppliers.

Table XII shows the distribution of export orders among industrial countries which supplied 90 per cent of the identifiable orders financed by I.D.A. down to the middle of 1970. The final column in the Table relates the orders they received to their contributions. Thus, for every dollar donated Britain received export orders to the value of $1.90. By reason of its traditionally close commercial connexions with the Indian subcontinent Britain has been well placed to benefit from the heavy concentration of I.D.A. financing in India and Pakistan. Among other big donors, Germany and Japan have also done well out of I.D.A. At the other end of the scale, the United States and France have obtained only between U.S. 50 to 70 cents of orders for every dollar contributed. Another $28 million can be credited to the United States from the cumulative total of I.D.A.'s administrative expenditure up to the middle of 1970. Even so, it is hardly surprising that I.D.A. could not escape the procurement restrictions which the United States has placed on so much of its total aid. It would not be puzzling either if the French government felt less than enthusiastic about I.D.A.

(4) The United Nations Development Programme.

In 1959 the United Nations (U.N.) established a Special Fund for financing pre-investment projects such as surveys of natural resources and the training of human resources. Seven years later it was merged with the older U.N. Expanded Programme of Technical Assistance to form the U.N. Development Programme (U.N.D.P.). The merger is the only notable attempt so far made to consolidate the growing profusion of international machinery.

The U.N.D.P. is the largest source of multilateral finance for promoting the transfer of skills and technical know-how and the investigation of potential investment opportunities. It depends

TABLE XII: INTERNATIONAL DEVELOPMENT ASSOCIATION
(I.D.A.)
CONTRIBUTIONS AND IDENTIFIABLE ORDERS
RECEIVED: TWELVE MAIN SUPPLIERS.
CUMULATIVE TOTALS TO 30TH JUNE 1970.

COUNTRY OF SUPPLY	CONTRIBUTION[1]		SHARE OF IDENTIFIABLE[2] ORDERS GENERATED BY IDA FINANCING		RATIO OF[3] IDENTIFIABLE ORDERS TO SUBSCRIPTION
	Amount $ Million	Share of Total Per Cent	Amount $ Million	Share of Total Per Cent	
Australia	63.98	2.15	20.0	1.40	0.65
Belgium	36.90	1.24	37.6	2.63	2.12
Canada	154.53	5.19	51.3	3.59	0.69
France	212.03	7.12	70.3	4.92	0.69
Germany (Fed. Rep.)	242.56	8.15	216.0	15.11	1.85
Italy	48.16	1.62	60.0	4.20	2.59
Japan	141.32	4.75	155.5	10.88	2.29
Netherlands	73.52	2.47	16.1	1.13	0.45
Sweden	104.23	3.50	36.5	2.55	0.73
Switzerland[4]	12.10	.41	26.9	1.88	4.59
United Kingdom	383.26	12.88	328.9	23.01	1.90
United States	1,112.29	37.37	273.3	19.12	0.51
TOTAL (Countries listed.)	2,584.88	86.84	1,292.4	90.42	1.04
TOTAL	2,976.55	100.00	1,429.4	100.00	

NOTES:

[1] Includes initial subscriptions plus supplementary resources provided by (i) the first replenishment which became effective in 1964, (ii) the second replenishment which became effective in 1969, except for Italy's share which was paid in December 1970, (iii) special additional contributions by Sweden, Denmark and Norway and (iv) an interest free loan made to the Association by Switzerland. The countries listed accounted for 86.84% of the resources available to I.D.A. to 30th June 1970 from subscriptions, contributions and the Swiss Loan.

[2] The cumulative total of I.D.A.. disbursements as of 30th June, 1970 was $1,741.6 million of which $312.2 million (17.9%) had gone to finance local

222

entirely for its funds on the voluntary contributions of governments and is, therefore, like I.D.A., a charge on their national budgets and taxpayers. In the ten year period 1959-1968 the cumulative total amounted to nearly $1.3 billion, about 90 per cent of which came from industrial countries. Over the same period the cumulative expenditure of U.N.D.P., excluding administrative costs, totalled just over $870 million or $87 million a year on average. Expenditure was divided equally between pre-investment and technical assistant projects. In the period 1964-68, however, the average annual expenditure rose to $128 million and the share of pre-investment projects to about 60 per cent. The reason why total expenditure fell well short of total contributions is that a significant portion of U.N.D.P. funds was earmarked for project expenditure after 1968.

The bulk of U.N.D.P. funds are spent on expert services, including those provided under pre-investment projects, and training fellowships. How much of this expenditure returns to the main donor countries depends, in the first place, on the number and value of the experts and fellowships they provide through U.N.D.P. The cost of experts and training fellows and the length of their appointments vary enormously. Then there is the question of whether their salaries should be credited to their country of nationality or to the host country or divided between the two. To mention these problems is to show why precise answers are impossible. Any estimate must necessarily rest on certain assumptions and different assumptions will give different results. Those selected by the author are set out in the notes to Table XIII. The estimates presented follow from the assumptions made.

In Table XIII the number of experts recruited by U.N.D.P. from each of the main donor countries has been multiplied by

---

expenditure or imports for broad development programmes where the sources of items purchased has not been identified. The balance of $1,429.4 million represents disbursements abroad on imports by I.D.A. borrowers. The countries listed thus account for 90.4% of the identifiable orders directly generated by I.D.A. financing.

[3] Percentage share of identifiable orders generated by I.D.A. financing divided by percentage share of total contributions.

[4] Switzerland is not a member of the World Bank Group, but in recognition of its loan to the Association and its importance as a source of capital for the Bank, countries receiving I.D.A. credits are permitted to make purchases in Switzerland as well.

TABLE XIII: U.N.D.P.: CONTRIBUTIONS AND ESTIMATES OF THE PROVISION OF MAJOR INPUTS FOR PROJECTS, BY COUNTRY AND SUPPLY: 1959-1968.

COUNTRY OF SUPPLY	EXPERTS		VALUE (b)	FELLOWSHIPS		EQUIP-MENT (e)
	(Number) (a)	Assuming Avg. Unit Value $12,600	Assuming Avg. Unit Value $6,300	(Number) (c)	(d) Value Assuming Avg. Unit Value $1,950	
		(000$)	(000$)		(000$)	(000$)
	(1)	(2)	(3)	(4)	(5)	(6)
Australia	1,121	14,125	7,062	445	868	1,045
Austria	301	3,793	1,896	245	478	415
Belgium	1,439	18,131	9,066	555	1,082	2,698
Canada	1,377	17,350	8,675	556	1,084	1,793
Denmark	891	11,227	5,613	3,679	7,174	2,667
Finland	261	3,289	1,644	268	523	213
France	5,065	63,819	31,910	3,550	6,923	8,177
Germany Fed. Rep.	1,553	19,568	9,784	1,623	3,165	15,797
Italy	1,067	13,444	6,722	1,984	3,869	4,759
Japan	523	6,590	3,295	752	1,466	8,455
Netherlands	1,744	21,974	10,987	1,132	2,213	4,241
Norway	828	10,433	5,216	217	423	1,813
Sweden	997	12,562	6,281	979	1,909	4,382
Switzerland	1,017	12,814	6,407	1,709	3,333	6,690
U.S.S.R.	1,410	17,766	8,883	3,679	7,174	9,308
U.K.	7,071	89,095	44,547	4,537	8,847	27,567
U.S.A.	4,282	53,953	26,977	3,854	7,515	37,942
Other Countries	13,806	173,956	368,924	17,205	33,550	14,347
TOTAL:	44,753	563,889	563,889	46,972	91,596	152,309

224

TABLE XIII: U.N.D.P.: CONTRIBUTIONS AND ESTIMATES OF THE PROVISION OF MAJOR INPUTS FOR PROJECTS, BY COUNTRY AND SUPPLY: 1959-1968.—(Continued)

COUNTRY OF SUPPLY	SUBCONTRACTS (f)	TOTAL VALUE OF MAJOR INPUTS (g)		CONTRIBUTIONS (h)	RATIO OF RECEIPTS TO CONTRIBUTIONS (i)	
		Cols. 2, 5, 6 & 7	Cols. 3, 5, 6 & 7		Based on Cols. 8 & 10	Based on Cols. 9 & 10
	(000$) (7)	(000$) (8)	(000$) (9)	(000$) (10)	(11)	(12)
Australia	1,053	17,091	10,028	10,652	2.22	1.30
Austria	101	4,787	2,890	5,832	1.14	0.69
Belgium	1,125	23,036	13,971	12,905	2.47	1.50
Canada	10,862	31,089	22,414	63,874	0.67	0.49
Denmark	2,561	23,629	18,015	44,194	0.74	0.56
Finland	62	4,087	2,442	5,160	1.10	0.65
France	18,240	97,159	65,250	31,653	4.25	2.85
Germany Fed. Rep.	2,471	41,001	31,217	68,070	0.83	0.63
Italy	7,025	29,097	22,375	20,598	1.95	1.50
Japan	2,581	19,092	15,797	23,297	1.13	0.94
Netherlands	4,274	32,702	21,715	52,562	0.86	0.57
Norway	1,022	13,691	8,474	31,545	0.60	0.37
Sweden	2,099	20,952	14,671	88,370	0.33	0.23
Switzerland	2,239	25,076	18,669	25,649	1.35	1.01
U.S.S.R.	—	34,248	25,365	31,500	1.50	1.11
U.K.	8,123	133,632	89,084	94,240	1.96	1.31
U.S.A.	16,527	115,937	88,961	513,268	0.31	0.24
Other Countries	6,685	228,538	423,506	114,370	2.76	5.12
TOTAL:	87,050	894,844	894,844	1,237,739	—	—

Notes to this table appear on following page.

225

NOTES:

(a) Refer to the number of experts, classified by their nationality. The number of sub-contractors' personnel and consultants under the Special Fund component are excluded. An expert was counted once for each calendar year that he was in the field (regardless of the man months served).

(b) Number of experts multiplied by estimated unit value of $12,600 and $6,300 per expert. The higher average unit value assumes that the expert's "nationality" can be credited with his full earnings. The lower average unit value assumes that only half the expert earnings should be credited to his nationality, the other half being credited as a "return" to "other countries", which are the recipient countries.

(c) Refers to the host country of study of fellows. A fellow was counted once for each time he visited a country for study, irrespective of the duration of the visit.

(d) Assumes that host countries can be credited with all the money spent on fellows; i.e. an average of $1,950 per fellow.

(e) Refers to orders placed for purchase of equipment.

(f) Refers to awards made for sub-contracts which consist mainly of personnel services.

(g) Refers to sum total of sub-contracts, equipment, fellowships and the two estimated values for experts.

(h) Refers to voluntary pledges. Only countries contributing more than $5 million have been separately listed.

(i) Calculated from ratio of value of inputs provided by each country to the total value of all the inputs provided divided by ratio of individual country contributions to the total value of contributions. The formula is:

$$\frac{i_n}{I} \div \frac{c_n}{C}$$

where: i = value of major inputs provided by each country.
I = total value of inputs provided by all countries.
c = contributions of each country.
C = total value of all contributions.

The formula has been calculated on the basis of the two estimates for the values of inputs in columns (8) and (9).

(j) Excludes $7,931,000 in awards to "international consortia"; these contracts involve participation by contractors from two or more countries.

an average unit cost of $12,600 per expert. The category "Other Countries" are the recipients of U.N.D.P. assistance and it is worth noting that they provided nearly 30 per cent of the experts recruited in the period 1959 to 1968. Column 2 credits the nationality of the expert with his full earnings, while Column 3 assumes that half the earnings are spent in recipient countries, which seems more plausible. The Pearson Commission, it will be remembered, reckon that each $100 spent on technical assistance probably represents only $20 in foreign currency. Fellowships have been valued at an average unit cost of $1,950 and the whole of the amount credited to the host country. Equipment orders and sub-contracts admit of precise accounting. The total cumulative value of all these inputs of U.N.D.P. projects in the period 1959-1968 adds up to $895 million which is close to the cumulative expenditure of $870 million reported earlier.

In Columns 11 and 12 of Table XIII the contributions of the main donors are related to their receipts from U.N.D.P. The ratios set out in the final Column are probably more realistic than those in the preceding Column. The results provide only a rough indication of how much of U.N.D.P. expenditure returns to the main contributors but, even so, some interesting differences emerge.

Australia, Belgium, Britain, France, Italy, Switzerland and the Soviet Union received back more than a dollar for every dollar contributed. France tops the list with $2.85 of receipts for every dollar contributed, mainly because its share in the total value of experts (Column 3) and fellowships (Column 5) is conspicuously greater than its share in total contributions (Column 10). Much of the return to France stems, of course, from U.N.D.P. projects in French speaking Africa. Sweden and the United States are at the other end of the scale for precisely opposite reasons. Their share of experts and fellowships is notably smaller than their share in total contributions, which largely explains why they received only about U.S. 24 cents for every dollar contributed. Excluding experts and fellowships from the calculations and considering only equipment orders and sub-contracts, raises the Swedish ratio to 0.38 and the American one to 0.55. As in the case of the World Bank Group, a large proportion of U.N.D.P. administrative expenditure accrues to the United States. The cumulative total for the period 1959-1968 is estimated at

$31.5 million, which increases the American ratio from 0.24 to 0.32.

Interestingly enough, there is a significant, though not high, correlation between the I.D.A. ratios of orders to contributions and the U.N.D.P. ratios of receipts to contributions. With the exception of France, the countries which tended to do well out of I.D.A. also did well out of U.N.D.P. and conversely.

Apart from the assumptions underlying the estimates, Table XIII is not in any case a complete indication of the returns to donor countries from U.N.D.P. activities. For one thing, the calculation credits half the earnings of the experts to recipient countries and it is a fair presumption that the bulk of these foreign exchange receipts are respent in industrial countries. More importantly, U.N.D.P. projects can and do lead to follow-up investment. For instance, it is known that 46 surveys, feasibility studies and research projects, undertaken at a total cost to U.N.D.P. and recipient countries of $60 million, had by 1968 stimulated commitments of about $2 billion in follow-up investment from public and private sources both domestic and foreign.[1] Available evidence suggests that 50 per cent at least of this investment will be financed by industrial countries and multilateral sources, the World Bank especially. That is perhaps a truer glimpse of the business which U.N.D.P. activities help to open up for industrial countries, than a rough calculation of how much of its own expenditure they get back.

(5) The European Development Fund.

When the European Economic Community (E.E.C.) was launched in 1958 it set up a European Development Fund (E.D.F.) to channel aid to the politically dependent territories, mostly African, of its member countries. The E.D.F. was intended to supplement their own bilateral aid programmes. It was initially to run for 5 years with total resources of $581 million. France and Germany each contributed one-third of the total, Belgium and the Netherlands 12 per cent each and Italy 7 per cent.

Within a few years, however, many of the dependent terri-

[1] *The Work of the United Nations Development Programme.* U.K. Ministry of Overseas Development. Information Department. Occasional Paper No. 1. November, 1968.

228

tories of Africa achieved their political independence. The Community thereupon negotiated a new form of association with 18 states of Africa and Madagascar and the outcome was embodied in the Yaounde Convention of 1963. Under this agreement the E.D.F. was renewed for another five years and its resources increased to $730 million.[1] France and Germany again contributed one third each but the share of Italy was increased compared with the First Fund and that of Belgium and the Netherlands reduced.

The E.D.F. is clearly a major source of development finance for Africa. Its total resources in the first ten years were equal to those of U.N.D.P. over the same period. But what particularly makes E.D.F. unusual is that its funds, the eligible recipient countries and the general area of its operations are all agreed in advance for a five year period. This facilitates long term planning and avoids the annual political struggle for funds which national aid administrations are compelled to wage. On the other hand, E.D.F. has not avoided the considerable lag between commitments and disbursements which characterises so many other aid operations.

The E.D.F. provides most of its aid in the form of grants and mainly for schemes of rural modernisation and social investment such as public works, transport, communications, education, health and training. The contracts it finances are won through competitive bidding but only suppliers from within the E.E.C. and its Associate States are eligible to tender. Table XIV shows their share of the orders placed up to the end of 1970.

Since the bulk of E.D.F. aid goes to French speaking African countries it is not surprising that the share of France should be over 40 per cent. German suppliers had very little experience of such markets and were slow at first in tendering for contracts, with the result that the share of Germany under the First Fund was less than 7 per cent. A continuation of this situation might well have threatened Community harmony and the future of E.D.F. A special effort was, therefore, made to inform German business of the opportunities E.D.F. offered, with the result, as Table XIV shows, that by the end of 1970 the German share

[1] Another $70 million was contributed by the European Investment Bank. Under the second Yaounde Convention, signed in 1969, the resources of the E.D.F. were increased to $1 billion, of which the member governments contributed $900 million and the European Investment Bank $100 million.

TABLE XIV: European Development Fund
Contributions and Orders Received to 31 December, 1970.

| Country of Supply | FIRST FUND (1 January, 1958-31 December, 1962) | | | | SECOND FUND (1 June, 1964-31 May, 1969) | | | | FIRST AND SECOND FUND | |
| | CONTRIBUTIONS | | GOODS AND SERVICES SUPPLIED | | CONTRIBUTIONS | | GOODS AND SERVICES SUPPLIED | | GOODS AND SERVICES SUPPLIED | |
	Amount $ mil.	Share of total Per Cent	Amount $ mil.	Share of total Per Cent	Amount $ mil.	Share of total Per Cent	Amount $ mil.	Share of total Per Cent	Amount $ mil.	Share of total Per Cent
Belgium	70.0	12.0	17.1	3.7	69.0	9.5	31.8	7.9	48.9	5.6
France	200.0	34.4	202.8	43.7	246.5	33.8	160.3	39.6	363.1	41.8
Germany	200.0	34.4	30.9	6.7	256.5	33.8	90.5	22.4	121.4	14.0
Italy	40.0	6.9	65.1	14.0	100.0	13.7	40.9	10.1	106.0	12.2
Luxembourg	1.25	0.2	1.5	0.3	2.0	0.3	3.4	0.8	4.9	0.6
Netherlands	70.0	12.0	22.8	4.9	66.0	9.0	19.3	4.8	42.1	4.8
Associated States and Dependent Territories	—	—	123.6	26.6	—	—	58.0	14.3	181.6	20.9
Third Countries	—	—	0.4	0.1	—	—	0.5	0.1	0.9	0.1
TOTAL:	581.25	100.0	463.8	100.0	730.0	100.0	404.7	100.0	868.9	100.0

230

of orders under the Second Fund had risen to 22 per cent. The share of Belgium also rose, while that of France and Italy fell. Finally, it is worth noting that the recipient countries themselves have obtained over one-quarter of the orders financed from the First Fund and 14 per cent so far of those from the Second Fund.[1]

The Return Flow of Debt Service Payments

One further point needs to be made about the burden of aid. The capital repayments the industrial countries receive on their past lending obviously improve their capacity to provide new resources. This is recognised by measuring the transfer of resources as a net flow. The 1 per cent of G.N.P. target and the Pearson Commission's target for official development assistance both refer to net flows. So do the figures presented earlier.

What the figures and targets do not take into account, however, is the investment income, profits and interest payments, the D.A.C. member countries receive from the Third World. The amount is hard to calculate exactly because the available data is full of gaps and ambiguities. But the order of magnitude is clear enough. For the period 1964-67 the annual average works out at $5.8 billion.[2] A preliminary estimate puts the net total in 1969 at $7 billion, which is double the amount in 1960.[3]

Around 70 per cent of this return flow consists of profits and dividend payments to private investors in D.A.C. member countries. Most of this comes from the heavy concentration of private foreign investment in the oil and mineral exporting countries of the Third World. Only a relatively small proportion is due to private foreign investment in industrial expansion, though it looms large in the outflow of countries like Argentina, Brazil and Mexico. Another part of the return flow consists of interest payments on short and medium term private debt. For the period 1964-67 these payments are estimated to have averaged $700-900 million a year.[4]

[1] The second Yaounde Convention gives a price preference of up to 15 per cent for project tenders submitted by enterprise in the recipient country or in other Associated countries of the same region.

[2] World Bank: Annual Report 1970.

[3] U.N.C.T.A.D.: Review of International Trade and Development 1970. Sales No. E.71.II.D.5.

[4] World Bank: Annual Report, 1970.

231

Government lending also generates a return flow of interest payments. During 1964-67 the donor countries received roughly $500 million a year in interest on official loans outstanding.[1] By 1969 the figure had risen to $635 million, which is of the same order as the aid Third World countries received that year from private voluntary agencies.[2] Much of the interest on official loans comes from countries, such as India, Pakistan and Brazil, for example, which began to borrow heavily in the fifties. The United States, Britain, Germany, France and Japan received more than 90 per cent of the total in 1968. The U.S. share alone was over 50 per cent.[3] The rising proportion of official aid in the form of loans and the expiry of grace periods on loans made in the early sixties, means that their interest income will grow even more rapidly in the seventies. A similar trend is apparent in the case of multilateral financing.

In 1968 the return flow of interest payments to the multilateral lending agencies amounted to over $250 million. Most of this went to the World Bank whose income from loans to less developed countries rose from $125 million in 1964 to $224 million in 1969. For every dollar of interest it received from these countries in 1964, it disbursed $3.40 in new loans to them. By 1969 the ratio had fallen to 2.88. In other words, the net transfer of resources financed by the World Bank had steadily declined in recent years. The same can be said about the net amount of resources provided by industrial countries.

In 1969, for example, the net flow of financial resources from D.A.C. member countries totalled $13.6 billion (Table V). But more than half the flow was offset by the return flow of investment income. Put another way, the net amount of new resources they provided that year was less than half their net outflow of capital to the Third World. The net flow of official aid similarly overstates the net provision of new resources by the amount of interest received on past official lending. It follows that the burden of aid, however estimated, must be correspondingly less.

It is worth remembering, moreover, that Third World countries pay the amortisation and interest charges on their borrowing, their debt service charges in short, in convertible currency. The

[1] loc. cit.

[2] O.E.C.D., Development Assistance: 1970 Review.

[3] U.N. The External Financing of Economic Development, 1970. Sales No. E.70.II.A.3.

balance of payments of donor countries thus gain from tying when the aid is provided and from the receipt of convertible currency when debt service payments are due. Tying, however, is an overvalued expedient which prejudices their longer term economic interests. Nor are their rapidly rising receipts of debt service payments a pure gain. For if Third World countries did not have to make these payments they could afford to buy more goods and services from industrial countries. The real gain is, therefore, less than the dollar value of these receipts, just as the real cost of the aid provided is less than its nominal value.

The foreign exchange earnings of most Third World countries have not kept pace with the rise in their debt service payments which explains why their imports have not grown as fast as their foreign exchange availabilities. In fact, their outflow of profits, interest, and indigenous capital has been increasing faster than their total inflow of resources. In 1968 service charges on external public debt preempted about 10 per cent of the Third World's export earnings. In a growing number of cases the proportion is much higher. In 1968, for example, it was around 20 per cent for Pakistan, Brazil and Peru and a quarter or more for Argentina and Tunisia.[1]

Unfortunately for poorer countries, the structure of international indebtedness is isolated from the structure of internal indebtedness. Within countries the real burden of debt can be reduced through inflation and tax allowances. But the dollar cost of, say, a heavy truck in international capital markets cannot be reduced in this way. There is no international authority to offer a tax allowance and in money terms the prices of the primary products exchanged for the truck has not risen in recent years; but the prices of manufactured goods certainly have. When it comes to international price inflation the poorer countries have lost out.

Of course, their external debt problem is much more complicated and should really be viewed in the context of their whole economic performance. Even so, it is disturbing that the average terms of official development assistance should actually have hardened in recent years. A given flow of aid on harder terms constitutes a smaller amount of real resources than the same nominal flow on softer terms. To put the point another

[1] World Bank: Annual Report, 1970.

233

way, the longer the loan maturity and the lower the rate of interest, the longer the period of net resource transfer and the larger its aggregate value. More assistance on highly concessional terms is, therefore, a frequently recommended way of sustaining the momentum for growth of Third World countries while easing their burden of debt service payments. The Pearson Commission recommended that aid should also be used to reschedule existing debt obligations over a longer period. The economic effect of this would be similar to the provision of new aid on more concessional terms. On both counts, however, the cost of aid to donor countries would rise, a prospect they will hardly welcome. This should encourage them to pursue other solutions as well. One line of approach speaks for itself.

The whole problem would obviously be more manageable if the export earnings of Third World countries were rising more rapidly. It is because the additional output their borrowings helped to finance has largely gone into home consumption, that their foreign exchange earnings are being increasingly preempted by debt service payments. A more rapid growth in these earnings would therefore benefit the donor countries in three ways. Firstly, it would temper the need to transfer large amounts of resources on highly concessional terms and thereby lessen the cost of their own aid programmes. Secondly, it is the only way they will ever be repaid the huge sums they have already lent to the Third World. Thirdly, it would mean that Third World countries could afford to buy more of their goods and services. Donor countries would do well, in other words, to direct their aid and trade policies towards encouraging and facilitating the growth of exports from less developed countries. It is in this direction that they can most advantageously pursue their own economic self-interest in the development of the Third World.

Appendix

TABLE: A-I

EXPORTS OF INDUSTRIAL COUNTRIES TO THIRD WORLD COUNTRIES.
(Given in Billion U.S. $ and as a % of Total Exports)

Destination Origin	Year	Total World $	Total World % of Total	Third World $	Third World % of Total	THIRD WORLD Latin America $	Latin America % of Total	Developing Africa $	Developing Africa % of Total
Industrial Market Economies	1955	60.48	100	16.67	27.6	5.66	9.4	4.22	7.0
	1960	85.45	100	21.79	25.5	6.64	7.8	5.32	6.2
	1965	128.18	100	26.99	21.1	7.17	5.6	6.22	4.9
	1969	193.19	100	37.46	19.4	10.21	5.3	7.67	4.0
U.S.A.	1955	15.43	100	5.69	36.9	3.30	21.4	0.36	2.3
	1960	20.40	100	7.08	34.7	3.55	17.4	0.50	2.5
	1965	27.19	100	8.92	32.8	3.73	13.7	0.77	2.8
	1969	37.46	100	11.13	29.7	4.81	12.8	0.86	2.3
Canada	1955	4.39	100	0.34	7.7	0.16	3.6	0.02	0.5
	1960	5.55	100	0.42	7.6	0.19	3.4	0.03	0.5
	1965	8.11	100	0.60	7.4	0.30	3.7	0.04	0.5
	1969	13.75	100	0.84	6.1	0.41	3.0	0.04	0.3
Western Europe	1955	35.29	100	9.00	25.5	2.00	5.7	3.46	9.8
	1960	51.52	100	11.61	22.5	2.59	5.0	4.28	8.3
	1965	79.03	100	13.02	16.5	2.75	3.4	4.49	5.7
	1969	118.72	100	17.41	14.7	4.13	3.5	5.51	4.6
E.E.C.	1955	18.92	100	5.05	26.7	1.21	6.4	2.26	11.9
	1960	29.73	100	6.71	22.6	1.56	5.2	2.95	9.9
	1965	47.90	100	7.46	15.6	1.63	3.4	2.92	6.1
	1969	75.69	100	10.18	13.4	2.44	3.2	3.56	4.7

235

	Year								
E.F.T.A.	1955	14.03	100	3.72	26.5	0.67	4.8	1.16	8.3
	1960	18.50	100	4.55	24.6	0.91	4.9	1.24	6.7
	1965	26.10	100	5.01	19.2	0.87	3.3	1.42	5.4
	1969	35.62	100	6.31	17.7	1.30	3.6	1.71	4.8
U.K.	1955	8.30	100	2.84	34.2	0.32	3.9	0.92	11.1
	1960	10.21	100	3.37	33.0	0.48	4.7	0.93	9.1
	1965	13.23	100	3.50	26.5	0.45	3.4	0.98	7.4
	1969	16.89	100	4.03	23.9	0.58	3.4	1.03	6.1
Japan	1955	2.01	100	1.16	57.7	0.18	9.0	0.17	8.5
	1960	4.05	100	2.05	50.6	0.28	6.9	0.29	7.2
	1965	8.45	100	3.64	43.1	0.41	4.9	0.67	7.9
	1969	15.99	100	6.82	42.7	0.80	5.0	0.86	5.4
Australia/ New Zealand	1955	2.45	100	0.27	11.0	0.01	0.4	0.02	0.8
	1960	2.79	100	0.37	13.2	0.02	0.7	0.02	0.7
	1965	3.91	100	0.57	14.6	0.04	1.0	0.04	1.0
	1969	5.11	100	0.85	16.6	0.06	1.2	0.04	0.8
U.S.S.R.	1955	3.43	100	0.09	2.6	0.02	0.6	0.01	0.3
	1960	5.56	100	0.40	7.2	0.10	1.8	0.10	1.8
	1965	8.17	100	1.21	14.8	0.43	5.3	0.33	4.0
	1969	11.66	100	1.68	14.4	0.65	5.6	0.41	3.5
East Europe (except U.S.S.R.)	1955	4.98	100	0.29	6.5	0.12	2.7	0.07	1.6
	1960	7.41	100	0.47	6.3	0.13	1.8	0.09	1.2
	1965	11.54	100	0.88	7.6	0.17	1.5	0.28	2.4
	1969	15.85	100	1.22	7.7	0.29	1.8	0.32	2.0
Total Industrial Countries	1955	68.39	100	17.05	24.9	5.80	8.5	4.30	6.3
	1960	98.42	100	22.66	23.0	6.87	7.0	5.51	5.6
	1965	147.89	100	29.08	19.7	7.76	5.2	6.83	4.6
	1969	220.69	100	40.36	18.3	11.15	5.1	8.40	3.8

Table continues on following page.

236

TABLE: A-I—(Continued)

| Origin | Year | THIRD WORLD — Developing Asia | | | | Non-Third World | |
| | | Middle East | | Asia, Other | | | |
		$	% of Total	$	% of Total	$	% of Total
Industrial Market Economies	1955	1.46	2.4	4.55	7.5	43.43	71.8
	1960	2.24	2.6	6.37	7.4	63.27	74.0
	1965	3.24	2.5	8.70	6.8	100.73	78.6
	1969	5.12	2.7	12.02	6.2	155.04	80.3
U.S.A.	1955	0.38	2.5	1.47	9.5	9.61	62.3
	1960	0.52	2.5	2.19	10.7	13.32	65.3
	1965	0.82	3.0	3.09	11.4	18.27	67.2
	1969	1.25	3.3	3.47	9.3	26.32	70.3
Canada	1955	0.01	0.2	0.08	1.8	4.06	92.5
	1960	0.02	0.4	0.11	2.0	5.14	92.6
	1965	0.02	0.2	0.15	1.8	7.50	92.5
	1969	0.04	0.3	0.22	1.6	12.91	93.9
Western Europe	1955	0.96	2.7	2.10	6.0	26.08	73.9
	1960	1.52	3.0	2.53	4.9	39.61	76.9
	1965	2.06	2.6	2.96	3.7	65.93	83.0
	1969	3.22	2.7	3.38	2.8	100.77	84.9
E.E.C.	1955	0.46	2.4	0.94	5.0	13.72	72.51
	1960	0.81	2.7	1.14	3.8	22.77	76.6
	1965	1.09	2.3	1.45	3.0	40.14	83.8
	1969	1.72	2.3	1.82	2.4	65.15	86.1
E.F.T.A.	1955	0.45	3.2	1.15	8.2	10.29	73.3
	1960	0.63	3.4	1.34	7.2	13.95	75.4
	1965	0.87	3.3	1.41	5.4	21.06	80.7
	1969	1.34	3.8	1.47	4.1	29.16	81.9

U.K.	1955	0.36	4.3	0.98	11.8	5.46	65.8
	1960	0.47	4.6	1.11	10.9	6.83	66.9
	1965	0.62	4.7	1.11	8.4	9.73	73.5
	1969	0.97	5.7	1.03	6.1	12.73	75.4
Japan	1955	0.08	4.0	0.72	35.8	0.83	41.3
	1960	0.14	3.5	1.31	32.3	2.00	49.4
	1965	0.28	3.3	2.20	26.0	4.82	57.0
	1969	0.55	3.4	4.45	27.8	9.17	57.3
Australia/ New Zealand	1955	0.02	0.8	0.16	6.5	2.17	88.0
	1960	0.04	1.4	0.19	6.8	2.40	86.0
	1965	0.06	1.5	0.29	7.4	3.31	84.7
	1969	0.06	1.2	0.47	9.2	4.26	83.4
U.S.S.R.	1955	0.03	0.9	0.02	0.6	3.29	95.9
	1960	0.06	1.1	0.11	2.0	5.15	92.6
	1965	0.09	1.1	0.37	4.5	6.69	81.9
	1969	0.34	2.9	0.28	2.4	9.16	78.6
East Europe (except U.S.S.R.)	1955	0.03	0.7	0.05	1.1	4.15	92.6
	1960	0.07	0.9	0.13	1.8	6.83	92.2
	1965	0.15	1.3	0.28	2.4	10.59	91.8
	1969	0.34	2.1	0.28	1.8	14.66	92.5
Total Industrial Countries	1955	1.52	2.2	4.62	6.8	50.87	74.4
	1960	2.37	2.4	6.61	6.7	75.25	76.4
	1965	3.48	2.4	9.35	6.3	118.00	79.8
	1969	5.79	2.6	12.58	5.7	178.85	81.0

Notes to this table appear on following page.

NOTES TO TABLE A-I

SOURCES: *UNCTAD Handbook of International Trade and Development Statistics.*
U.N. *Monthly Bulletin of Statistics, March and May 1971.*

NOTE:

a) Third World = Latin America,
Developing Africa
Middle East
Asia
Rest of World Category in source table
(includes small Pacific Islands)

b) Industrial Market Economies = U.S.A.
Western Europe,
U.K.
Canada
Japan
Australia & New Zealand
South Africa

c) The difference between the total world figures and the sum of the Third World and non-Third World is due to the statistical difference between reported imports and exports.

d) Non-Third World includes Industrial Market Economies plus Eastern Europe, U.S.S.R., China Mainland & Other.

e) Total Industrial Countries = Industrial Market Economies
U.S.S.R.
East Europe (Except U.S.S.R.)

239

TABLE: A-II

STRUCTURE OF INDUSTRIAL COUNTRY EXPORTS TO THIRD
WORLD TOTAL.

(Percentage Distribution)

SITC	DESCRIPTION	1955	1965	1969
0, 1, 22, 4.	Food, Beverage & Tobacco	13.3	14.3	11.9
2–(22+27+28)	Agricultural Raw Materials	3.0	3.0	2.8
27–8	Minerals, Excluding Fuels	0.5	0.7	0.7
3	Fuels	3.5	2.2	1.9
67	Iron and Steel	7.8	6.4	6.2
0.68	Non-Ferrous Metals	1.2	1.7	1.5
5	Chemicals	9.7	10.5	10.7
6+8–67–68	Other Manufactures	27.7	21.6	21.2
7	Machinery and Transport Equipment	33.2	39.7	43.1
	TOTAL:	100.0	100.0	100.0

SOURCES: U.N.C.T.A.D. *Handbook of International Trade and Development Statistics.*
U.N. *Monthly Bulletin of Statistics,* March and May, 1971.

240

TABLE: A-III
PERCENTAGE SHARE IN EXPORTS OF INDUSTRIAL COUNTRIES TO THIRD WORLD COUNTRIES.
(Billion U.S. $ and as % of Total Imports)

DESTINATION ORIGIN	YEAR	THIRD WORLD		LATIN AMERICA		DEVELOPING AFRICA		MIDDLE EAST		ASIA	
		$	% of Total	$	% of Total	$	% of Total	$	% of Total	$	% of Total
Total Industrial Countries	1955	17.05	100.	5.80	100.	4.30	100.	1.52	100.	4.62	100.
	1960	22.66	100.	6.87	100.	5.51	100.	2.37	100.	6.61	100.
	1965	29.08	100.	7.76	100.	6.83	100.	3.48	100.	9.35	100.
	1969	40.36	100.	11.15	100.	8.40	100.	5.79	100.	12.58	100.
U.S.A.	1955	5.69	33.4	3.30	56.9	0.36	8.4	0.38	25.0	1.47	31.8
	1960	7.08	31.2	3.35	48.8	0.50	9.1	0.52	21.9	2.19	33.1
	1965	8.92	30.7	3.73	48.1	0.77	11.3	0.82	23.6	3.09	33.0
	1969	11.13	27.6	4.81	43.1	0.86	10.2	1.25	21.6	3.47	27.6
Canada	1955	0.34	2.0	0.16	2.8	0.02	0.5	0.01	0.7	0.08	1.7
	1960	0.42	1.9	0.19	2.8	0.03	0.5	0.02	0.8	0.11	1.7
	1965	0.60	2.1	0.30	3.9	0.04	0.6	0.02	0.6	0.15	1.6
	1969	0.84	2.1	0.41	3.7	0.04	0.5	0.04	0.7	0.22	1.7
Western Europe	1955	9.00	52.7	2.00	34.5	3.46	80.5	0.96	63.2	2.10	45.4
	1960	11.61	51.2	2.59	37.7	4.28	77.7	1.52	64.1	2.53	38.3
	1965	13.02	44.8	2.70	34.8	4.49	65.7	2.06	59.2	2.96	31.7
	1969	17.41	43.1	4.13	37.0	5.51	65.6	3.22	55.6	3.38	26.9
E.E.C.	1955	5.05	29.6	1.21	20.9	2.26	52.6	0.46	30.3	0.94	20.3
	1960	6.71	29.6	1.56	22.7	2.95	53.5	0.81	34.2	1.14	17.2
	1965	7.46	25.7	1.63	21.0	2.92	42.8	1.09	31.3	1.45	15.5
	1969	10.18	25.2	2.44	21.9	3.56	42.4	1.72	29.7	1.82	14.5

241

E.F.T.A.										
1955	3.72	21.8	0.67	11.6	1.16	27.0	0.45	29.6	1.15	24.9
1960	4.55	20.1	0.91	13.2	1.24	22.5	0.63	26.6	1.34	17.2
1965	5.01	17.2	0.87	11.2	1.42	20.8	0.87	25.0	1.41	15.1
1969	6.31	15.6	1.30	11.7	1.71	20.4	1.34	23.1	1.47	11.7
U.K.										
1955	2.84	16.7	0.32	5.5	0.92	21.4	0.36	23.7	0.98	21.2
1960	3.37	14.9	0.48	7.0	0.93	16.9	0.47	19.8	1.11	16.8
1965	3.50	12.0	0.45	5.8	0.98	14.3	0.62	17.8	1.11	11.9
1969	4.03	10.0	0.58	5.2	1.03	12.3	0.97	16.8	1.03	8.2
Japan										
1955	1.16	6.8	0.18	3.1	0.17	4.0	0.08	5.3	0.72	15.6
1960	2.05	9.0	0.28	4.1	0.29	5.3	0.14	5.9	1.31	19.8
1965	3.64	12.5	0.41	5.3	0.67	9.8	0.28	8.0	2.20	23.5
1969	6.82	16.9	0.80	7.2	0.86	10.2	0.55	9.5	4.45	35.4
Australia/ New Zealand										
1955	0.27	1.6	0.01	0.2	0.02	0.5	0.02	1.3	0.16	3.5
1960	0.37	1.6	0.02	0.3	0.02	0.4	0.04	1.7	0.19	2.9
1965	0.57	2.0	0.04	0.5	0.05	0.6	0.06	1.7	0.29	3.1
1969	0.85	2.1	0.06	0.5	0.04	0.5	0.06	1.0	0.47	3.7
U.S.S.R.										
1955	0.09	0.5	0.02	0.3	0.01	0.2	0.03	2.0	0.02	0.4
1960	0.40	1.8	0.10	1.5	0.10	1.8	0.06	2.5	0.11	1.7
1965	1.21	4.2	0.43	5.5	0.33	4.8	0.09	2.6	0.37	4.0
1969	1.68	4.2	0.65	5.8	0.41	4.9	0.34	5.9	0.28	2.2
Eastern Europe (except U.S.S.R.)										
1955	0.29	1.7	0.12	2.1	0.07	1.6	0.03	2.0	0.05	1.1
1960	0.47	2.1	0.13	1.9	0.09	1.6	0.07	3.0	0.13	2.0
1965	0.88	3.0	0.17	2.2	0.28	4.1	0.15	4.3	0.28	3.0
1969	1.22	3.0	0.29	2.6	0.32	3.8	0.34	5.9	0.28	2.2

SOURCES: U.N.C.T.A.D. *Handbook of International Trade and Development Statistics.*
U.N. *Monthly Bulletin of Statistics,* March and May, 1971.

TABLE: A-IV

PERCENTAGE SHARE THIRD WORLD REGIONS IN CATEGORIES OF EXPORTS FROM INDUSTRIAL COUNTRIES—YEARS 1955 AND 1965.

SITC	DESCRIPTION	THIRD WORLD			LATIN AMERICA		
		1955	1965	1969	1955	1965	1969
0, 1, 22, 4	Food, Beverages & Tobacco	100	100	100	27.4	19.3	19.0
2−(22+27+28)	Agricultural Raw Materials	100	100	100	37.6	28.9	24.7
27 + 28	Minerals Excluding Fuels	100	100	100	54.3	45.6	36.6
3	Fuels	100	100	100	35.7	36.7	37.4
67	Iron and Steel	100	100	100	40.5	26.9	27.8
68	Non-Ferrous Metals	100	100	100	38.2	30.6	32.3
5	Chemicals	100	100	100	37.2	34.6	33.9
6+8−67−68	Other Manufactures	100	100	100	27.2	21.5	21.1
7	Machinery and Transport Equipment	100	100	100	41.9	30.0	31.9

243

SITC	DESCRIPTION	DEVELOPING AFRICA			MIDDLE EAST			ASIA		
		1955	1965	1969	1955	1965	1969	1955	1965	1969
0, 1, 22, 4	Food, Beverages & Tobacco	26.8	23.8	21.4	9.6	12.1	11.3	27.4	35.2	37.9
2-(22+27+28)	Agricultural Raw Materials	20.5	17.4	15.4	10.0	12.6	13.8	30.5	38.5	42.0
27 + 28	Minerals Excluding Fuels	14.8	11.3	12.1	4.9	8.7	7.9	16.0	32.3	41.1
3	Fuels	38.0	23.9	29.8	5.3	5.7	7.0	13.2	26.5	19.0
67	Iron and Steel	7.1	19.8	20.4	10.4	14.1	14.6	27.4	35.8	33.1
68	Non-Ferrous Metals	15.2	13.5	14.4	6.3	7.8	13.0	32.5	45.1	38.6
5	Chemicals	20.5	19.5	18.6	5.8	9.2	9.9	30.2	31.5	32.4
6+8-67-68	Other Manufactures	30.3	27.8	22.6	9.7	14.8	16.2	28.5	28.3	31.8
7	Machinery and Transport Equipment	24.0	24.4	21.3	8.7	11.1	14.5	22.5	30.4	27.8

SOURCES: U.N.C.T.A.D., *Handbook of International Trade and Development Statistics.*
U.N. *Monthly Bulletin of Statistics,* March and May, 1970.

TABLE: A-V

PERCENTAGE SHARE OF CATEGORIES OF EXPORTS FROM INDUSTRIAL COUNTRIES TO THIRD WORLD COUNTRIES.

Origin	Year	Category SITC	Food & Bev. & Tobacco 0, 1, 22, 4	Agricultural Raw Materials 2−(22+27+28)	Minerals, excl. Fuels 27, 28	Fuels 3
U.S.A.	1955		34.8	34.6	55.6	37.1
	1965		47.4	41.8	57.4	33.1
	1969		40.3	35.0	46.4	33.1
Canada	1955		5.4	3.5	11.1	0.2
	1965		4.8	4.6	13.3	0.2
	1969		4.0	3.2	19.2	0.4
Western Europe	1955		45.6	44.4	25.9	50.1
	1965		31.2	25.6	19.5	26.8
	1969		32.7	25.4	20.4	31.7
EEC	1955		26.6	14.5	12.3	38.0
	1965		18.2	10.5	12.8	17.7
	1969		17.4	13.5	12.8	23.4
EFTA	1955		16.0	18.9	11.1	11.8
	1965		10.4	9.7	5.7	7.0
	1969		10.4	11.9	0.8	6.2
U.K.	1955		10.8	6.6	9.9	10.5
	1965		6.0	3.5	4.1	6.1
	1969		6.0	4.4	—	5.5

Japan	1955	2.3	2.5	1.2	1.2
	1965	2.1	8.5	2.6	3.4
	1969	6.3	13.4	—	5.7
Australia/New Zealand	1955	8.8	6.4	1.2	1.4
	1965	7.8	7.6	1.5	2.6
	1969	7.6	10.3	—	2.8
U.S.S.R.	1955	0.5	0.6	—	2.8
	1965	3.7	6.9	3.1	30.1
	1969*	7.2	12.7	4.9	24.1
Eastern Europe (except U.S.S.R.)	1955	0.6	6.6	1.2	6.4
	1965	1.9	3.9	—	2.0
	1969†				
Total Industrial Countries	1955	100	100	100	100
	1965	100	100	100	100
	1969	100	100	100	100

Table continues on following page.

246

TABLE A-V—(Continued).

Origin	Year	Iron & Steel 67	Non-Ferrous Metals 68	Chemicals 5	Other Manufactures 6+8−67, −68	Machinery & Transport Equipment 7
U.S.A.	1955	18.7	15.2	33.6	22.1	38.0
	1965	16.6	28.5	29.1	19.0	29.0
	1969	15.5	25.6	27.5	18.4	26.4
Canada	1955	1.0	8.9	2.1	1.2	1.2
	1965	1.8	9.9	1.9	1.6	1.2
	1969	1.1	10.6	1.0	1.6	1.8
Western Europe	1955	60.4	11.5	57.2	58.7	54.0
	1965	46.5	11.8	55.6	57.6	47.8
	1969	37.3	37.6	53.9	48.4	45.9
EEC	1955	44.4	56.5	31.4	32.4	29.1
	1965	33.7	38.0	35.1	27.9	26.7
	1969	27.3	18.8	34.2	26.7	26.4
EFTA	1955	15.7	28.8	25.2	24.4	24.9
	1965	12.2	20.5	19.8	20.7	19.7
	1969	9.5	15.4	18.2	18.3	17.5
U.K.	1955	14.1	24.6	19.2	16.9	20.8
	1965	10.0	15.6	13.2	12.9	14.8
	1969	8.1	10.4	11.0	10.7	11.8

247

Japan	1955	16.7	13.1	3.7	13.8	3.8
	1965	26.4	10.8	8.9	20.3	12.7
	1969	34.8	13.3	11.9	24.6	17.0
Australia/New Zealand	1955	0.2	5.2	0.4	0.2	0.8
	1965	0.8	5.3	0.6	0.8	0.5
	1969	2.5	5.6	0.6	1.0	0.6
U.S.S.R.	1955	1.5	—	0.1	0.4	0.1
	1965	3.3	4.0	1.2	1.6	5.3
	1969*	7.2	6.0	4.0	4.8	7.6
Eastern Europe (except U.S.S.R.)	1955	0.9	0.5	1.0	2.1	1.7
	1965	3.3	1.0	2.7	4.2	3.1
	1969†					
Total Industrial Countries	1955	100	100	100	100	100
	1965	100	100	100	100	100
	1969	100	100	100	100	100

SOURCE: U.N.C.T.A.D., *Handbook of International Trade and Development Statistics.*
  * These figures include Eastern Europe.
  † Eastern Europe figures are included in the figures for the U.S.S.R.

The Great Experiment

Science and Technology
in the Second United Nations
Development Decade

The day I began the preparation of this booklet was the same day that I received the June 1971 issue of *Science and Public Affairs* (the old *Bulletin of the Atomic Scientists*). The Bulletin contained two articles which, considered together, were so germane to the problem of science and development that I have used them as the theme for this introduction. They not only provided a vivid illustration of how fast development can proceed when stimulated by the judicious application of science and technology but, at the same time, they both stressed the momentous effects of the social and economic changes that always follow in the wake of such a development. Such effects may be just as desirable as the new technology itself. Or they may serve to push a society in directions which neither its people nor its government particularly want. And this, of course, is the central paradox of scientific development: how to exploit the rich fruit of science and technology in a way which provides both material and social progress at a time when we are all agreed on what material progress means but when we are far from agreed about the best means of social progress.

The Green Revolution . . .

The first of the articles was by Norman E. Borlaug, Nobel Peace Laureate for 1970. For 26 years Borlaug has been associated with an inter-disciplinary research study in Mexico designed to improve agricultural yields. The results that he and his team produced must be counted as among the most significant of any that have emerged over the past two decades. For what was devel-

249

oped in Mexico were new genetic strains of wheat which give higher yields, have a broader spectrum of resistance to disease, are insensitive to variations in day length and can adapt to a wide range of different ecological conditions. But the work at the International Maize and Wheat Improvement Center in Mexico City did not stop there. It went on to show in detail how these new strains could best be farmed—how the crops should be rotated, the ground prepared, the fertilizer spread and the grain harvested.

The results of this programme were spectacular. Even by 1948 wheat yields began to climb, and by 1956, Mexico's wheat production became self-sufficient. Over the past 26 years the average national yield climbed from 750 kilos per hectare to nearly 3000. The maximum yields reached 4500 kilos and then, when the introduction of yet newer, short stalked varieties became possible, climbed to 9000 kilos per hectare. Nor did the pay-off stop there, for these were the wheat strains first introduced into India and Pakistan in 1963.

In six years Pakistan's wheat production rose from 4.6 to 8.4 million tons and she became self-sufficient in wheat production in 1968. India's production rose over the same period from 12.3 to 20.0 million tons. Similar, if somewhat less spectacular, advances have been made with new rice strains in both countries. One result has been economic: Indian and Pakistani wheat farmers have been able to increase their net income from $37 per hectare to $162 per hectare. Together those countries have been able to bolster their joint GNPs by more than $2000 million in three years from increases in wheat production alone. The extra production made it possible in 1969/70 to sink 70,000 tubewells in India which promised to provide irrigation for a further 1.4 million hectares of productive land. All this shows something of the return that has been achieved from a small research programme started nearly a quarter of a century ago in Mexico. In that country alone, up to 1964, the return on investment was estimated at 750 per cent per annum. If the last six years work, and the effects in India, Pakistan and other countries were now included, the over-all return would be incredibly high even in simple economic terms. In human terms, it would be incalculable.

But Borlaug dwelt on more than just the direct agricultural and economic changes produced by the new varieties. He stressed as well the fact that the new wheat responded much better to fertilizer. For instance, every pound of nitrogen in fertilizer produced an increase in yield of 10 kilos of grain from the old wheat. In the new wheat, the same amount of fertilizer has produced 20 to 25 more kilos of grain. One result has been that India plans a five fold increase in fertilizer production over the next four or five years. The new wheat has also stimulated demand for tractors, threshing machines, pumps and storage facilities. This in turn has liberated bullocks for use in preparing ground for the next crop. Some Indian farmers now harvest three crops a year, producing 12 tons of food grain per hectare a year where previously they produced only 2.5 tons. Thus more food has meant more employment and the beginning of a qualitative change in the way of life. In Borlaug's own words to the Nobel Foundation:

". . . brick houses are beginning to replace those made of rammed earth. More electricity is being used to light the houses and to drive the motors on the wells. There has also been a rapid increase in demand for consumer goods. The purchase of transistors and radios for use in the villages has increased rapidly, and thereby the government can for the first time effectively reach the remote villages with educational programs. Sewing machines, bicycles, motor scooters and motor-cycles are coming to the villages, and truck and bus service between villages is improving".

In conclusion, Borlaug stressed that all these advances have given man "only a breathing space" in the battle against the relentless tick of the population clock—a tick which now provides the world with 2.2 more people every second but which threatens to increase to 2.7, 3.3 and 4.0 every second by 1980, 1990 and the year 2000. Unless that tick can be slowed, he claimed, and the resulting millions better educated, better housed, better clothed, better employed and better doctored, then man would degenerate sooner from environmental diseases than he would from hunger.

. . . and the Development Dilemma

It was from this point that the second article in the *Bulletin*, by the distinguished US geochemist Harrison Brown, took off. Brown described the brute economic facts of today's world in harsh terms. It was a world, he claimed, in which most people were either very rich or very poor—about 1000 million people had an average per capita GNP of $2300 a year while the culture of poverty, embracing 2500 million people, could command only $180 a year, 13 times less. Yet the per capita rate of increase for the rich was four per cent, while for the poor it was two per cent. The implication, he said, was that it would take 130 years for the poor to reach the levels of those who now consider themselves rich. But by then the rich would be approaching a per capita GNP of nearly $1 million a year.

Such a future is neither desirable nor possible. And the fact that it is not indicates the scale of change which we shall all, rich and poor alike, experience over the next two or three decades. Our job is to ensure that that change is made in peace and harmony and Brown made it quite clear that the way the rich countries provide the poor with massive amounts of armaments did not augur well for the future. In 1969, he pointed out, the military expenditure of the poorer countries was $26 billion, some $8 billion more than those countries' total expenditure on public education and health.

Brown then dealt with the 'black box' approach to development —the idea that all that is required is to pour money or technology into one end of a box labelled 'development process' and out would come at the other end a fully developed country. Money and technology may well be essential but they are by no means sufficient. And to illustrate the point, Brown chose the specific example of agriculture:

"As crop yields increase, new problems emerge. One must always be on the look-out for new pests which might get out of control. As output per man-hour increases less farm labour is needed and the surplus people migrate to the cities. As nutrition improves, infant and child mortality is lowered and the rate of population growth increases. The urban areas, unable to provide jobs for the migrants, become inundated by vast slum areas and the local government finds itself unable to expand community services as rapidly as people move in. On the farm increased production strains storage facilities and distribution systems".

Thus we can see how a partial answer to one agricultural problem can spawn a whole host of new problems. Depending on

252

one's viewpoint, one can interpret these secondary effects as in themselves beneficial (as Borlaug does) or as a necessary evil of the development process (as Brown does). One may argue, of course, that it is better for a developing country to have to struggle with these new problems than to undergo successive failures in trying to solve the old ones. But either way the new problems exist, and they cannot be left to look after themselves.

There are two obvious lessons to be learnt. The first is that scientific development cannot be a piecemeal affair. To boost agricultural yields, for example, will remain an important goal for many years to come. But the good it can do will be undone if a corresponding effort is not made to improve the chances of employment, lower fertility, provide better storage and distribution systems for grain and alleviate the fate of those who suffer from urban blight. And in doing each of those things, other secondary effects will appear which in their turn will require further attention. If that appears a vicious circle, it is at least a less vicious one than the circle of poverty, misery and malnutrition in which most of the world is currently trapped.

The second lesson concerns the nature of the technology which the developing world uses in the name of progress. In India, at the present time, a well placed tube-well now will do far more good than plans for a huge nuclear desalination plant to be erected within five years. The demands of the developing world are not the same as were those of the developed world even a hundred years ago, and they are much different from today's demands. We should beware of over-sophistication, and of trying to solve the Third World's problems with technology that was designed for quite different purposes. The developing world needs its own technology, and it will have to be produced to order and not bought off the peg from another country. At the same time, we should not blind ourselves to the obvious fact that some bits of very·advanced technology may be ideally suited to development. The atom, the computer and even space technology may have a role to play in development which must not be neglected.

How, then, are we to proceed? We must first beware of false fears—because, as one wit has put it, "if we had stopped to think through all the implications of inventing the wheel, we would probably never have done it". Yet we also know that science and technology are no magic panacea—that the pouring of ever greater funds into their bottomless coffer will not necessarily lead us to

253

that Golden Age where man can live in dignity and peace and with a full stomach. This new knowledge—scarcely older than a decade or so—is supremely important, as important perhaps as the promise of science itself. It is, as we shall see, the guiding light that illuminates our plans for using science and technology in the Second Development Decade that is now starting.

1960-1980: *The Critical Decades*

Beneath these broader philosophical issues lie a host of more practical yet equally difficult problems. If science and technology are to catalyse and speed development in the way that they might, the present distribution of world scientific talent seems far from ideal. In 1966, for every 100,000 people living in Africa, only 0.2 obtained science degrees. The comparable figure for Asia (including Japan) was 2, for Latin America 1.4 and for the Arab countries it was 3. Yet in Europe 13 people per 100,000 received science degrees and for North America the figure was 37. And, more important, the numbers of technicians and other scientifically trained workers are even more heavily weighted towards the developed world.

This drastic imbalance would be less serious if the developed world's research interests were directly related to the needs of the Third World. In general, they are not. On the contrary, many developed countries spend more than one-third of their total research and development funds in areas of military interest. Much of the rest goes in research of interest mainly to advanced types of consumer society. Thus of the estimated $65,000 million which the developed world spends annually on research and development, literally all but a few million goes into areas unlikely to benefit the developing countries in any immediate or direct sense. The argument that all research ultimately benefits everyone is now known to be false. Even if it were true, we should have to recognize that the problems of development are so large and so urgent that a laisser-faire, or rather a laisser-innover, attitude is hopelessly inadequate for our current predicament.

So two objectives emerge: to stimulate more research in the Third World, and to orientate more of the developed world's research into areas of interest to developing countries. How is this to be done? And how is the balance to be struck between these two objectives? Furthermore, how are these demands for new knowledge to be meshed with the quite obvious fact that development could be speeded by a better use in the Third World of that enormous amount of technical knowledge that already exists? So much of this knowledge lies unexploited because it is unknown to those who need to know it. A great deal more lies unexploited because it would cost too much to exploit it. The remainder lies unused because those who would use it do not have the technical manpower available to put it into effect. To answer those questions is to move away from the concerns of scientific research and into areas calling for economic and educational wisdom. Thus is the bridge established between scientific technology and all those other financial, economic and social issues which lie at the heart of the Second Development Decade. It is on the building of these bridges that all our hopes for progress will ultimately rest.

Quite obviously, it is no one nation's job to ponder these matters alone. The problems concern the Earth's family of nations and hence it is to the United Nations that we look for an institution capable of grasping the nettle. The time when they first began to do so dates back to 1961, the year in which the UN Economic and Social Council decided to stage a large conference to explore ways of harnessing recent advances in science and technology development. The conference, known as the UN Conference on the Application of Science and Technology for the Benefit of the Less Developed Areas (more conveniently shortened to UNCSAT), met in Geneva in 1963. There, more than anywhere else, was it first realized just how complex the overall problem was. As a result, the UN Advisory Committee on the Application of Science and Technology to Development (ACAST) was created the next year.

During its meetings in the 1960s, this committee was to define and refine the whole notion of scientific development. It began the slow process of identifying likely areas of relevant and important breakthroughs, of assessing the relative merits of generating new knowledge or applying known technology and of charting the directions and distortions of mainstream scientific research. By May 1966 it was led to reject the notion of piecemeal progress and to call instead for a World Plan of Action—a plan which would help to turn priorities in the right direction, identify needs which might be met by scientific technology and specify the institutional and financial resources that would be needed. This plan was published in 1971 and, together with ten earlier reports pre-

255

pared by the Committee, provided the major scientific input to the UN plan for a Second Development Decade.

This ten year period, which began on 1 January 1971, is probably the crucial period of the 20th century for improving the quality of life on Earth for two-thirds of the human race. Official UN strategy for the Decade is quite blunt about the problem: ". . . the level of living of countless millions of people in the developing part of the world is still pitifully low. These people are often still undernourished, uneducated, unemployed and wanting in many other basic amenities of life. While a part of the world lives in great comfort and even affluence, much of the larger part suffers from abject poverty, and in fact the disparity is continuing to widen. This lamentable situation has contributed to the aggravation of world tension".

The main goals of the Decade include an average annual rate of growth in gross product of the developing countries of at least six per cent. If population growth can itself be held back to 2.5 per cent, then gross product per head will increase by 3.5 per cent a year—sufficient to double the average income per head within two decades. These figures in turn imply an average growth rate of 4 per cent in agricultural output and 8 per cent in manufacturing output.

The ways in which these goals can be achieved have been carefully set out in the UN publication "International Development Strategy". They depend to a large measure on the developed countries providing financial resources of at least 1 per cent of their gross products by 1972, and on a whole series of fiscal, social and legal measures. But a crucial part of the overall strategy must depend on what use is made of science and technology.

In what follows I shall first discuss the eight specific areas in which it is thought that better use of existing technology and the generation of new knowledge could make a singular impact. These are: natural resources, food and agriculture, industry, transport and communication, housing and urban development, health, scientific education, and population and fertility. We shall then examine the more general problems of institutional change, science policy, financial resources and manpower which alone can translate our brightest scientific hopes into reality—a reality in which we may be able to discern the end of the world's overlong division into opposing camps of the rich and the poor, the hungry and the well fed, the ill and the healthy. Even then, we shall not

256

have a Utopia. But we shall at least have a global community in which all men can live their lives, for better or for worse, on an equal footing.

The Scientific Priorities

(i) Natural Resources: Spaceship Earth Needs Careful Management

The planet Earth is a fragile spacecraft. Tiny in relation to the Sun round which it makes it annual journey, it yet carries with it an incredible chemical bounty. Only a minute fraction of it is available for man's use—a slim segment extending a few miles above and below the Earth's crust, no thicker in relation to the whole than is the skin to the apple. Yet it is on this skin that man has built all his material aspirations. From it he extracts air to breathe, fossils to burn, minerals to fashion and rocks to build with. From it some nations have turned themselves into rich and thriving industrial giants, leaving others without the knowledge or the power (and sometimes without the desire) to a simpler but usually harsher existence. The problem of development is very largely the problem of natural resources. Not that the resources are particularly unequally spread—but they are unequally exploited.

For instance, it is estimated that in the United States there are currently some ten tons of steel in use for every member of the population. Comparable figures for other metals are 160 kilos of copper, 140 kilos of lead, 100 kilos of zinc, 18 kilos of tin and 110 kilos of aluminium. To transport these and other minerals and their products, about 15,000 ton-kilometers of freight are moved per person every year. To provide the energy for the mining, distribution and production of these goods, and to cater for domestic consumption, every individual consumes energy at the rate equivalent to burning ten tons of coal a year. The disparity is revealed most clearly by the last figure. Other developed countries burn the equivalent of 5 to 8 tons of coal a year per head. The world average, however, is only about 1.5 tons. Hence, energy consumption in the vast majority of developing countries is even less than this, even though they supply many of the raw materials on which the prosperity of the developed world is based.

We are not yet approaching the point at which most of these

257

materials are likely to become exhausted. Much of the world's reserves lie in areas which have yet to be geologically explored and one of the first priorities for the next decade must be extensive geological mapping in the underdeveloped areas. This will require teams of highly qualified manpower conversant with all the new scientific tools now available to the geologist. New airborne and space techniques, including magnetic and radar survey, are likely to become extremely important. And once new reserves are identified, developing countries will have to make careful studies of how those reserves can be rationally exploited. Our recently developed ecological conscience insists that the globe's resources are precious things, not to be lightly disposed of. What is needed must be taken but it must be taken in such a way that waste takes as small a toll as possible. That, too, will require a degree of scientific planning which has been noticeably absent in the past, even in the developed areas. The emphasis is on trained manpower, careful exploitation and wise decision making.

One of the likely trends of the 1970s is that we shall seek our new resources not only in the conventional places but also in some quite novel ones. One of these is that vast watery resource that covers 70 per cent of the Earth's surface—the oceans. It is currently thought that the 300 million cubic miles of sea water contain, in theory, sufficient minerals to meet world needs for at least a century. And even in 1969 the value of the minerals harvested from the sea amounted to more than $7000 million. Today, 17 per cent of the world's oil comes from off-shore oil wells. By 1980 a third of it will come from beneath the ocean floor. To add glitter to the prospect, scientists estimate that the three very hot and salty undersea 'pools' found 2000 metres below the surface of the Red Sea alone contain brines worth over $2300 million in gold, copper, zinc and silver. But ocean exploration will be of interest to more than jewellers. The seas contain vast amounts of almost every known and important mineral resource.

For the developing countries, this bounty should prove particularly attractive. As recent UN debates have shown, there is considerable confusion as to who, legally, owns which parts of the oceans. Coastal states have clear legal rights only to the coastal regions. For the rest, an international regime should be established which will enable the developing countries to take a major share of ocean resources. In support of this noble ideal, Malta has recently issued a postage stamp bearing the slogan "Sea's Bed for the World's Good".

258

Yet many difficult technical problems remain to be solved. Mineral extraction from deep water is expensive—the cost of establishing an off-shore oil field currently more than doubles as the depth is increased from 30 to 180 metres. Furthermore, most of the oceans have yet to be satisfactorily surveyed. Work by the International Hydrographic Bureau currently suggests that, for the preparation of small scale charts, data from 15 to 20 per cent of the oceans are insufficient and from 40 to 50 per cent of the oceans they are virtually non-existent. At an informed guess, 80 per cent of the ocean still has to be adequately charted and surveyed.

Nor should our plans for the oceans overlook the most common of its constituents—water itself. Desalination will become increasingly important in the 1970s and the traditional techniques of distillation, freezing and electrodialysis are under active research. Two newer methods—desalination with nuclear or geothermal power as the energy source—hold promise for the more instant future. In the next decade it is proposed that up to 20 new experimental desalination plants should be set up—ten in Asia, seven in Latin America, and three in Africa—at a cost of some $40 million. This technique of obtaining drinking water— or even slightly brackish water for irrigation—will of course come into its own where salt water is the only possible source.

In other areas, greatest emphasis must be put on new hydrographic surveys. It is estimated that the ground water hidden within the top half mile of the Earth's crust is equivalent in volume to 130 years flow of all the rivers in the world. Little of this is currently being tapped and indeed plans for doing so in the future must be laid with great care. The use of ground water can easily become the equivalent of 'mining' a non-renewable resource—with the result that the supply dries up or that subterranean water movements bring about an unwelcome flow of salt into the area, making the water unusable. But advances can be made. Under the Sahara, for instance, there is a deep artesian basin of some 800,000 square miles with fresh water reserves of an estimated 30 million cubic metres. A survey and development programme has been worked out for this area, and the United Nations Development Program will contribute $800,000 towards its cost.

It has been estimated that cloud seeding to catalyse rainfall could increase world precipitation by 15 per cent. While such 'global fiddling' with the world's weather system has dangerous implications, this is a technique which could transform agricultural patterns in a dry country. It is hoped that within the next decade some 20 river basins will be identified over which the effects of seeding technology can be accurately gauged.

Finally, it is recommended that at least $18 million be spent on research and development into techniques for minimizing water wastage, and that four new water management centres be set up, along the lines of the UNDP project at Kuwait, at a total cost of $82 million. The research needed to solve the problem of water wastage by evaporation and seepage is urgent. It is estimated that in some rivers in arid zones water loss through evaporation can amount to 40 per cent. Seepage itself may account for a 30 per cent loss and at the same time lead to a rapidly rising water table and finally to water logging and the problems of rising salinity and alkalinity.

Laboratory experiments have shown that if thin monomolecular layers can be spread over water surfaces, evaporation can be reduced by 50 to 70 per cent. However, on areas much bigger than an acre the quantity saved rapidly falls off and the film becomes much more difficult to establish. This technique appears promising but more research is needed on the design of an effective water evaporation control system. Seepage also needs further study, particularly as the lining of canals and rivers to prevent seepage may have a positive effect on weed growth and help reduce the snail populations which carry the fluke diseases and bilharziasis. Other ways by which the water economy can be improved are by the careful re-use of treated industrial or domestic water for irrigation and the breeding of drought resistant and salt tolerant crops.

One other natural 'resource' deserves special mention: the world's weather. Economic calculations have long since shown that the return from investment in meteorological research and forecasting is inordinately large. Accurate predictions have been known to save entire crops from the effect of a sudden frost or a torrential downpour. And this is an area where research is already moving fast and broadly in directions which will benefit the developed and the less developed alike. Two new international programmes, the World Weather Watch (WWW) and the Global Atmospheric Research Program (GARP), have recently been started. The latter is concentrating on models which will describe the entire atmospheric system (or a large part of it) while WWW is greatly increasing our knowledge of the weather as it happens, particularly by the application of the very newest techniques. As an example, it is planned that for the Global Observing System 40 new radiosonde/radiowind stations should be set up and programmes at 95 existing stations expanded. The number of merchant ships making meteorological observations should be doubled and five to ten new ocean weather stations set up, mainly in the southern hemisphere. Some 20 regional meteorological stations should be built in addition to the three world centres already operating in Moscow, Canberra and Washington, D.C. Storm warning radar stations are needed at five sites in the Caribbean. All this will require a considerable increase in appropriately trained specialists and most of the UN agencies are already involved in extensive educational and training programmes. Some of this work will also overlap with the need to lessen the effects of natural disasters, a subject currently under intensive UN study.

Finally, we turn to what is probably the single most significant of all resources: energy. If our plans for the Second Development Decade are successfully carried through, energy demand in the developing countries will rise 8.4 per cent per annum. In the next ten years, then, a further 124,000 megawatts of generating capacity will have to be installed. And if we take the figure of $200 per kilowatt as the rough capital cost of installing and transmitting this power, an investment of no less than $25,000 million will be called for.

One important and cheap way of generating energy is to use the Earth's own geothermal sources—as has recently been done in Chile, Taiwan, El Salvador, Guadeloupe and Turkey. And in the next decade all the unconventional sources of energy should be the subject of considerable research—an efficient fuel cell running on a cheap fuel such as kerosene is needed, as are more efficient means of converting solar power into mechanical or electrical energy. Tidal power, too, can be a novel and cheap way of producing energy where the coastal situation permits. A little used source of a conventional fuel over the next decade is likely to be shale oil but so far the world's vast reserves have remained unexploited through want of an economic technology.

Nuclear energy, of course, is already becoming an important source in the developed world. Developing countries can and should begin to assess and exploit their reserves of uranium and, later, thorium. Such exploitation is expensive and no country should devote more than 15 per cent of the total recoverable value to the search for new fields. Furthermore, the minimum size of ore worth exploiting is about 2000 tons of contained uranium oxide; this means that a developing country must be prepared to spend a capital sum of between $3.2 million and $8 million in finding, evaluating, mining and milling operations.

Nuclear reactors themselves can be economic if operated on a large scale. In effect, this means that the plant must be capable of providing at least 500,000 kilowatts of electrical energy and it must be connected to a grid system with a capacity of at least ten times as much. As a result nuclear power holds promise only for a rapidly developing country where the growth of energy consumption is large and where the reactor is to be the first in a series which will lead to a carefully planned nuclear power grid. Nuclear energy is not something to be undertaken lightly; the capital and hidden costs are very high and the demand on technical manpower is heavy.

Obviously, success in this or in more conventional fields will not be achieved unless a sufficient number of experts is trained, means set up for improving the flow of technical ideas relating to energy production and distribution, and national institutes brought into being to study the long-term implications of their country's economic development plans and policies.

(ii) *Food and Agriculture: More Food from More Land*

It does not need a skilled writer or a clever statistician to show how alarming the world food problem already is, and how much worse it will get in the next decade if current trends are not changed substantially. Today nearly half the world goes hungry and more than half of it is malnourished. To achieve anything like a satisfactory situation we need an immediate increase of 30 per cent in world cereal production.

But this is not the only problem: between 1965 and 1985 another 1000 million people, mostly living in the developing world, will be added to the world total. If plans for economic development proceed to schedule, this will mean that world food demand will increase by 142 per cent over the period 1962-85.

Our recent history provides a grim comparison. The per capita food available in the developing world over the first six years of the 1960s showed no increase at all; in fact, it fell by 0.1 per cent. The gross food production in the world as a whole during 1956-66 rose by only 2.7 per cent per annum. Yet our plans call for an average increase of 4.0 per cent per annum up to 1980. How can this be achieved? If current trends in the developing world were to continue, it would, by 1985, have to be importing food from the developed world worth $26,000 million a year. Even that is a hypothetical situation for the developed world would not have that amount of food to sell nor would the developing world have the foreign exchange to buy it with if it did. How, then, can the trends be altered?

Basically, there are two ways: to increase yield and to increase acreage. Both possibilities have been extensively studied in the UN Indicative World Plan prepared by the Food and Agriculture Organization, on which plans for the Second Development Decade lean heavily. During the next ten years, for instance, it is planned to bring a further 40 million hectares of land under cultivation, most of it coming from permanent pasture, a lesser amount from forests and some 10 per cent from waste land. By then 730 million hectares of arable land will be in use out of the world's estimated total potential of 1150 million hectares.

Another broad approach is to extend the area of land under irrigation from 95 to 133 million hectares, at a growth rate of 3.5 per cent a year, and at a total cost of $30,000 million.

Although population pressure tends to encourage the exploitation and improvement of new land, neither will happen of their own accord. Probably the best catalyst is the establishment of pioneer pilot projects in which the feasibility of the idea is established by the use of technical innovation, provision of services, successful farming and disposal of the produce. If such projects are to work, they cost about $850-1000 per hectare, or $3-10 million per project, and most of the money has to come from foreign aid.

The complementary technique of increasing yield will come largely from the use of improved genetic strains, as described in the introduction. However, these new strains need to be extended to much larger areas, and the yields themselves still further improved for such crops as wheat, maize and rice. Furthermore, there is still a research gap with regard to winter and durum wheats, upland, swamp and deep water rice, millet and sorghum. New international research programmes will be needed for this. Equally important will be improvement in the yield of starchy roots and tubers, which are the staple food of some 80 million people in tropical Africa alone. FAO estimates that by 1980 research costs for all food crops should have increased to $325 million, of which 45 per cent will have to be in the form of foreign aid.

Concurrent with this, of course, will be the allied developments also mentioned in the introduction. Fertilizer expenditure over the decade will rise from $3,200 to $7,200 million, pesticide expenditure from $400 to $1200 million, and mechanization will increase sharply but should be of a type which does not displace labour. The practice of multicropping, one of the best means of increasing both yield and nutritional balance, will have to be greatly extended from those few areas where it is already practised.

Perhaps the major problem with livestock is that so little of it ever ends up on anyone's table. In some countries calf mortality runs as high as 50 per cent and fertility rates in adult cattle may be as low as 30 per cent. Here the application of existing technology is required but it must be coupled with improved breeding programmes. These measures alone could, at an estimated cost of $86,000 million over the decade, raise production of beef, veal and cow's milk to a level commensurate with demand. Control of foot and mouth disease would do much to improve Latin America's meat exports and control of trypanosomiasis in Africa would help open up much new land; the tsetse fly still holds sway over 4 million acres of Africa with the result that much adequate farming land there is still unexploited; camels, pigs and cattle are all affected. The introduction of industrial methods of rearing pigs and poultry are to be given high priority in the next decade.

A third important source of food will be the oceans. Here, three areas warrant particular attention: the fishing vessel themselves, the exploitation of unconventional ocean foods, and the development of aquaculture or fish farming. At the simplest level, much could be done if small existing fishing fleets had outboard motors and if larger vessels were made more efficient. Then there is a whole panoply of new devices which is already spreading slowly from the advanced countries: sonar detection methods, very deep water trawls and refrigeration at sea are among the most important. Gross investment in vessels for the decade is estimated at $2500 million, with a further $500 million for harbour development.

The world's oceans are already quite heavily fished—so much so that some stocks are becoming increasingly difficult to find. But there are many smaller species not yet touched: perhaps unique among these are the Antarctic krill with a potential annual catch of more than 50 million tons. These novel resources will, however, need new equipment and here an international effort is required. This is less true of aquaculture where the technique has been well proven for trout and for carp, and for shell fish in Asia and in the Near East. Here the main problems to be overcome concern the supply of qualified personnel, and the economic and legal problems which have perpetually dogged the history of fish farming.

The forests are another biological resource of great potential. Although tropical forests contain 80 per cent of the world's broadleaved wood, they currently supply only 30 per cent of industrial consumption. Here modern mechanized methods of timber harvesting and distribution are called for and it is proposed to establish experimental extraction areas of 10-20,000 hectares, requiring a capital investment of about $1,500,000 and costing $1 million a year for a five year period. The use of tropical forest wood also implies that mills have to accept mixtures of perhaps 50 or 100 different species. Programmes to develop products made of mixed woods are to be expanded. Total cost of all forest programmes for the decade is estimated at $280 million.

The overall cost of the total agricultural programme proposed in the FAO's Indicative World Plan amounts to $232,100 million. Of this the developing countries will have to find $192,100 million; aid from the advanced countries is estimated at $21,500 million, from the international sector $14,500 million and from the private sector $3,900 million. Even more important, it is suggested that the share of all aid which goes to agriculture should be raised from the 12 per cent it was in the First Development Decade to 18 per cent. Here, if anywhere is a clear indication of the United Nations' determination to tackle the problem of starvation—a problem which makes all other forms of development meaningless if it is not resolved.

(iii) Industry: The Alternative Way

The developed world owes its wealth primarily to industrialization—and in particular to heavy industry. Iron and steel, chemicals, electrical equipment, bricks and cement are the very backbone of the industrial giants. The existence of these industries itself gave rise to prodigious amounts of research, leading first to mechanization and then to automation. Capital costs are now incredibly high and the labour component is being reduced to the minimum possible.

But it was natural that when the Third World began its slow progress to development, it should seek to copy the one known method of success. Indeed, the developed world aided and abetted this process, thinking at one and the same time to help the underprivileged and to extract from them a share of their resources in return for technical assistance.

The World Plan has some strong things to say about this model of development. "The high rates of growth in population, large-scale migration of unskilled labour from rural to urban areas, and the slow pace and the relatively high capital intensity with which industrialization is taking place in the developing countries may lead to a massive build-up of unemployment in the years to come", it claims. And the results of the First Development Decade show that where capital-intensive technologies have been simply transferred to developing areas, the results have included "widespread and increasing unemployment and underemployment, growing internal inequalities and social tensions and stagnation in the traditional (typically rural) sector".

It seems, in fact, as though there are three distinct techniques of industrial development. The first embraces the simple transfer of existing industrial technology to the developing world. The second involves the adaptation of that technology to the special and often very different conditions that exist in the developing nation. And the third is reached when the country can itself begin the process of research which leads to the development of those new industries most suited to it. At this stage the process becomes self-propelling, and the developing country itself generates the new ideas and manpower required for each new industry.

Regrettably, most industrial development in the Third World has been of the first kind. The third is hardly in evidence anywhere, with a few possible exceptions such as India. It is estimated that in Pakistan, for instance, less than one per cent of the industrial programme stems from the research carried out by Pakistan's Council for Scientific and Industrial Research.

266

UNESCO has estimated that in 1963 only 71 of Africa's 3428 research workers were involved in industrial research.

One key concept unites the objectives of both techniques two and three. That concept is appropriate technology. Those two words embrace a philosophy of development which is new, exciting and full of promise. In one sense they are the key to the World Plan of Action. They imply an attitude to industrialization so different from what has gone before that their implications merit spelling out in some detail.

First, they implicitly recognize the natural differences that exist between, say, Chad and Sweden or between Thailand and France; countries with different sizes, different climates and different reserves need different techniques. They recognize, too, that the developed world's industries were often based on substantial imports or on artificial substitutes for those imports when they became either scarce or too costly. And they imply that the developing world need not—indeed should not—seek to copy the industrial pathways of the developed world. Such a conclusion today comes as something of a relief when the developed world is learning to its cost the heavy environmental price it has had to pay for its industrial development. And it perhaps spares us that lingering background fear that the world is heading for some awful crisis of uniformity and conformity. Appropriate technology means that industrial development can mean other things than smoking factory chimneys, oil pollution, social alienation and the worst effects of mass production. Instead, it can mean diversity, choice, craft industries, new and needed products and an alternative means of achieving the wealth that typifies the heavily industrialized nations.

The two essential ingredients to appropriate technology are local natural resources and cheap manpower. It is on these that the new industries for the developing world should be built up. Some specific examples will make the point clear. One important natural resource of the developing world—and one that often goes to waste—are agricultural by-products. But rice hulls, peanut shells, bagasse, sawdust and tobacco stems could, with the help of the appropriate technology, provide the food additive glutamate, furfuraldehyde for plastic production, ethyl alcohol for industrial chemicals as well as paper, building board and fuel briquets. In the same way, with cheap labour, new plants to process low grade ores can provide minerals at competitive prices, earn useful foreign exchange and act as a fruitful source of employment.

It is estimated that two thirds of the world's livestock are in developing countries. Currently used primarily as a source of meat, milk or wool, they could however form the basis of a thriving industry of hides and skins. Good local preprocessing could improve their value by 75 to 100 per cent. In doing so it could retain a vital link with the land for those employed and provide jobs outside the more usual locale of the city or urban complex.

Other applications of appropriate technology appear less radical. For instance, research has shown that many of the static parts of machine tools need not be built of expensive cast iron but can be fashioned from cement concrete. Similarly many of the items of manufacturing equipment available from the developed countries need not be used for exactly the production process for which they were designed. Simple changes can open up new avenues which would have had no value in a capital-intensive, labour-saving economy. Nor need all machinery be new. Often it can be obtained second hand, in adequate working order, at a fraction of the cost when new. Often it is cheaper and preferable to service and repair old equipment than to buy new. Not only does the process save foreign exchange but it provides employment as well. Small scale industries, particularly forestry and textiles, have much to recommend them in developing countries. The resources are cheap, the equipment simple and the manpower contribution high. This being so they do not suffer the same disadvantages of scale that they do in developed societies, where scaling up is always held to produce economies. It usually does but only at great cost in flexibility and the burgeoning bureaucracy which always seems to expand faster than the industry it is meant to serve.

None of this should be held to imply that appropriate technology is a magic panacea. It involves some stiff problems. First and foremost, it can be interpreted as 'second class development' —there is always a feeling that if industries do not suffer from the same over-complexity and grossness which they have assumed in the developed world, they are not true industries. No misapprehension could be more unfortunate; it may well be that in time we shall see the course followed by today's industrialized nations as 'second-class development'. Today's developing countries really could pave the way for first-class development. Secondly, appropriate technologies cannot be designed on the back of an envelope. They require clever thinking and original minds. Furthermore, it is not yet anyone's specific job to design them. Certainly, there is no profit incentive for industries in the developed world to produce them, and the World Plan recommends that public bodies should begin to direct some of their funds towards solving the very tricky but highly challenging problems that are presented by a totally different concept of industrialization.

At the same time, we have to recognize that some of the advanced world's technology is already 'partially appropriate'. Iron and steel, for instance, are likely to be essential in any conceivable form of industrial development. But there could, for instance, be enormous benefits if a means could be found of using Indian coal in iron and steel production. Similarly, nearly all Latin American countries import both coking coal and steel, although their own reserves of coal are estimated at more than 94,000 million tons. From here it is a short step to the mechanical engineering industries where capacity in the developing world is still low. The priorities in many countries are clear: first, manufacture of agricultural machinery—such as tractors and small engines; second, manufacture of machine tools, motor vehicle components and parts and pipe; and, third, development of electrical machinery and appliances, heavy steel fabrication, shipyard facilities and industrial tractors.

But what flows from all this may again be quite different. In many countries markets will be small and the need is for multi-purpose machinery and non-specialized casting workshops. The catalytic role that such developments could play in helping the textile and forest-based industries—supremely important in many developing countries—should not be under-estimated. The chemical industry presents a separate problem; its growth rate may be particularly attractive to developing countries but the appropriate technology for the natural resources available has to be designed. Priorities may include petroleum, oil and natural gas products, complex fertilizers, ammonia and nitrogen plants.

Two things remain to be stressed. One is that the industries of the developing world will vary greatly from region to region and from country to country. There is no over-all master plan that can be deployed. The second point is that, contrary perhaps to previous development ideas, research can and must play a crucial role in industrialization. The idea that industries of all kinds already exist in the developed world, and that all that needs to be done is transfer them, is totally misleading. Research and development usually accounts for only 5 to 10 per cent of the total cost of innovation and hence is well worth the expenditure. "During the Decade", the World Plan states, "the development stages of pioneering applied research must take priority for all developing countries bent on successful industrialization. UNIDO recommends that Governments of developing countries earmark at least 0.5 per cent of their national budgets for industrial research, once there is assurance that existing research facilities are properly co-ordinated and the required personnel can be made available".

(iv) *Transport and Communication: Moving People, Goods and Ideas*

To a casual visitor, perhaps the thing that most simply distinguishes the less developed country is its lack of transport. The modern industrial state thrives on its transport—cars and lorries, roads and railway tracks, trains, ships and aircraft are the constant preoccupation of the developed world. Yet in the developing countries, often with much greater distances to span, these are noticeable in their absence. What transport systems do exist function irregularly and inefficiently, even compared to the developed world's far from perfect standards. And it almost goes without saying that without better transport all the improvements that can be made in the next ten years in economic growth, productivity and individual incomes will count for very little.

The role that science and technology can play in solving this situation is not straightforward. There is a view in the developed world that we already have all the transport we can afford—and that quite possibly we have too much. And in nine cases out of ten the problems of developing transport systems for the poorer countries depend quite simply on the cash to buy them with coupled with some sound principles of management operation. Quite certainly, transport research comes low in the list of priorities. And even technology transfer does not present the problems it does in other areas: the technology is well known and easily discovered. So my aim here is simply to present a selection of scientific and technical ideas which may accelerate transport development, bearing in mind that the principal problems are more properly the concern of the financial and economic aspects of the Second Development Decade.

One area of great interest is road development. It is highly unlikely that we shall see any new breakthroughs in road design or construction. But there is an important gap—how to build feeder roads, linking main arterial trunk roads with smaller towns and villages. The problem is to build these roads with local materials, such as sand and gravel, using local labour and yet produce a surface able to withstand harsh tropical conditions—which may be alternately very wet and very dry. There is a research need here, and it is closely coupled to the nature of the vehicle that will operate on the new surface. In the developed world we know to our cost what an ergonomic disaster the modern motor car is. Designed for five people when it normally carries an average of little more than one, designed to cruise at 80 miles an hour when it spends a large proportion of its time in a garage or traffic jam, and endowed with over complicated engineering that gives rise to breakdowns at the most inconvenient moments, it is a product that the developed world might well have hesitated to export. And of course it is vastly more unsuited to conditions in the developing countries. There is clearly a need for the development of a totally different type of motor vehicle. One cannot help wondering, too, whether such a development might not yield substantial exports to the developed countries themselves.

A number of similar problems might be neatly solved by new transport technology. The World Plan lays special emphasis on hydrofoil and hydrojet boats, hovercraft with their remarkable ability to cross water or unprepared terrain, and on the transport of gas, liquids and solids in slurry form by pipeline. All these techniques are in use in the developed world but because they arrived on the scene late in the day, they have perhaps not played as important a role as they might in a country so far without substantial investments in already existing transport systems. And in this context natural waterways look particularly attractive, with their relatively low capital cost, high labour maintenance requirements, simple technology and large bulk capability.

It is estimated that internal transport development for the poorer countries over the decade will cost $242 million, half of which will have to come from domestic sources and $48 million from multilateral assistance. Research and development will account for $61 million of this, education and training $75 million, scientific and technological information $34 million and institution building $72 million. These costs, however, do not include external transport systems.

Foremost among these is ocean shipping. Here the trend in the developed world to larger and larger vessels, with their inflexibilities, labour saving potential and social hazards, do not necessarily warrant copying. There is a considerable advantage to be obtained from plying smaller ships. Nor should the modern trend towards containerization always be followed, though here the choice is more difficult. A modern container vessel of suitable size would cost a developing country about $6 million compared to half that for a pallet ship and a little less for a conventional liner. Furthermore, container ships involve substantial harbour work. Experience in the developed world suggests that two container berths with an annual through-put of 50,000 containers would cost $4 million. Before embarking on a containerization programme, then, a developing country would have to calculate its return on investment very carefully, adequately weighing the social cost of diminishing the docking force. On the other hand, in spite of their cost of over $20 million a vessel, LASH (lighter aboard ship) vessels do appear attractive. Carrying with them their own barges—easily constructed within a developing country—they are efficient means of handling bulk cargoes where docking facilities are poor and where there can be a direct link with inland waterways.

Air transport cannot yet rival the cheapness of freight movement by air or rail or the flexibility and convenience of motor transport. Nor can it be envisaged that developing countries immerse themselves in the immensely costly business of aircraft research, development and production—an activity which only a handful of the more developed countries engage in now. But aircraft do have certain advantages for developing countries.

They are unmatched for passenger and mail delivery over long distances, for transport over rough terrain and may well hold the key to the development of areas that simply cannot be reached by any other method. When, and if, the short take-off and vertical take-off models become economic they will undoubtedly be of great value in areas where landing strips can be built only with difficulty or at great cost. So there is a case for the aircraft in development; it is one which rests inevitably on the application of very advanced technologies, requiring large teams of very highly trained personnel. But the decision to open up aviation links can open up development possibilities where none previously existed. Aircraft freight transport can also provide new markets for old goods, particularly perishable ones.

If the aircraft is the most expensive form of travel, the transistor radio is certainly the cheapest. It is important to realize that telecommunications are in reality an alternative form of transport in which ideas rather than people are transported from place to place. Furthermore, the transistor industry is something which can be developed quite cheaply. The aim in the next decade should be for more developing countries to be able to market their own transistor radios at no more than $5 a set. In special situations it may be advisable to produce a superior set, with frequency modulation for improved reception. A rediffusion system is often very attractive, with one sensitive tuner in each village wired to loudspeakers in every home. For example, in South Korea the average cost of a village system, with a 50 to 500 watt amplifier, some 250 speakers and 15 to 20 miles of wire, has worked out at about $900.

The educational benefits of radio can be greatly extended by television but only at much increased cost. This cost needs to be compared with the alternative of training special teachers and establishing them in remote areas. Mass education through television can be economic, as has been shown in Algeria, Chile, India, Jordan, Nigeria and Singapore. It may become cheaper still as communication satellites become more common, and the experiment being undertaken between India and the US space agency (NASA) should soon provide useful information on the technique. Other studies are under way in Argentina, Chile, Colombia, Ecuador, Peru and Uruguay, and UNESCO is already playing a valuable role in evaluating this form of "alternative education".

Another aim of the Second Development Decade is to make the telephone available to at least 80 per cent of the rural population. To do this will require many new telecommunications systems with problems of quite a different nature to those experienced in the developed world. The need for standardization in telecommunications is so great, however, that after study the

International Telecommunications Union has recommended that wherever possible equipment which is already available be used rather than new equipment designed. This development, bringing the isolated into touch with the outside world, will go hand-in-hand with the aim of establishing one post office per 3,000 to 6,000 population or every 20 to 40 square kilometers before the end of the development decade. Again, the emphasis must be on clever use of existing technology rather than new research breakthroughs—though postal communication in the developed world is fast being modernized and automated. For the developing countries, the simple idea of the mobile post office van is of much more relevance.

(v) *Human Settlements: Eliminating Urban Blight*

Between now and the year 2000, it is estimated, we shall have to construct twice as many human habitations as have been erected in the whole of human history. The problem has a three-fold origin: the lamentable state of human shelter today; the rapidly increasing size of the total population; and the flood of people that daily moves off the land and into the towns and cities.

Today cities are expanding at an average outward rate of two metres a day, including weekends. In the Second Development Decade an average of 90,000 people a day will enter the towns and cities of Africa, Asia and Latin America—a total of 325 million all told. By 1980 41 per cent of world population will be urbanized and in some countries urban growth will be running at over 10 per cent. No less than 18 cities in Latin America will have passed the million mark. Buenos Aires alone will have more than 9 million inhabitants.

Such statistics defy even the most vivid imagination. Without adequate action, the situation that will shortly exist in most of the developing world's cities will be catastrophic—even today 79 per cent of the families living in Calcutta do so in one room, typhus and dysentery are endemic in nearly all the shanty towns of Latin America, only 45 per cent of Brazil's municipalities have reliable water supplies and only 34 per cent have sewage systems. In most cities of the poorer countries unemployment runs at nearly 30 per cent. Of those that are employed nearly half are often lumped in that euphemistic category known as the 'service

274

sector'. Barbara Ward, who has prepared a special study of urbanization for the United Nations, tells us that we should have no illusions as to what that means. "In the main it includes all the myriad odd-job men who live on the rim of starvation in the run-down slums and miserable fringe settlements of the great urban jungles". She concludes that the city is the symbol of a development process that has thus far been patchy and at best partially successful. "The cities", she writes, "are where the evils come to a head in monstrously visible gatherings of human misery".

So what has gone wrong? How has the city, the very symbol of Victorian success and progress, come now to represent the lowest depths of squalor to which the human race has sunk? The answer is historical. In Europe and the United States, the accumulation of an agricultural surplus freed man from the land. Simultaneous mechanization and industrialization provided new jobs which benefited from concentration. People moved from the land, where they were not wanted, to the cities where they were. Population growth was extremely low and such expansion of the work force as there was could easily be absorbed by the new and thriving manufacturing industries.

In the developing world the situation is much different. There is no agricultural surplus or, where there is, it is of very recent origin. The movement to the cities began much earlier and was the result not of the land needing fewer people but of population growth providing an excess of labour. They trooped to the towns and the cities to find neither work nor money but hunger and deprivation. Whereas in Europe the proportion of the work force employed in manufacturing industry was often three times the proportion of people living in towns and cities, in the developing countries the reverse is true. In 1951 in Colombia, for instance, 45.8 per cent of the population lived in towns of more than 20,000 people but only 9.9 per cent of the work force was employed in manufacturing industry. Nor can this trend be corrected as easily as was the case in the 19th century. Much manufacturing industry was then labour intensive and it cost only the equivalent of six months salary to provide the equipment to find a man work. Today the cost is nearer 350 months salary in the developed world.

Clearly some new urban strategies are called for. But there are few good models to work from. The city crisis includes developed as well as developing and it hardly makes sense for countries a hundred times less well off to ape the failures of the developed world where cities are no less the symbols of the different types of failure which progress has brought in its train. But there are some pointers. New urban complexes are best situated remote from the existing ones and near new sources of raw materials. Such a city can encourage development rather than symbolize its failures. Linear cities and subsidiary centres can be located close to agricultural regions where they can act as a catalyst to agricultural growth, stimulate light industry and provide farm necessities. The advantage of high population clusters can then be exploited—family planning, medical services, communication and education are all easier in such a situation, providing the population is well housed and well employed.

The key to the future undoubtedly lies in planning and study and a willingness to recognize that any solution to the city problem will surely involve radically new concepts of urbanization. To this end are needed training and research centres, new housing finance systems, an international campaign to arouse public concern over urban blight, and a decision by developing countries to invest 5 per cent of their national incomes in housing and urbanization (a considerable increase which would still leave the developing countries a long way behind the developed world). Finally, a United Nations publication has estimated that roughly $1000 million a year in seed money will be needed to enable mobilization of sufficient domestic resources to confront the annual cost of housing and basic utilities for 80 per cent of the urban populations of Asia, Africa and Latin America. These were estimated at $5865 million a year. This level of support would represent a three fold increase in international assistance.

From this most appalling of problems to the building of individual houses may seem to trivialize the issue—yet houses are principally what cities are made of, and shelter is only equalled in its primary importance with food. During the First Development Decade the goal was for developing countries to produce ten new housing units per 1000 population annually. In the event, no more than two or three were built. Failure to reach the magic figure of ten in the Second Decade would be far more catastrophic in its effect, and the goal has been given far greater priority. This time it can be realized if the quite specific recommendations of the Decade are followed up and acted upon.

One of the keys will be industrialized building methods—particularly the mass production off-site of specific items of the house. The repetition of building operations in long sequences in this way has been known to reduce costs by 20 per cent. Standardization of units is essential—and cost saving—for this type of operation and good management itself can lower costs by 20 to 30 per cent. In addition much can be gained with a little additional research and the choice of local building materials deployed in a labour intensive way.

Because transport costs are so high, research is needed into lightweight building materials. If wood, metals, clay and cellular concrete could be made less fragile—and hence more easily transported—industrialization could proceed faster. Other areas of concern are the problems raised by the curing and setting of concrete in tropical areas and thermal insulation in cheap building projects. There are also abundant supplies of cereal husks and vegetable fibres, fly ash, slag and garbage in the developing countries. With suitable binders, all these materials could become an important source of building material—given adequate research.

Accordingly, the World Plan recommends the training of 1000 research workers, at a cost of $6 million provided from external sources, in industrial building materials and techniques. Short training courses are planned for 40,000 workers for every 10 million inhabitants. External sources should be asked to provide $500,000 a year for undergraduate and graduate fellowships in industrial building—enough to cover about 100 fellowships a year. Seminars, lectures and publications may cost another $20 million over the decade and it is proposed to set up two national institutes in both Africa and Latin America at a cost of $24 million from external sources and $16 million from domestic sources. A series of pilot and demonstration housing programmes should also be run at an estimated cost of $15 million, 40 per cent to be spent in Asia, 25 per cent in Africa and 35 per cent in Latin America.

All this will help—and it will be aimed particularly at the problem of finding the appropriate building technology for each nation. The technologies used now are far from appropriate—some African nations, for instance, import 58 per cent of their building materials. Imported materials in the ECAFE region average 30 per cent of construction costs. All this is a monumental waste of foreign exchange which only leads to instability

277

in the building industry. Local materials are quite vital to developing nations' housing programmes and brick production needs to be sharply increased because clay is often available and brick making is a labour intensive industry. Similarly, lime may prove a better cementing material than Portland cement if techniques can be evolved to make it more manageable. Timber production, particularly, can answer many of the problems of the building industry and many developing countries have enormous timber reserves lying unexploited while they import special foreign timber for housing.

(vi) *Health: Priorities in the Never-ending Battle*

· There is no discernible upper limit to the amount that the health of the human race could be improved. Not only is the field for new research and application unlimited but highly effective and well tried techniques of public health have yet to spread throughout most of the world. For this reason, if plans for the next decade are to be effective, they have to be highly selective. Careful study for the World Plan has produced a list of six priority areas: water supply, communicable diseases, vector control, nutrition, education and training, and population and fertility. This last is considered so important that it forms a separate programme in itself.

Today, two-thirds of the world population lack an adequate supply of safe water. Mainly for this reason cholera, enteric fevers, dysentery, and diarrhoeal diseases are never far from the surface in developing countries. They affect some 500 million people a year and cause 5 million infant deaths a year. Of these cholera is probably the most serious, and its effects are amplified by conditions of high deprivation and population density. By 1980, therefore, it is planned that 40 per cent of the urban population in developing countries should be provided with piped water and the remaining 60 per cent given access to nearby public fountains. Bad as the situation now is in the cities, it is much worse in rural areas where probably no more than 10 per cent of the population has a safe and adequate water supply. An interim target would be to double this by 1980.

Little research will be needed in this programme. Instead the World Plan recommends that some 50 'pre-investment projects' be funded through the Special Fund of the UNDP at a total cost of $40 million. Another $5 million should be spent on fellowships for those whose job it is to manage and engineer water supply systems. $2 million has been estimated for scientific and technical information—such as seminars, training courses and the publication of manuals—and $3.75 million for the establishment of five applied research institutes in Africa, the western Pacific and south-east Asia. All told, the cost of this water supply programme is estimated at $9,100 million—60 per cent for Asia, 25 per cent for Latin America and 15 per cent for Africa. The urban programme will require the largest share—$7,100 million—and of the total between one third and one quarter will have to come from external sources.

Of the communicable diseases, it is planned that smallpox should be totally eradicated before the end of the Second Development Decade. It is still endemic in 27 countries and, at a cost of $0.12 per vaccination, the programme will cost $347 million (of which all but $50 million come from the countries affected). In addition, eradication needs a continuing vaccination programme for at least two years estimated at $50,000 to $150,000 a year per million people. Malaria, which was once endemic in 146 countries, cannot be totally eliminated by 1980, particularly in Africa, but it is hoped that by then it will have been eradicated in 83 countries and nearly eradicated in a further 23. The total cost would be $2050 million, of which $310 million will come from external sources. A further $16 million will be spent on training projects, $120 million to strengthen research institutes and $15 million on pilot projects.

African trypanosomiasis, affecting people as well as animals, is preventing the development of a stock-raising industry in large areas of Africa. It can be controlled only by elimination of its vector, the tsetse fly, and only at some cost. By 1980 it is hoped to reclaim 100,000 square miles at a cost of $40 million. A further $1 million should be spent on fundamental research and $2 million on applied research into control and elimination of the fly—including study of the techniques and effects of releasing into the tsetse population males which have been sterilized by radiation or chemical methods. A further $280,000 should be spent on providing four training fellowships a year. The American form of this disease (Chagas' disease) is transmitted by large reduviid bugs living in poorly constructed sheds and houses. At the moment control by spraying is laborious and

279

inefficient and the main concern is for further research (budgeted at $5 million). A similar situation exists for the tropical virus diseases, which include yellow fever. Here it is planned to strengthen the already existing 9 reference centres and their 6 collaborating laboratories by the expenditure of $970,000 as capital costs and $5.2 million as recurring costs. Schistosomiasis, which currently affects 200 million people and acts as a strong brake on socio-economic progress, should also be the subject of intensified research ($800,000). A further $300,000 is budgeted for research and training fellowships, and the World Health Organization will continue to sponsor the investigations of 33 researchers in 15 different countries.

The remaining disease singled out for special attention is leprosy. In 1965 it was estimated that there were more than 10 million cases of which about one fifth received treatment. Since then a million more cases will have arisen, mainly because some 2000 million people live in areas where the disease is endemic (the disease is most common in Asia but even Europe had 52,000 cases in 1965). Prospects for control are not good and research should be given top priority by the provision of an additional $500,000 per annum over the ten year period. What is needed is a breakthrough in either therapy or immunization, coupled with an improvement in the socio-economic conditions which so often lead to contraction of the disease.

The third area of priority is the control of the various insects, rodents and other animals which carry human disease or act as reservoirs of it. Basically, only three species are currently extensively studied and during the next decade a further ten should be added to the list at a cost of $5 million. Research must also concentrate on the need to find new insecticides as resistance is developed to previously efficient ones and on the possibilities of using the predators and parasites of the vectors as control weapons. In addition it is planned to create a field unit to study vector control under differing ecological conditions at a cost of $1.2 million and to extend research in genetics, biochemistry and toxicology relevant to vectors at a cost of $2 million for 1971-80.

Among the new research institutes planned are one for the study of the *Aedes* mosquito in the Caribbean and one for *Filariasis* in Latin America. A sub-unit of the East African *Aedes* Research Unit will study the rural vectors of yellow fever in

Ethiopia. The black fly, triatomid bugs and the mosquito vectors of Japanese encephalitis may also deserve individual units. Cost of these would be $6 million and a further $2.4 million will be allowed for two new insecticide testing units, one in the western Pacific. Finally, two new institutes are recommended for the study of rodent control at a cost of $7 million over the decade.

Nutrition, already mentioned under food and agriculture, is the fourth priority area, and the chief research objective is the development of new protein weaning foods. Protein-calorie malnutrition is perhaps the commonest disease in the world, taking a particularly savage toll among the young and leading in turn to both physical infection through weakness and probably to mental impairment in later life. Some $10 million will be required for research and a further $5 million to try to close the gap between the demand and supply of nutritional and other experts. The 100 fellowships which this sum will buy will not be nearly sufficient and a further five nutritional research and advice centres should be established, at a cost of $52.5 million. Another 30 nutritional units should be established in the health ministries of developing countries at a cost of $9 million.

None of these priorities areas, of course, detract in any way from the normal demands and improvements expected in various national health services. These depend for the most part on the establishment of efficient health teams—doctors, dentists, midwives, pharmacists and social workers, for instance. The lack of such manpower now poses one of the most substantial blocks to world health improvement. In the highly developed countries there is often a ratio of one doctor to 500 people. But in Latin America it is nearer one to 2500, in Africa south of the Sahara one to 20,000 and in some Asian countries it reaches one to 30,000 (though the average is one to 6000). In the developed world there is about one medical school to every 3 million inhabitants. Progress here has been substantial in Latin America, and in India where the number of schools rose from 60 in 1960 to 91 in 1969. But in Asia and particularly in Africa the problem is almost catastrophic. In 1960 37 African countries could between them boast only seven medical schools. True, those same countries, now with a population of 215 million, currently have 19 schools but most are of recent origin. Twenty such countries still have no medical school at all. Hence the plan to establish 30 new medical schools in developing countries should not be regarded as over-ambitious—and ten of these should be in Africa and they should be operating before 1980. Only if these plans are successful can the powerful new methods of health improvement—so direly needed throughout two-thirds of the world—bring about their desired effect. Without them a life of disease and misery will continue to be the lot of most of mankind.

(vii) *Science Education: Beware the Ivory Tower*

The central thesis of this publication is that science and technology have a decisive role to play in the Second Development Decade. If this is true, science education and the production of scientific manpower are as vital to the process as pilots are to flying or people are to cities. No new research programme, no development project, no scientific management scheme has any hope of success without qualified personnel. It is true that a partial success for a limited time could be achieved by importing to the developing countries all the qualified people that were needed from the developed world (if they could be spared). But, again, the thesis here is that true development can be achieved only by the building up of an indigenous scientific ability—and this subject is of such importance that it is discussed separately on page 48.

But once we recognize this, we strike out into uncharted territory. Without wishing to detract from some substantial successes already made, science education has hardly begun in the developing world. We know it only from our experience of the developed world, and at the current time that experience is hardly encouraging. Certainly there is no model means of science education that could possibly be used as a blue print for developing countries. In one sense, the developed countries have been over-zealous in their approach to science education, certainly in the non-socialist countries. The emphasis has been on higher and higher levels of specialization and the achievement of a doctor's or master's degree, taken after three or more years of post-graduate study, has become a kind of starting point for most scientific careers.

The result has been unfortunate, and how unfortunate we are only now beginning to realize. For one thing, the process has hardly produced well-rounded individuals with broad cul-

282

tural and scientific interests and abilities. Specialization has seen
to it that communication between scientists of different disciplines has become more and more difficult at the very time
when we realize that almost all practical problems require inter-
disciplinary teams. This extreme specialization has also done
wild things to the labour market. The glut of graduates and
post-graduates is such that they have to take jobs considerably
below their abilities—thus many large companies are now no
longer content with fully qualified secretaries but insist that
those secretaries also have a university degree. Another result has
been serious unemployment of graduates, particularly in the
United States with the slowing up of the space programme, but
also in the United Kingdom and other countries. It is small
wonder that in these countries there is a swing away from science
in the schools; the well-known example of those physicists with
Ph.D. degrees who now earn their living as cab drivers is upper-
most in many people's minds.

Meanwhile, the broad population in many advanced countries
remains as scientifically illiterate as ever. Furthermore, acute
shortages of scientific manpower are building up at a lower level.
Technicians, nurses, social workers, scientific administrators and
the like are all in short supply. In short, scientific education in
much of the developed world is in turmoil and many of the
young are shunning those bold new plate-glass universities which
were designed for them because they do not see what is going
on inside to have much relevance to the kind of life they want
to lead. Just as in the Middle Ages, the rationale of scholasticism
for its own sake has been judged wanting.

For this reason, plans for science education for the next decade
in the developing world have quite different priorities. First, they
stress education at the secondary level as the most important
priority. Secondly, they involve the establishment of an educational process in all its ramifications and complexities, with great
importance being attached to new equipment and special types
of training for teachers, course designers, science administrators
and the like. The emphasis is on getting the system right—that
is, the course, the techniques, the teachers and the institutions—
rather than trying to process hundreds of thousands of students
through ill conceived educational programmes which end up being
nearly useless. The table below shows how the main funds for
the decade should be spent, and it presents a graphic demonstra-

tion of the priorities. Note, for instance, that $16,000 million is budgeted for high level education compared to only $26 million for post-graduate research and advanced training. Some $300 million should be spent on further education for those already in jobs. The other large sums involved are $400 million for teacher training, $280 million for projects to improve educational techniques, and $100 million for the establishment of ten regional centres for educational innovation. Note, too, the highly detailed way in which the budget is drawn up. Thus sums are included in the plans for teaching experts from the developed world something of the nature of the country they are going to work in, for Teacher Associations and even for the training of people whose job it is to design scientific and educational courses.

However, the philosophy of the programme cannot be wholly deduced from the table. For instance, much effort is attached to primary education, and to removing any discrimination to imparting scientific knowledge to the fairer sex at the earliest opportunity. Such programmes do not need expensive equipment. As J. S. Goldstein has put it, "The scientific study of soils, of mosquitoes and flies, of rainfall and sunshine, or animal behaviour are all examples of contexts which are directly and obviously relevant to national goals and priorities, and yet provide ample scope for the introduction and exploration of scientific ways of thinking".

Again, though the importance of secondary education has been emphasized, its nature also has to change. All too often secondary education has been regarded as a step towards the university, with huge wasted resources because the majority of students never go to university. The World Plan of Action asserts that there is an urgent need "for redesigning secondary education as a comprehensive and terminal unit". At the university itself, there is need for expansion of numbers and of the proportion of students studying science and technology. Thus in 1963, per million population, Africa has 220 higher education students, Asia 2740, Latin America 1990 and West Europe 3500. Furthermore the proportion studying science or technology was 19.5 in Africa, 16.2 in Asia, 27.1 in Latin America and 33.4 in West Europe. Even of those, far too many were involved in pure science rather than in scientific subjects of more direct national relevance.

Of various new educational techniques, radio and TV are of special importance in spite of their high capital cost. Experience

Principal Funds Needed for Science Education
($ million)

SUBJECT	Total	UN agencies	Bilateral agencies	Developing Countries
NATIONAL PLANNING				
Manpower units	20	(mainly from developing countries)		
S and T educational bodies	65	21	8[1]	36
ANALYSIS AND DESIGN				
Educational improvement projects	280	80	160	40
Preliminary investigation	9	3	6	—
Technical assistance	7	4	2	1
Continuing S and T education	55	15	30	10
Public understanding	11+	3	8	n.a.[2]
PERSONNEL				
Design of teacher training courses	15	4.5	4.5	6
Teacher training	400	80	80	240
Special fellowships	50	20	20	10
Training of course designers and science administrators	10	2	8	—
Training for high-level personnel	60	24	30	6
In-service teacher training	18	7.2	3.6	7.2
Professional associations	2.5	0.5	0.5	1.5
OPERATION				
High-level training	16,000	2,000	6,000	8,000
30 national centres for educational equipment	150	40	80	30
Data collection and analysis	8	3.2	2.4	2.4
Further education	300	50	100	150
Post-graduate and advanced training	26	4	20	2
RESEARCH AND DEVELOPMENT	28	5	20	3
INTERNATIONAL AND REGIONAL CO-OPERATION				
International store-houses of information	14	4	—	—
Information gathering	14	6	5	3
International meetings etc.	9	4	3	2
Federations of Teacher Assocs.	13	4	8	1
INGOs	2	2	—	—
Cultural education for experts	30	10	donor c'ntries:	20
10 regional innovation centres	100	30	50	20
10 strengthened institutes in developed countries for training	80	—	—	80

[1] From advanced countries.　　[2] Not available.

in Thailand, for example, shows that an audience of 800,000 people can be instructed at a cost of less than one per cent per student hour by radio. An extensive television educational scheme in the Ivory Coast may contain many lessons when the results are more fully known. So, too, will the Open University in the United Kingdom. So that the results of these and all other innovative educational ideas can be stored and assessed, the United Nations should fund the establishment of store-houses of information in each major scientific area.

In conclusion, I shall quote two statements from the World Plan of Action which seem to me to spell out most clearly the philosophies that lie behind the educational programme and its differences from education in the developed world. First, "The implementation of the action programmes in the food and agriculture sector, for example, will require widespread rural education, and the growth of a literate peasantry". And second, "In general the need will be for large numbers of technicians, fewer technologists and a reasonable number of technologically minded managers and entrepreneurs". Nothing could be more different from the priorities which the developed world has erroneously followed and nothing could be more badly needed by those countries in such desperate need of development.

(vii) *Population: Slowing the Relentless Tick*

The essential characteristic of the developed world over the past two or three centuries has been growth. Almost every main parameter—from energy consumption to speed of travel, from the volume of sewage treated to the size of the research budget— has been growing exponentially, doubling in size on average every 30, 20 or even 10 years. The developing world has not shared that growth or, if it has, has begun to do so only recently with the inevitable result that it lags far behind the developed world. Lags, that is, in almost every respect save one—population. The tragic paradox of our age is that while growth has done so much for the few, population growth—or at least 80 per cent of it—now occurs in those countries deprived of the major benefits of other kinds of growth. During the Second Development Decade the population of the developing world* will climb from 1760 million to 2320 million—an increase of 560 million.

* Defined here as the market economies of Asia, Africa and Latin America except Japan, Uruguay and Argentina.

286

In this Decade the world will have the highest rate of population growth it has ever had—and perhaps ever will. Not only does this present a serious challenge to the task of providing food, but it will weaken every other development effort equally. Unless it takes steps to reduce fertility, almost every developing nation runs the risk of seeing hard won progress being used only to maintain more people at the same, constant, low level.

So far, 30 of the developing countries—with about two-thirds of the population of the developing world—have established population policies aimed at controlling growth and reducing fertility. About five more countries per year are expected to evolve a policy during the Decade. But even for the few countries remaining without a population policy in 1980, it will be important to establish family planning activities as a health and welfare measure: high fertility poses a serious and immediate health problem for both the woman and her children. The World Plan of Action has therefore attempted to calculate the costs of population programmes throughout the developing world over the next decade, even though the basic principle that individual nations must make their own decisions about the need for population policies remains inviolate.

Undoubtedly the best way of providing family planning is as part of a maternity care programme. Although family planning need only be directed at fertile couples—which comprise about one sixth of the total population—costs have been worked out on a per capita basis for the whole population. It is estimated that, over and above what is already being spent, a further $0.2 per head a year over the Decade will need to be spent to provide adequate family planning within the context of maternity care programmes. This does not include the training of the appropriate personnel—itself an immense task. It is estimated that to provide for a population 80 per cent of that of the developing world would require more than 50,000 doctors, 200,000 paramedical workers and 350,000 field workers. This is sufficient for a population comprising 260 million women of reproductive age. But many other experts—including statisticians, demographers, teachers and social workers—are required. The total training cost is likely to be about $0.12 per capita per annum.

To these principal areas have to be added other less direct concerns. In 1969, for instance, in a special statement on the Second Development Decade, the United Nations Administrative Committee on Co-ordination stated that in every country steps needed to be taken to provide each family with access to family planning services. Access is no good unless there is knowledge of the existence of such services. Therefore a mass educational programme is called for. So, too, are social policy measures of reducing fertility such as legislation favouring a rise in age of marriage, the education of girls, improvement in the status of women and so on. All this must be accompanied by adequate census information including the collection of demographic statistics. When we add to this the need both for biological research in reproductive physiology and the development and testing of new contraceptives, as well as economic and social research on questions of population size and control, we arrive at the following breakdown in total costs:

| | Average annual costs | |
	($ million)	($ per capita)
Family planning within maternity services	400	0.20
Training of (a) family planning personnel	160	0.08
(b) other personnel	80	0.04
Mass communication activities	100	0.05
Overhead expenses, incentives and family planning through other than maternity services	160	0.05
Statistical, educational and informational activities	120	0.06
Basic biological research	100	0.05
Other research	40	0.02
TOTALS	$1160 million	$0.58

Bearing in mind uncertainties in the estimates, it is concluded that the cost for the Decade would fall between $10,000 and $13,000 million, or $1000 to $1300 million per year and $0.50 to $0.65 per capita per year. In 1970 total similar expenditures came to $180 million (of which $100 million came from the developing countries). The average per capita expenditure was $0.10 a year. The grim conclusion is that even if this figure can be increased by a factor of five or six, only modest results can be expected during the Decade, and the results thereafter will be highly speculative. During the next 15 years we cannot expect substantial declines in birth rate and a minimum goal for the 1970s must be to hold the rate of population increase down to its present level. But we do know that without this massive expenditure in the 1970s, the prospect for the 1980s and 1990s will be nothing short of horrific.

The United Nations has obviously a special role to play in this programme and the recent United Nations report "Human fertility and national development" has outlined greatly expanded population briefs for the United Nations organizations. Detailed objectives are outlined in the World Plan of Action and a huge range of specific actions, projects and programmes is being developed within the United Nations agencies. And although it is difficult for the United Nations to anticipate how its Member States will react to new proposals in this area, it has made a rough calculation of the kind of support it should provide:

	Costs for 1971-80 ($ million)
Statistics	24.1
Research	68.0
Training	142.8
Communications, education, information	12.2
Advisory services	75.8
Technical meetings	12.5
Equipment and supplies	9.6
TOTAL	$345.0 million

In addition, the United Nations calculates that a further $300 million will be required for general programme support and a further 10 per cent of the cost of the expanded activities will be needed for strengthening the various United Nations agencies to enable them to carry out this ambitious programme. Thus the total United Nations requirements for the Decade will exceed $700 million, starting from considerably less than $70 million a year and working up to more than $100 million by 1980.

It would be possible to describe how this money should be spent in great detail. In this context, however, it may be better to stress two general and related points. The first is that research accounts for a rather small proportion of the total cost. This reflects the fact that we already have a technology available which could be used to halt the population explosion. What is required is action. As one population expert has put it: "If

289

your house is burning down, you don't take time off to sort out the chemistry of combustion". The second point is the enormous gap that exists between the United Nations contribution of $700 million for the Decade and the required total of between $10,000 and $13,000 million.

Let there be no confusion about one point: the house *is* burning down. There are, of course, many political dimensions to the question of population control. The very idea is itself seen in some quarters as a political plot by the developed world to prevent development so that the developed can continue their own highly developed way of life. I can respect the motivations of those who argue this case but, as a scientist, I am also aware of a much bleaker and ultimately more final cause for concern. We live on a planet whose diameter has not changed for hundreds of millions of years; it has not grown as its human population has grown and it will not do so in the future. In spite of space travel, we thus live in a closed world. It is true, of course, that we can manipulate that world, extracting from it materials we need and substituting synthetic ones for them when that becomes more convenient. But all this activity depends on the Earthly supply of raw materials and, if population growth continues, they will ultimately be exhausted. At the present rate of progress, we can continue in the same manner for perhaps another century or so providing we accept some shortages of some materials within the next few decades. But the real cause for concern is that we have already tapped a substantial fraction of the resources available. Another few decades of unrestricted population growth will change our planet beyond recognition and—quite possibly—beyond survival.

One concrete example will have to suffice. At the current rate of growth we could burn up all our theoretical supply of fossil fuels within 170 years. Long before we do that, however, we would so have overladen the atmosphere with carbon dioxide that, like a greenhouse, the Earth would become insufferably hot (the high temperatures recorded on Venus are largely the result of a carbon dioxide rich atmosphere). This dilemma can be resolved by using nuclear technology instead of burning valuable fossil fuels—but this adds a new paradox: were our exponential rate of growth of energy production to continue to increase as it has for the last few hundred years, we would within only 60 years produce so much unavoidable waste heat that it would

290

be equivalent to five per cent of the incoming solar radiation. And if that happened the Earth's ambient temperature would rise with untold and unforseeable effects.

Thus there are limitations. We will soon be faced with a choice of restricting and even decreasing standards of living for an expanding population or of improving living standards for a relatively static population. This is why we must close the gap between the costs and the funds of population programmes in the 1970s. And this is why we close this description of the eight main areas of scientific priority for the Second Development Decade in the way in which we began it: "The planet Earth is a fragile spacecraft"—and that indisputable fact should be recognized in all our actions over the next decade.

Undermining the Knowledge Barriers

From what has been said, it is clear that the scientific priorities in development are by no means all a matter for research. Many of the problems are already technically solved and, in principle, all that is required is to put those who need to know in touch with those who already do know. But in a sense this is where the problems really begin. Today there are well over three million books in print, there are 50,000 scientific journals publishing 3 million articles a year, there are over 12 million patents and a further quarter of a million appear annually. Small wonder, then, that some people claim that it is quicker to do a piece of research than check through all the literature to see if some one else has already done the same thing. The problem is acute, and worsening, in the developed world. In the developing world, where even survival may depend on finding the right piece of knowledge at the right time, it is nothing short of a nightmare.

If there is not to be a complete or partial collapse of our information systems—and there are already signs of that in the technically advanced countries—there will have to be some radical new thinking in the next decade. The first partial solution to the information explosion was the development of abstracting services, enabling interested parties to scan for what they wanted in a more efficient way. But the volume of the abstracts themselves soon led to the need to publish abstracts of the abstracts. Then came the computer, with its near infinite memory, into which could be fed all the key words of an article title and which could be told to print out only those article titles known to be of interest to the user. And here we approach the essential tragedy of the information explosion: it is not that the volume of useful information has grown exponentially but that the volume of irrelevant information has reached such enormous proportions. The problem is essentially knowing what to reject and how to reject it to arrive at those unique pearls of wisdom which alone may settle the question at hand.

And although we set such high store today on the value of knowledge, we have slipped far from the ideal of the Enlightenment that knowledge should be free for all to use as best they can. So much research is subject to commercial or military classification that it is difficult to estimate how many solutions to how many problems remain under lock and key. Furthermore, knowledge has itself become the subject of a mammoth industry, available only to others at a price—usually a high one. It is true that both West Germany and Japan won through to prosperity at least partially by paying that price—in the form of the purchasing of licenses and patents and know-how. But other countries have paid the price with less success. In 1966, for instance, the cost of royalties and other technical services to Colombia was at least $20 million, or 0.4 per cent of its gross domestic product. The costs of foreign consultancy and other services for Pakistan are thought to be over $100 million a year. And in general these costs seem to be doubling about every five years. According to one estimate, if in the developing world payments for patents, trademarks, licenses and know-how were to increase by 20 per cent a year—as they did in Japan during 1957-65—the total would rise to some $1500 million in 1980, and to much more if all the hidden costs were included.

So the information gap poses two quite separate problems to developing countries: first, to identify those pieces of relevant knowledge more or less freely available to anyone who can find them; and, second, to afford to pay for that specially selected knowledge to which someone else already holds the title. For the first there can be no substitute for effective action by governments themselves. Probably every country would benefit from the setting up of a national technology transfer centre, closely linked on the one hand with the appropriate planning authority and on the other with industry and the universities. The nature of such centres would vary from country to country but they would all have one thing in common: an aggressive attitude to information. It is not sufficient for a centre of this nature to collect information—it has also to bring it to the notice of potential users and to encourage them to make their requests known. And each of these centres should tie in with each other and be well connected to a coherent international system.

After a pilot study of those centres of this type which already exist—in different types of country and meeting different types of need—it is proposed that several experimental technology transfer centres be established. Furthermore, it appears that the problems that such centres will pose—if they are to become the dynamic type of institution which is required—merit the setting up of an international institute devoted to research on the centres and to the training of personnel to serve on them. This might best be done through the UN Centre for Industrial Development.

The way to answer the second problem is much clearer. The cost of privileged technical information to the developing world must be drastically reduced. Restrictive practices that surround so many licensing agreements must be removed and there must be an international trend towards liberating the flow of information from the stranglehold of market demands and private profit that has done so much to delay the Third World in its progress towards industrialization. But the means of doing this are far from clear. The problem itself has received scant attention compared, for instance, to the no more important problem of trade barriers. The objective for the Second Development Decade must be to bring the 'knowledge barriers' tumbling down by eroding their foundations with careful research aimed at quantifying the problem and exposing its worst excesses. Once we recognize the importance of the situation, we may be well on the way to its cure.

Finally, one point should be stressed that is often forgotten. Technical knowledge is not the same thing as personal knowledge. The frontiers of every scientific field are manned by an 'invisible college' only a few score strong. These are the men who produce the new ideas and who usually know—months and sometimes a year or more ahead of publication—what is new and what is important. Their knowledge comes from conversations, from letters and from international meetings. So it is in every field. The visit is worth a hundred articles, the personal friend a hundred bibliographies—computerized information can only ever be second best.

According to one good estimate, 98 per cent of all the research and development carried out outside the socialist countries is performed by the developed countries. The developing world contributes a mere 2 per cent. Even that would not be so alarming if the developed world's research were relevant to the Third World. But, as the figures for the OECD countries show, this is far from being the case. Defence, space and atomic energy claim more than half of the OECD countries' expenditure on research and development. A further 26 per cent goes into the 'economic field'—that is, mainly into industrial research related to products for the consumer society and to advanced engineering. A further 22 per cent goes on fundamental and welfare research. That leaves only 1 per cent for research into the specific problems of developing countries. Statistically, then, hardly any one is concerned with the research problems of the Third World.

Furthermore, the kinds of research practised in the developed world tend to aggravate the situation still further. The fashionable research fields, almost by definition, become those of little direct concern to developing countries. As a result, there is great temptation for the few scientists that those countries do possess to work in areas remote from their own, more pressing needs. And much of the work in the developed world is actually detrimental to developing countries. For instance, about $1000 million per annum is currently spent on research and development into synthetic fibres and other materials. As a result the importance of natural rubber, cotton and vegetable oils has greatly declined in world trade. In short, the current direction of scientific research in this area—and in some others—has actually worsened the situation for the developing countries.

Perhaps for the first time, this particular nettle of discontent has been firmly grasped. "Each highly developed country should", ACAST claims, "devote at least 5 per cent of its own internal non-military research and development expenditures to research for lesser developed countries by the end of the Second United Nations Development Decade". This principle, if not the actual figure, has already been accepted as part of the strategy for the decade.

If it can be achieved by 1980, it will mean that an extra $2250 million will be made available annually for research on Third

World problems. Put another way, it means that a further 75,000 highly trained scientists and engineers would become available to help tackle the key problem of scientific development. It is hard to imagine any more specific or more powerful catalyst to world development.

But can it be achieved? The target is certainly ambitious. It would amount, in effect, to cutting the military research of the developed world by about one eighth by the end of the decade. If even that seems a lot, it amounts to less than a 2 per cent cut per annum in military research and development over the next eight years, with the money saved being invested in Third World research. And if the goal of general and complete disarmament could be translated into reality, the money available in this area could probably be greatly increased.

There is another reason for optimism. Much of the current criticism of science in the West concerns the vast sums spent on military matters to the detriment of other, more pressing social problems. In the past few years the tide of opinion has swung decisively against science for its own sake, against science for the military and against science for private profit. There is a growing concern both within the scientific community and without, from the young and from the more experienced, that science should be put to responsible uses and that it should be relevant to the very real problems of our time. Viewed in this light, a 2 per cent switch from the military towards development may be less than the minimum needed to satisfy the demands of those who are not convinced that the industrialized nations scientific priorities are always right. By 1980 the critics may well be demanding more. And if their demands are not met by 1980 there may be dire consequences not only in the developing world but in the wealthier countries as well.

There is another, often overlooked, reason why such a trading in of military research for development progress would be wholly desirable. The mass migration of scientific talent from the developing to the developed world became known in the 1960s as the brain drain. The outflow now approaches about 40,000 people a year and as such constitutes a greater negative movement of manpower than is the positive effect achieved by technical assistance from developed to developing. But what is much more rarely pointed out is that in the 1960s the brain drain was, ultimately, often a movement of scientists and engineers from the civil laboratories of the developing world to the military laboratories of the developed world. It is not, of course, true that the Third World researchers often went to work directly on military projects. But their presence in the host country certainly made it possible for more of that country's scientists to work on military affairs than would otherwise have been the case. To reverse that trend now would, in fact, be doing no more than repaying the substantial debt which military laboratories already owe the developing countries.

The Essential Ingredient: Third World Science

The development "gap" embraces a multitude of evils: the differences in prosperity, standard of life, nutrition, housing, transport and communication that demarcate the fortunate one third of the world population from the less fortunate majority. But properly defined it also includes another gap which is, in some sense, a cause of all the other gaps. This is the scientific gap, reflected in the fact that the developing countries spend an average of 0.2 per cent of their GNP on research and development compared with between 1 and 3 per cent for the developed world.

Were our efforts during the coming development decade to be concentrated solely on technology transfer, the scientific gap would remain and even grow bigger. We would in effect be adding yet one more item to the list that distinguishes the "haves" from the "have-nots". This in itself is good enough cause to explore the means by which developing countries can accelerate their own scientific efforts. But there are others.

Technology transfer is not a one way process. Before a country can gain an adequate idea of what there is to be transferred, and of how it can be adapted to its own particular needs, it must possess a body of scientifically literate people. On them will fall the task of guiding their country's modernization in the light of what is, and what is not, technically feasible. Nor is this a job that can be easily handled by scientists from the developed world. Understandably, their whole orientation is towards a highly developed society and they tend to see in new science and technology the glitter that holds promise for their own societies. More often than not, such ideas will require subtle or wholesale changes before they become relevant to a developing country. One particular area of concern are the social and economic changes that flow in the wake of technical change. True development requires very careful study of these disturbing influences. And thus it is that social science—often regarded even in the developed world as something of a luxury—becomes one of the basic necessities of life to a developing country. Close co-operation between natural and social scientists working in a country's indigenous institutions are the hallmark of success for any development project.

There are other, more cultural reasons why developing countries should mount their own scientific efforts. An adequate research basis, of course, is essential to any major plan for higher education. In the long run—though here the data are sometimes confusing—it will have a markedly beneficial effect on economic growth rates. Even over and above this, as the World Plan of Action points out, "there is increasing evidence that the impact of a local scientific elite on national development is of much greater importance than it was hitherto believed to be. It is nowadays recognized that excellence in scientific research—regardless of its relevance to national development goals—not only enhances a nation's cultural status and prestige, but also sets standards of creativity, truth, honesty, independence of judgment, clarity and logic which are among those most needed by a complex modern State".

There are pitfalls, too. If a nation is to develop its own scientific effort, how is it to assess the relative merits of pure and applied research? In short, how is it to direct its own science policy when that subject is even now a matter of heated controversy in the developed world? There are no quick answers, no simple blueprints to follow. But there are some general points on which the World Plan lays great stress.

First, there must be fundamental research and it must be of high quality. Low standards lead only to negative results when passing from basic research to application and they tend to isolate the laboratory from world scientific centres. What are needed are a few centres of excellence doing work that ranks with that carried out anywhere else in the world. Such centres need not be large, numerous or particularly expensive—but they must be there.

Second, these centres are too often linked more with government than with universities. Their catalytic effect on the educational process may thus be lost and their fundamental work may become directed towards national priorities. There is a delicate balance to be achieved here, for there can be no question but that most scientific research in a developing country should be applied in nature. It should be directed towards solving those particular social and economic problems which are of most concern to that nation. If developing countries could achieve this delicate balance by the 1980s, they are indeed likely to find themselves on par or even ahead of science policy in the developed world. Much of the present "crisis" in science in the developed world stems from a reorientation of policy—a clear decision having been made that, while some science for science's sake is necessary, by far the larger part can and should be related to national needs. But the cries of anguish currently echoing round university campuses in countries such as the United States and the United Kingdom merely attest to the difficulty of changing science policy once it has been established. The developing countries have a clear chance to cut out a painful stage in the development of scientific effort.

These are generalities but the Second Development Decade embraces some quite specific advice as to how an indigenous scientific effort can be built up. The most important is that developing countries should aim to spend 0.5 per cent of their gross national product on research and development. This, of course, is an average figure. Some of these countries already spend about 0.4 per cent in this way and they will have no difficulty in reaching the target. Others spend much less than 0.2 per cent and they will not be able to achieve it. But should the average reach 0.5 per cent, then on the estimated GNP of the developing countries in 1980—about $500,000 million—no less than $2,500 million will be available for developing countries' research. Actually, per head of population the sum spent will still be fairly small as the developing world will number nearly 2,500 million by then ($1 per head per year). For contrast, the United Kingdom, with a population of about 50 million, today spends roughly the same amount on research and development. ($50 *per capita* per year—but over one quarter goes to defence.)

There are a number of corollaries. It is suggested, for instance, that the growth rate for research should be about 15 per cent. This will take the bigger spenders over the 0.5 per cent target but will not bring the small spenders up to it. This is as it should be. A growth rate of more than 15 per cent is now generally felt to be unmanageable—neither the institutions nor the manpower can be generated sufficiently quickly to make best use of the increase in funds.

Nor do these figures include what are generally called scientific and technical services—that is, the whole range of activities such as mapping and public health measures which do not call for research but do call for specific scientific and technical knowledge. The World Plan of Action suggests that by 1980 their funding too should have increased to 0.5 per cent of GNP—bringing the total scientific and technical indigenous effort to about 1 per cent of GNP. Assuming the cost of a scientist in a developing country to be about $12,500 a year, this will mean that the developing countries will by 1980 be employing about 400,000 of their own scientists and engineers. And we have already examined some of the problems such an expansion in the work force will raise, and what means are available to meet them.

The Second Development Decade embraces another target: that by 1980 the developed countries should be spending 1 per cent of their GNP on foreign aid. The World Plan of Action suggests that 5 per cent of this should be in direct support of science and technology. As well as devoting 5 per cent of their own research efforts towards the problems of development, the developed countries would then, over and above this, be providing 0.05 per cent of their GNPs to promote science and technology in the developing countries. It is estimated that this fraction will be worth about $1,250 million by 1980, of which $750 million would go towards the provision of scientists and engineers working in the developing countries. This sum would cover the costs of about 20,000 such "specialists". The other $500 million would be used to pay for scientific and technical laboratories and their equipment.

To summarize, then, we have one specific Second Development Decade target for the developing countries to spend 0.5 per cent of their GNPs on research and development, providing a total of $2,500 million or 200,000 scientists and engineers. The World Plan of Action recommends that the same amount be spent on scientific and technical services. It also recommends that the developed world spends 0.05 per cent of its GNP on direct scientific and technical aid, providing 20,000 specialists and $1,250 million a year by 1980. Finally, it suggests that developed countries spend 5 per cent of their non-military research and development funds in areas of direct relevance to developing countries, thus providing some 75,000 researchers or $2,250 million to deal specifically with the problems of development.

The grand total, if all this can be achieved, looks something like this. By 1980 the scientific effort expended by or for the developing world will total about $8,500 million and will involve a technical manpower of about 500,000 people. It is a grand plan and nothing like it has ever been tried before. In a very real sense, it will constitute the greatest scientific experiment ever attempted.

Getting it Done: There is No Alternative

This experiment, like all others, will stand or fall on how it is put into practice. We have the theory; we have the scientific master-plan; and we know in general terms the specific steps that need to be taken. It remains to turn the goals to reality, and to do it within a tightly defined schedule.

Much will depend on the operation of the United Nations machinery. The World Plan of Action has still to be submitted to the UN General Assembly. If and when it is approved, the UN agencies must examine those parts of it which they can take care of within their normal budgets and those other parts for which they will need additional funds. The United Nations Development Programme must be asked to specify which parts of the programme it can take on and the World Bank must be approached to see which programme it might assist. The various regional plans have to be worked out in final detail and specific proposals for bilateral projects have to be put before the developed nations. ACAST has suggested that a special World Plan of Action fund or account will have to be set up within the United Nations Development Programme.

It would be possible to spell out these and many other administrative matters in great detail. In this context, however, I believe it more valuable to examine briefly the nature of the choice that lies before us: shall we see to it that the developed world is now finally provided with a chance to make its own way into the twenty-first century? Or shall we let the idea, like so many other good ones, go by default—trusting in luck, a certain amount of foreign aid and the dedication of the few to see us through?

The plan is not a particularly cheap one. It cannot be implemented merely by a tiny readjustment of the developed world's expenditure which no one need notice. It will require changes and expenses that we may all feel. But if the cost is considered great, it is tiny in relation to the alternative. For if we do not begin to close the development gap by the 1980s, if we do not provide the developing world with its scientific chance of attaining equality through its own efforts, some grim prospects lie before us. We can expect to see famine on a scale never before experienced. We can expect poverty magnified beyond recognition. We can expect wars to become more frequent and their effects, amplified by deprivation, to touch on or destroy the lives of hundreds of millions.

It would be folly to imagine that such events could occur without major repercussions within the developed nations. Today modern communications see to it that we all share something of the sufferings of others. In many countries of the developed world Governments are on the defensive even now against the charges of the young that the world is not as it should be and that not enough is being done to put it right. I do not believe that this attitude is going to change with time but that, on the contrary, it will deepen and harden as every year goes by unless action is taken.

This, then, is the "strategic" argument for scientific development: our very survival may depend on it. In deploying it, I am conscious that it is neither the best reason for development nor the most moral. There are surely deeper reasons, that lie closer to the soul, for *knowing* that the development gap must be diminished, and quickly at that.

But to me one of the most compelling reasons of all concerns the way we have used science in the developed world. The great majority of our scientists are concerned with the stockpiling and improvement of the weapons of death or with quite trivial matters which serve only to prolong the life and the absurdities of the consumer society. Neither activity adds much to our chance of survival or our sense of purpose. Even were the world not so sharply divided into the rich and the poor, one would have to conclude that our scientific priorities were far from wise. A new emphasis on science for development, then, promises two things—hope for the developing and saner priorities for the developed. This use of science means development—in its real sense—for us all. There can be no more encouraging conclusion and no better reason for total commitment to the aims of the Second Development Decade and the scientific plans on which it may stand or fall.

About the Authors

The late MAX F. MILLIKAN was Professor of Economics and Director of the Center for International Studies at the Massachusetts Institute of Technology. He was also the President of the World Peace Foundation, a trustee of the Carnegie Endowment for International Peace, and a member of the Indian Investment Centre Advisory Committee, the U.S. Chamber of Commerce Foreign Policy Committee, and many groups dealing with economic development. His books and articles on the subject of economics and international affairs include (with W. W. Rostow) *A Proposal: Key to an Effective Foreign Policy,* and (with Robert N. Gardner) *The Global Partnership: International Agencies and Economic Development.*

SIR ARTHUR LEWIS is James Madison Professor of Political Economy at Princeton University and President of the Caribbean Development Bank. He was Principal (then Vice-Chancellor) of the University of the West Indies, Professor of Political Economy in the University of Manchester, and Lecturer at the London School of Economics. He has held various official positions, as Director of the Colonial Development Corporation, Deputy Managing Director of the U.N. Special Fund, and Director of the Central Bank of the Industrial Development Corporation, Jamaica. His writings include books and articles on development and on economic planning.

JOSEF PAJESTKA is Director of the Institute of Planning, Poland, Professor of Economics at the University of Warsaw, and Vice-Chairman of the Polish Economic Society. In 1965 he served as a member of a panel of experts in Uganda; he was head of the Polish Delegation to the Economic Commission of the Council for Mutual Economic Assistance in 1964-65. In 1963 and 1964 he participated in meetings of the Economic Commission for Europe Senior Economic Advisers, and, in 1963, in the United Nations Conference on the Application of Science and Technology for the Benefit of Less Developed Areas. He was a participant in the United Nations Seminar on Industrial Programming in 1963 and a member of the United Nations Group of Experts on Economic Projections in 1962. In 1960 he was a member of the International Labour Organisation Panel of Experts on Employment and Economic Development, and also Economic Adviser to the Iraqi Ministry of Planning. His writings and publications include *On Economic Development of Poland* (1963-1965), *Studies on Development Patterns of Developing Countries* (1962), and *Capital Invest-*

ment, Employment and Economic Development (1961).

JEAN-MARIE DOMENACH is the editor of the Parisian monthly review *Esprit* and general editor of a series of works published by the Editions du Seuil. He has lectured in various foreign countries and taught in several American universities. In addition to a great many articles, he has written a number of books, the most recent of which is entitled *Le Retour du Tragique* (The Return of Tragedy).

DAVID WIGHTMAN is Professor of International Economic Organisation at University of Birmingham, England. He has frequently served as a consultant to international organizations on work in the economic and social fields. He is the author of *Economic Cooperation in Europe, Toward Economic Cooperation in Asia,* and various articles and booklets on international economic affairs. He cooperated with Gunnar Myrdal in the research and writing involved in the study, *Asian Drama: an Inquiry Into the Poverty of Nations.*

ROBIN CLARKE has served as editor of the scientific publication *Discovery* and as editor of *Science Journal.* Mr. Clarke has written and published three books, *The Diversity of Man, We All Fall Down,* and *The Science of War and Peace.* As a science writer, Mr. Clarke is very concerned with the direction in which science and its technologies are leading society and is presently working on a publication on current trends of scientific research.